The Jewellery of Roman Britain

The Jewellery of Roman Britain

Celtic and Classical Traditions

Catherine Johns

UCL PRESS

First published in 1996 by UCL Press

UCL Press Limited
University College London
Gower Street
London WC1E 6BT

The name of University College London (UCL) is a registered
trade mark used by UCL Press with the consent of the owner.

British Library Cataloguing in Publication Data
A catalogue record for this book is available from the British Library.

ISBN: 1-85728-566-2 HB

Typeset in Garamond.
Printed and bound by Butler & Tanner Ltd, Frome, England.

To Alun and Lyn

Contents

Acknowledgements

An attempt to summarize a complex subject is generally based on a combination of direct personal experience, discussion with other researchers and wide reading of published specialist work, and it can therefore be very difficult to acknowledge fully and fairly all the influences that lie behind a particular interpretation. My own views on the jewellery of Roman Britain as set out in this book have been formed during nearly thirty years of working in the British Museum and learning from the artefacts themselves and from the knowledge of colleagues within and outside the museum. Many friends and colleagues who are experts on aspects of jewellery history quite unconnected with Roman Britain have widened my horizons beyond the limitations of archaeology and the Classical period, and I hope I have learned well from their insights; I thank them all sincerely.

Some of my debts will be obvious from the bibliography, and I should like to mention in particular the work of Reynold Higgins, who died while this book was in preparation. I owe a special debt of gratitude to those friends who have not only published indispensable books and articles and discussed relevant themes with me over the years, but have willingly and generously taken on the task of reading the whole or parts of the manuscript in draft and have thus improved my text and saved me from some errors; namely Martin Henig, Jennifer Price, Val Rigby, Jack Ogden, Lindsay Allason-Jones and Ralph Jackson. Any mistakes that remain are my own responsibility.

Though the sources of the illustrations are acknowledged in the usual way, I should like to add more personal thanks to the following colleagues in various museums who have been so helpful in obtaining photographs for me: Lindsay Allason-Jones, Chris Delaney, Joanne Freeman, Jenny Hall, Elizabeth Hartley, Sue Margeson, Nigel Meeks, Bill Milligan, Andrew Oddy and Michael Ryan.

Together with the publishers, I should also like to express my gratitude to the Society of Jewellery Historians for a contribution towards the cost of the colour plates. (The Society may be contacted at the Department of Prehistoric and Romano-British Antiquities, British Museum, London WC1B 3DG.)

Word-processors have made writing easier, cats are a welcome distraction, and music makes the whole process bearable; hence, thanks to Amstrad, to Riley and the late Dynamo, and to the sounds of reggae and classic rock. Finally, Don Bailey has as ever put up with my throes of composition, and given me moral support and the benefit of his vast knowledge of the ancient world and its material culture.

Catherine Johns

List of illustrations

Colour plates

Map of Britain

The map shows the approximate positions of sites mentioned in the text.

- Traprain Law
- Hadrian's Wall
- Backworth
- Corbridge
- Great Chesters
- Whitby
- Malton
- York
- Chorley
- Gainsborough
- Lincoln
- Brancaster
- Snettisham
- Thetford
- Hoxne
- Wroxeter
- Icklingham
- Rhayader
- Felixstowe
- Dolaucothi
- Castlethorpe
- Baldock
- Colchester
- Carmarthen
- Oldcroft
- Verulamium (St Albans)
- Caerleon
- Cardiff
- London
- Havering
- Bath
- Silchester
- Warlingham
- Faversham
- Canterbury
- Richborough
- Amesbury
- Odiham
- Wiveliscombe
- Low Ham
- Hod Hill
- Winchester
- Kimmeridge

Introduction

The gold and silver jewellery of the Greek and Roman world represents a pinnacle of artistic and technical achievement. This fact is recognized in many of the books devoted to the history of jewellery, but the Roman provinces, including Britain, tend to receive at most an oblique comment in such works. This book is the first general survey devoted to the jewellery worn in Roman Britain. In this short introductory section my aim is to define the scope of the subject and the way in which it will be surveyed in the chapters that follow.

Traditional definitions of "jewel" and "jewellery" refer to ornaments of high monetary value incorporating precious metals and gemstones. This interpretation was followed by the leading Classical jewellery historian, the late Reynold Higgins: in the final paragraph of his indispensable book *Greek and Roman jewellery* he wrote:

> Bronze brooches, richly decorated with champlevé enamel, are also found in the former Celtic areas of the Empire. It may be objected that such articles have no place in a survey of this nature, since, being of bronze, they are not truly jewellery, and, being predominantly Celtic, they are not truly Roman. They do, however, merit a passing mention, if only for their attractive and novel appearance.[1]

I propose to take a broader approach, based on what prehistorians usually call "personal ornament". This unromantic technical term, deliberately colourless, is designed to encompass decorative items made of any material, and to avoid implications of intrinsic worth. Yet ordinary English usage has surely long overtaken such pedantic scruples: in conversation, few people would hesitate to use the word "jewellery" to describe personal ornaments of base metal, glass, wood, plastics and other substances that are not intrinsically precious. It is in this wider sense that I shall use the term here, as an equivalent to the useful German word *Schmuck.*

Jewellery is an adjunct to clothing, a notoriously difficult subject of study for the archaeologist dealing with ancient periods. Actual garments rarely survive because of the perishable nature of organic materials, and representations in art of people in contemporary dress may be stylized, misleading or ambiguous. Fashions in dress and adornment and their significance in the perceptions of wealth or status are sometimes regarded as frivolous or superficial subjects, but this is a false judgement. Throughout recorded history, and no doubt in prehistory as well, the ways in which persons of both sexes have covered and decorated their bodies with clothing and ornaments have been of profound importance and significance in defining their place in society. The choice of clothing and jewellery cannot fail to make a statement, whether deliberate or inadvertent, about the wearer, and this statement is perceived by other members of the same society.[2] The study of personal ornament is therefore an important one in trying to understand the values of past societies.

There are numerous ways of classifying jewellery types, and the most useful approach will depend on the nature of the culture being studied. An obvious classification that can be applied to jewellery of most early periods is based on a distinction between objects that are purely decorative, like earrings and necklaces, and those that have a practical function, for instance the buckles and brooches used for fastening clothing. Archaeologists dealing with prehistoric periods can sometimes only guess at the way in which certain gold ornaments were worn or used because the incomplete and patchy knowledge of the society simply does not include enough information to provide a context. Some of the beautiful gold artefacts of the British and Irish Bronze Age, so-called "tress-rings" and "cuff-fasteners", may indeed have been used to adorn hair or clasp clothing, but might equally well have been earrings or nose-rings, or have served a purpose we cannot even envisage. However, the jewellery of the Roman period is extremely familiar and accessible to us; most of the items are so similar to those which we still favour that replicas of Roman jewellery can be worn today without causing any comment other than admiration for their attractive design.

We can often recognize practical function from archaeological evidence alone, since the form of a brooch or pin declares its use as a fastener, but jewels that appear to be merely decorative may also have had important symbolic functions, such as designating the marital status of their wearer, and these abstract, but equally meaningful, purposes can be inferred only in the presence of some additional knowledge about the society in which the item was current – hence the problems in interpreting Bronze Age jewellery. We shall consider these symbolic values in more detail in due course. The Classical world has left a rich legacy of written information that helps us to interpret surviving artefacts on many levels, but the traditions of the native populations of the Roman provinces are far less well documented. One of the main themes in this book concerns the presence of both Roman and Celtic elements in Romano-British society, and we must remember that inferences which are based on Classical writings do not necessarily apply precisely to the mixed society of a remote Roman province with its own distinctive traditions.

Another form of classification seeks to define distinctive varieties of jewellery worn by people of different sexes, ages or social groupings. For instance, in some societies the wearing of certain types of jewellery may be confined to persons of specific ethnic backgrounds. This kind of information can sometimes be deduced from the archaeological evidence alone, but inferences founded on interpretation of the ornaments buried with the dead, usually an important source of archaeological data, must be treated with reservations, a point that will be fully discussed in the next chapter. The selection and purchase of jewellery may be controlled by many factors, including wealth, fashion and sometimes legal restrictions such as sumptuary laws, but there is still a major element of personal choice involved. In spite of the limitations that may have governed the choice of personal ornament, we can still assume that a man or woman in the Roman period would have selected a ring or a brooch with care, and that the choice would reflect individual preference as well as the buyer's place in society.

One of the simplest methods of organizing data that consist mainly of numerous small artefacts is to use the typological approach of the archaeologist, dealing in turn with rings, brooches and so forth and describing their variations and chronological development. This is the system that I propose to use here since it is the most direct and effective way of familiarizing the reader with the full range of personal ornaments in use in Roman Britain. But if the objects are to be understood not only as a catalogue of interesting and sometimes beautiful trinkets but also in their wider role as part of the material evidence for the nature of Romano-British society, it is necessary first to elaborate on some of the points made above about the use and meaning of jewellery and also to look at the limitations which are imposed on us by the nature of archaeological evidence. It is also important to be reasonably familiar with the Celtic and Classical elements that came together to create the provincial Roman society of Britain in the first four centuries AD. Chapters 1 and 2, then, are intended to set the scene and provide the background against which the jewellery itself must be assessed and interpreted.

In the subsequent chapters, devoted to specific items of personal adornment – finger-rings, necklaces, brooches and so forth – the principal types current in the early, middle and late Roman periods in Britain will be described and illustrated, as will some exceptional and rare types.

Common, simple styles that are found throughout the Roman period, and which therefore have no special value to archaeologists as dating evidence, will also be discussed. My objective is not to provide a textbook that can be used to identify and date any item of Romano-British jewellery (an aim which would be virtually doomed to failure) but to help the reader acquire a good general knowledge of the range of jewellery favoured by the inhabitants of Roman Britain at all social levels and at all dates within that formative period in the history of the island.

Chapter 1

The nature of jewellery and the nature of the evidence

Meaning and symbolism in jewellery

The reasons for buying and wearing jewellery may appear to be self-evident and to have changed little over the centuries. Probably most people would initially quote appearance as the principal motivation: metal and other ornaments are regarded as beautiful in themselves, and are thought to enhance the appearance of the wearer. While this is true as far as it goes, it is only part of the story. Jewellery is still heavily loaded with symbolic values and associations, and there is every reason to believe that these factors were at least as important in antiquity as they are today, if not more so.

At its most basic, the wearing of precious-metal jewellery provides evidence of the owner's wealth. The ornaments may have an actual intrinsic value that can be directly related to the value of currency in those societies that use coinage. Closely linked with this is the use of jewellery as a badge of status or rank in the form of special items that symbolize authority or even a particular profession or calling. For women, the status of being adult and married is one that is defined in most societies by specific types of personal ornament that may not be worn by unmarried girls; the question of wealth is often interconnected. Finally, amuletic jewellery, designed to express religious or superstitious beliefs and to offer some kind of protection to the wearer, is, and always has been, extremely widespread. We can point to modern analogies for all these classes of jewellery, and we can be sure that they existed in some form in the Roman period, but there are quite severe limitations on the inferences we can draw from surviving ornaments themselves. Some meanings can be revealed only if written sources describe them.

Jewellery as visible wealth is exemplified in some modern Islamic contexts by the wearing of actual coins in headdresses and other ornaments. Such ornaments may themselves indicate the adult, married woman, and the gold may include dowry money, brought into the marriage by the wife, and often legally distinguishable from the joint wealth of a couple. Jewellery incorporating coins was fashionable from time to time in the Roman period, as it still is today, and indeed the display of intrinsically valuable jewellery to indicate the wearer's wealth remains a frequent function of jewellery in modern Western society; so much so that there is a widespread urge to imitate precious materials in such a way as to deceive the observer and present an appearance of affluence at no great expense to the owner. Our modern low-purity gold is part of this phenomenon, but because 9-carat is called "gold", its status is ambivalent. In Roman and in modern times, gold and silver have been simulated by the gilding and silvering of base metals, and by using bronze, iron and tin in such a way that they look superficially like gold and silver. Glass was, and remains, the material principally used for imitating gems, though the appreciation of hardstones in antiquity was based on qualities other than those which constitute their greatest appeal today (in general, colour was prized rather than sparkle). The monetary value of precious-metal jewellery has often been combined with the symbolism of permanence and affection which is carried by some jewellery to produce a very powerful amuletic effect.

Most societies have defined gold as an exceedingly precious material, and its use as a medium of exchange and an absolute standard of value has become interwoven in a rather complex fashion with its use as a decorative metal. This perception persists today in spite of the fact that much modern gold jewellery, although officially sanctioned by hallmarks, is of comparatively low purity: 9-carat gold contains only 37.5 per cent gold, with 62.5 per cent of alloying metals. The importance of the symbolic image of permanence and high quality, even when belied by low prices, was vividly illustrated by a widely reported news story of 1991 in Britain. Light-heartedly and with engaging honesty, the head of a major chain of high-street jewellers admitted in a speech that his firm's products were of a low quality commensurate with their modest and popular prices. The reaction of the public was intensely hostile, and the company suffered severely from reduced sales as a result. Even the most naïve buyers must have been aware at some level that gold jewellery which costs less than a good meal could not possibly be of heirloom quality. But they did not wish to face that fact. Disgruntled customers interviewed on the news media mentioned repeatedly that the admission by the chairman of the firm had undermined and even destroyed their pleasure in important gifts and symbols of affection and commitment such as wedding and engagement rings; it was abundantly clear that the jewellery was important as a physical embodiment, in the form of a precious and lasting object, of certain emotional and spiritual concepts; the devaluing of the actual gold ornaments reflected adversely on the ideas they symbolized.

Jewellery may also communicate information about the wearer's rank or calling, which is another aspect of his or her position in society. As we shall see in the next chapter, there is reason to believe that in the Celtic societies of pre-Roman Britain and Gaul the wearing of a torc around the neck may have carried specific messages of authority, while to Graeco-Roman perceptions circlets to be worn on the head indicated authority and triumph or victory. Wreaths, diadems and crowns have retained these meanings, to the extent that certain types of crown may be worn only by a royal ruler. In modern society, a jewelled tiara continues to convey a social message, but one that has become more focused within the last century or so. In the late eighteenth and nineteenth centuries such ornaments were appropriate jewellery for women attending balls and other formal evening occasions, so although their use was always restricted to the upper echelons of society, they might be said to have been in fairly regular wear. By the late twentieth century the number of women who possess a tiara, and the number of functions where such an article may properly be worn, are very small indeed, being virtually confined to grand occasions where royalty is present.

Examples abound of jewels worn as a mark of office, and there would undoubtedly have been instances of this in Roman Britain. Objects such as mayoral chains and bishops' rings are not intended primarily for decoration, however elaborately wrought they may be, but to advertise the role and the place in society of the wearer. Official significance of this kind has been postulated for some Roman ornaments. For example, late Roman crossbow brooches are thought to be badges of military or civilian authority. The point to remember is that our knowledge of such matters is likely to remain extremely limited and partial. We can infer special meanings for certain items, and we may well be right at least some of the time, but there are likely to be other objects that we pass over as purely decorative which in fact carried a clear and specific message to contemporaries.

One of the major classes of symbolic jewellery is that which indicates the married or adult woman; the two definitions are virtually interchangeable in most societies. It is and was the norm for married women to be distinguished from young girls by their costume and jewellery, and modern Western society is no exception. The wedding ring is still imbued with powerful connotations of personal status and commitment. As recently as a generation ago in Britain, most people regarded the presence or absence of a plain gold ring on the third finger of a woman's left hand as reliable proof of her married or single status: no married woman, it was thought, would be without such a ring, and few single ones would be brazen enough to wear one without legal sanction. The circular shape of a plain finger-ring, with no beginning or end, may be regarded as symbolic of eternity; formed of gold, a metal that does not corrode or deteriorate, this is a telling image of permanence. If the impact of such rings has diminished in the final decade of the twentieth century, it may be more attributable to changing perceptions of formal marriage contracts than to a weakening of the symbolic implications of rings. The wearing of wedding rings by men has gained ground in recent decades, but it remains optional and far less common than the woman's wedding ring.

This use of rings is so very familiar to us that it is easy to assume that Roman, and specifically Romano-British, practice was the same as today's, but there may have been other ornaments that were appropriate for displaying a woman's marital status. In modern Egypt, for example, some country women still wear gold or silver ankle bracelets (*khul-khaal*) to show that they are adult, married women.[1] Similar ornaments are known in other North African countries, and it is interesting to speculate on the underlying symbolism, which would appear to include hints of bondage or slavery: certainly these heavy precious-metal rings resemble shackles. With the development of feminist perspectives, they can more easily be perceived as symbolic of the traditionally subordinate position of women within marriage. If any of the bracelets and bangles (some of which may well be anklets) that survive from Roman Britain had such a meaning, we would have no way of knowing it. As an interesting aside, we might note that the wearing of an ankle-chain in Britain in the 1930s and 1940s was widely understood to signify a woman of easy virtue, or indeed a professional prostitute; this symbolism appears to have died out. In a very specific sense, we do not know whether the widespread practice of attributing the adult/wife meaning to a particular item of jewellery took different forms in the Roman and Celtic traditions. Finger-rings, as we shall see, were relatively uncommon items of jewellery in the pre-Roman Iron Age of Britain, and it follows that if British Iron Age women wore some special ornament that proclaimed them mature, it was not a ring. Some Romano-British women might well have followed the indigenous tradition.

It is not only the marriage contract itself that can be symbolized by a ring. Both today and in the past, a ring may be a record of betrothal in advance of the formal wedding, or may serve simply as an informal token of love or friendship. Certain late Roman and Byzantine rings are decorated with busts of a man and a woman, which, though not realistic portraits, are probably intended to represent the betrothed couple, but more common are rings that bear the device of clasped right hands (*dextrarum iunctio*), generally regarded as betrothal or marriage rings since the handshake signified a contract. The tradition of rings as gifts between lovers rather than specific marriage rings also goes back to the Roman period, and such gifts are identifiable by the inscriptions they bear. Phrases like

Figure 1.1 A gold ring from Colchester, set with a finely engraved garnet depicting Cupid with a herm and a goose. (Photo: British Museum)

amo te (I love you) appear on Classical jewellery as well as contemporary popular ornaments. Jewellery that openly declares material riches or social position is intended to be "read" and understood by others, but love-tokens, even if clearly displayed, have a more private, talismanic function, reinforcing the bond which they express. Medieval "posy rings", which bore a motto, often of a pious nature (a "poesie") were often inscribed on the interior of the band, and this is still a favoured position for personal dedications and messages of affection. Such inscriptions may be kept completely private, known only to the giver and the recipient of the gift. They may be regarded in much the same light as the amuletic jewellery which forms a wide-ranging class in antiquity and is still more important today than is commonly realized.

Amuletic jewellery

A great deal is known about pagan Graeco-Roman religion and mythology, and it is therefore not difficult to identify elements from these beliefs in objects such as engraved gems. Equivalent elements from Celtic beliefs are far harder to recognize and define, and we must frequently rely on guesswork. Once again, we find that there are modern parallels for the meanings and significance attached to personal ornament, although they may not be immediately obvious. It has already been demonstrated that the initial assumption, referred to above, that in modern society jewellery is worn only for its decorative value, is a very superficial judgement, and that wealth and various aspects of social status remain part of the system behind the choice and wearing of personal ornament. Yet religious and superstitious impulses also play their part even today.

The most obvious parallel in a modern European country is the wearing of a Christian symbol, namely a cross or crucifix. The extent to which the emblem is truly a statement of religious belief is very variable. The author well remembers, as a pupil in a very traditional and academic English girls' school many years ago, the popularity of gold pendants in the form of crosses or Stars of David. Only "religious" jewellery was permitted to be worn with school uniform, and many of the schoolgirls invoked their Christian or Jewish affiliations as an acceptable reason for wearing an article of adornment, even where the religious conviction was fairly lukewarm. The committed Christian may wear a crucifix solely as a reminder of his or her belief in redemption dearly bought by a saviour both human and divine; the mixed motivation of the person who wants to wear an attractive decoration which also has an acceptable symbolic devotional meaning is probably more common, and it is more than likely that there are even those who wear such pendants in spite of having only the haziest idea of their meaning. A London anecdote of the 1990s, surely based on fact, refers to a young saleswoman who offers the potential buyer the choice of a plain cross or one "with the little man on it".

Another example of Christian symbolism in modern jewellery is the St Christopher emblem. In the Middle Ages, numerous saints and martyrs, identified by distinctive attributes (often the instruments of their martyrdom), were depicted in applied art and were understood to have special powers of protection appropriate to their own individual histories. St Christopher has retained his significance as a patron saint of travellers even in late twentieth-century Britain. Travel is a frequent activity and a hazardous one in our society, but it is none the less hard to say why the image of this saint in particular is still widely perceived as apotropaic. It seems fair to assume that most of those who carry a St Christopher image on their person or in their car do so in a superstitious rather than religious spirit; the parallel with the use of religious charms in antiquity may be quite close.

The dividing line between superstition and religion will always be contentious, and will depend to some extent on the observer's own beliefs, but it seems appropriate to draw attention to some of the modern superstitious symbols in jewellery that have no apparent connection with religious belief.

Two that are particularly significant because they relate directly to ancient beliefs concern the zodiac signs and "birthstones". Jewellery that incorporates symbols from the twelve signs of the zodiac is so widespread that few modern Europeans think twice about it. A person's star-sign is casually regarded as a fortunate symbol, even by those who have little time for superstition and who would certainly not claim a deep-seated conviction in the efficacy of such a symbol in attracting good fortune. The history of the zodiac symbols extends well back into antiquity, and their appeal may be a combination of their venerable history and the distinctive and attractive appearance of many of the signs themselves.

The notion of "birthstones" sounds like the purest Victorian sentimentality, but it may be part of a tradition that goes back to ancient beliefs about gems. The symbolism and alleged mystic powers of crystals and coloured stones is still taken very seriously by many people today. Those without any belief in gem symbolism might still select a gem-set item of jewellery with a stone thought to be appropriate to their month of birth rather than one chosen only for its colour or reflective properties. Some of the meanings attached to certain gemstones in antiquity or the medieval period have been largely forgotten: amethyst is now regarded as the birthstone for February or for the star-sign of Aquarius, but few remember that it was once said to protect the wearer against intoxication. The significance lies not so much in the precise interpretation as in the fact that a mauve or purple quartz may still be regarded as having some special power. Some people also continue to be concerned about the negative symbolism of pearls ("pearls for tears") and of opals, though pearls also have an image of purity and innocence which still makes them popular for very young women and brides. Belief in the mystic powers of hardstone crystals is thus still present at various levels of consciousness, and even those who do not share it should be able to understand the way in which the Graeco-Roman world perceived these natural wonders.

Other symbols that are popular in modern jewellery were unknown to the ancients: horseshoes, four-leaved clover and heather now denote good fortune, as does the number 13 in some countries. Black cats are a post-medieval symbol of luck. Modern communications and advertising spawn unexpected and ephemeral images, such as cartoon characters, which are utilized in personal adornment and would be meaningless to an observer distanced by time or place from the culture concerned. The frequency of such images in contemporary life may not have been reflected precisely in antiquity, but similar circumstances, equally impossible for another culture to interpret, may have obtained. An example would be a visual image which referred to some folk saying or proverb that has not been preserved in the written record.

However, much of the imagery in Roman jewellery is perfectly straightforward for us to read and interpret. Most obvious are the representations of deities, usually on engraved gems which were set into jewels, typically rings. We find hardstones with depictions of most of the major gods and goddesses of Graeco-Roman mythology, and we can assume that the wearers would have exercised some conscious choice when they preferred one over the other. Animal or inanimate attributes of deities were often depicted on their own, and were understood to stand for a particular god or goddess: a panther or a wine-cup was as unmistakably a Bacchic device as a picture of the god Bacchus himself.

Some symbols were significant in their own right, and they will be discussed in more detail when referring to specific examples of their use in Roman Britain. Wheels and crescents were widely understood as solar

Figure 1.2 Gold snake-ring of type A i from Chesterford, Essex. British Museum. (Photo: author)

Figure 1.3 A very small gold ring from Faversham, Kent, with a phallus decorating the bezel as a good-luck device. British Museum. (Photo: author)

and lunar emblems, and jewellery incorporating these signs was found throughout the Roman Empire. The symbolism would have been meaningful to the native populations of the northern provinces as well as to those of Mediterranean origin. Direct phallic imagery, on the other hand, seems to have been absent in pre-Roman Celtic art but was an important vehicle for expressing apotropaic power which had a long tradition in Roman culture, and it began to appear in a variety of contexts, including jewellery, as provinces were romanized. Snake jewellery is another specific class of ornament with complex symbolic meanings derived entirely from Graeco-Roman thought but apparently accepted and adopted by Romano-Celtic wearers.

The nature of the evidence: materials

Before we turn to a survey of the types of jewellery worn in Roman Britain, and to the combined Celtic and Classical traditions that lie behind them, there is one more theme that needs to be explored to help our understanding of the subject as a whole. In the foregoing pages, I have already alluded to the special problems of interpretation that affect the study of archaeological finds, but the matter needs to be set out more fully.

Jewellery historians studying recent periods are able to base their conclusions on a combination of the surviving objects and the written and visual evidence relating to them. Some literary and pictorial evidence does indeed exist for the Roman period, but its relevance to a frontier province like Britain can be problematic. Documents ranging from the technical writings of Pliny to the biting satire of Juvenal mention jewellery in various contexts, and sculpture often depicts personal ornament in use, but the actual surviving objects still form the greater part of the data and this fact is a source of specific strengths and weaknesses. The jewels them-selves have existed since antiquity, and have usually been buried and unearthed, so that their state of preservation is often imperfect. The different materials and techniques used in the manufacture of jewellery are thus relevant not only for the specific study of technological history but also for their influence on this matter of physical condition.

In Roman times, as in most other periods, much of the finest work was carried out in the most precious metal, gold. The incorruptibility of gold enables it to survive the ages in virtually perfect condition, and gold objects therefore preserve for us a clear and accurate picture of their in-tended appearance when new. This circumstance also enables us to infer details about the methods used in the manufacture of the object, because traces of these processes survive undamaged by surface deterioration. Silver also frequently survives in good condition and appears much as it did in antiquity. Gold and silver jewellery, with or without gems, will therefore form a major part of the evidence considered in the following pages, but it would be impossible to gain any idea of the general taste in ornament that prevailed during the centuries when Britain was part of the Roman Empire if base-metal and non-metallic jewellery were excluded. Above all, the complex interaction between the two cultural traditions would be hard to perceive. On the whole, precious-metal jewellery was inclined to reflect Graeco-Roman ideals of design and symbolism, while Celtic taste tended to be more overtly represented in bronze ornaments. Many common types of Romano-British bronze brooch were probably never manufactured in gold or silver. The fact, noted by Higgins, that Celtic traditions appear to be more obvious in some of the non-precious ornaments adds to their interest and relevance if our wider aim is to understand more about Romano-British life and society.

Bronze, a mixture of copper with other metals, was extensively employed, especially for brooches. Numerous alloys of copper were in use in Roman Britain containing varying proportions of tin, zinc and lead; in many, perhaps most, cases, specific mixes of metal were very pre-cisely selected to suit the intended use and appearance of the object and the technology required for its manufacture. It is impossible to determine the exact composition of a metal without scientific examination, so a practice has grown up in the academic archaeological literature of refer-ring to all such metals as "copper alloys" unless analysis has taken place to define them as "bronze", "brass" or "gunmetal" (though these three desig-nations are in fact insufficient to cover the range of possibilities). This pedantic caution is quite unnecessary in view of the fact that in English the words "brass" and "bronze" have both traditionally meant copper alloy. Throughout this book, all copper alloys will normally be referred to as bronze.[2]

Figure 1.4 Pelta-shaped bronze brooch with coloured enamel decoration; from Castor, Northamptonshire. Width 4.2 cm. (Photo: British Museum)

A certain amount of imagination is needed to envisage the original appearance of bronze ornaments. We cannot say whether the metal was always brightly polished or whether it was sometimes allowed to develop a natural brown patina, but both these effects are quite different from the green surface that is the usual result of burial. The lustrous sage-green or dark green of many well-preserved ancient bronzes is beautiful in itself, and it requires a mental effort to remember that this effect was not desired or aimed for by the original manufacturers and owners. Some alloys would have closely resembled the colour and lustre of gold when new and well polished.

Iron was the appropriate metal for weaponry and for a whole range of everyday and specialized tools. Less obviously to us, it was also used for jewellery, although the manufacturing techniques required would have differed from those employed for bronze and precious-metal ornaments. A plough-coulter or sword-blade of iron, heavily rusted after two millennia underground, may still be recognizable and capable of being handled and studied, but a finger-ring or brooch of the same material may be too fragile and altered in appearance to be reconstructed, so our knowledge of iron jewellery is somewhat limited. We cannot even say for certain whether there may have been styles that were characteristic of iron jewellery, just as there are bronze ornaments of types that are apparently absent from the precious-metal repertoire. As with bronze, it is important to call to mind the appearance of iron when new and polished. It would have looked very like silver.

Britain's wealth in natural resources was actively exploited under Roman administration. Other metals available included lead and tin, both used on their own account and in the alloying of copper to make various types of bronze. Combined in the alloy known as pewter, lead and tin were extensively used in the later Roman period for metal tableware, but these metals are not particularly suitable for jewellery manufacture, and are rarely found in that form. Tin-plating on bronze was an important decorative technique, however, being used either to give an overall silvery appearance to a bronze object, or for partial plating to provide a colour contrast with the gold-coloured metal. Gilding and silver-plating were practised, and a range of other techniques was in use to provide colour contrasts in the completed ornament, principally enamelling. We shall consider the technology involved in Chapter 8.

Jewellery, in our definition, is not necessarily made of metal at all. Non-metallic jewellery includes items made of glass, bone, ivory, jet and shale, and amber, as well as the precious and semi-precious stones and pearls that were commonly used in association with metal. Wood must also have been used for inexpensive pins, beads and bangles, but its chances of surviving in a recognizable form are poor. The question of differential survival is always a central one in evaluating archaeological data, and must constantly be borne in mind when we try to envisage how popular or common certain artefacts were.

Glass is both fragile and re-usable, characteristics that militate against the survival of complete objects, but even so, we can say that it was widely used in Romano-British jewellery. Glass settings in place of hardstone, sometimes moulded in close imitation of engraved gems, are frequent finds, as are glass beads. The material was also used for bracelets and finger-rings. Beads, especially very small ones, can be difficult or impossible to reconstruct into their original associations – for example, some beads may have been sewn on to garments rather than strung as necklaces or incorporated into metal jewellery, and this fact could only emerge in the case of careful excavation of an inhumation burial.

Hardstones are most commonly represented in Romano-British jewellery by semi-precious quartzes such as amethyst, chalcedony and carnelian. Garnets and emeralds were widely used in Roman jewellery throughout the Empire, though the latter were not normally engraved. Sapphires also occur, but I know of no example of a diamond found in a piece of Roman jewellery from Britain, and rubies were virtually unknown. Pearls, however, were not only highly prized and frequently used, but were actually obtainable in British waters; they are listed alongside other natural resources of Britain by Tacitus.[3] Pearls do not survive burial very well, often perishing completely.

Jet and amber both had traditional uses in jewellery going back to the Bronze Age in Britain.[4] Added to their attractive appearance is the fact that both materials have electrostatic properties, which would undoubtedly have given them additional cachet as amulets. Elaborately carved amber items are not often found in Roman Britain and neither is coral, another material that was regarded by Romans as amuletic, but jet and similar black substances were extensively used for decorative pendants, beads, rings, pins and bracelets. Bone and ivory, too, were in common use, and were often intricately carved.

Figure 1.5 Two jet hairpins with faceted heads. From a Roman grave at Lincoln. Length 5.4 cm and 7.7 cm. British Museum. (Photo: author)

Wooden ornaments must have been commonplace in Roman Britain, but our knowledge of them is extremely limited. Beads, hairpins and bracelets are the most obvious items that might have been made of wood. Up to the present day, certain natural objects, such as shells and seeds, have served as beads, and it seems very likely that materials of this nature would have been employed in Roman Britain, but identification of jewellery of this kind would require a fortunate combination of circumstances.

The nature of the evidence: archaeological context

As I have already indicated, small Roman objects in museum collections and elsewhere have nearly all at some time been buried in the ground. They have come to light in various ways and circumstances, some of which provide more information than others. The inferences that can be drawn from objects that have been dug up are affected both by the circumstances in which they came to be in the ground and those in which they were removed from it. Older museum collections often contain items that have no recorded history, since many of the details that we now deem vital seemed unimportant to our forebears. Such objects may be closely classifiable and datable in themselves, and may therefore possess some intrinsic interest, but if we do not know where and how they were found and whether they were associated with other objects, their value in research is limited.

The principles behind the concept of archaeological association are sometimes misunderstood. Objects that were deposited together on a single occasion, for example as a cache or hoard or in a grave, or those that are found in a single level in a stratified site – that is, they were lost or discarded at about the same time on an occupied site – are said to be associated. If some of these items are intrinsically datable – coins come to mind – all the better, but even if they are not, the construction of a pattern of such associated finds helps to create a relative chronological framework. Associated finds and "sealed deposits" (those that cannot have been contaminated by later deposits, for example, finds that lie beneath an impermeable and undamaged floor level) are fundamental to the understanding of material culture and the development of specific types of artefact. Two Roman objects found in the same field at a similar depth on the same day are not *associated* in the archaeological sense.

There used to be only two ways in which archaeological finds came to light; by accident, while the finder was engaged in some manual activity, usually gardening, agriculture, or building work, or by design, during some form of archaeological research. Since the aims and principles of archaeological excavation have changed enormously over the last hundred years or so, deliberately excavated eighteenth- and nineteenth-century finds are often as poorly documented by our standards as those that were found by some unlettered farmworker, but this is not true of material found in more recent times. Excavated objects will be from a precise location and their relationship with other finds will be noted, while accidental finds may have little or no ancillary information. The principles of archaeological stratification and association were not fully established until the late 1920s, and we cannot expect all the information that we would like to have to be available in the case of material found in earlier times.

There is now a third method of discovery, and this is particularly relevant to our present subject, since so much jewellery is made of metal. The use of metal-detecting devices has developed into a popular leisure activity in late twentieth-century Britain, and treasure-hunting with such machines has become a major source of discovery of metal antiquities. Users of metal-detectors may have very different motivations. They range from the frankly dishonest individuals who hope to find objects of value that they can turn into cash, regardless of their legal ownership, to people who have a genuine interest in history and who liaise with professional archaeologists, refrain from damaging known sites, and do their best to record the location and archaeological associations of their discoveries. While the former kind of treasure-hunter causes untold and irreversible damage to the national heritage, members of the latter group come to understand that the objective is the increase of knowledge rather than an ever-increasing list of objects, and they can therefore make an important contribution to archaeological research.

According to its mode of discovery and the records made or neglected by the finders, the object that we ultimately examine in a museum collection may be able to provide us with an array of useful additional information or it may be a single and unprovenanced find that can be studied only in isolation. Even in the latter case, however, it may be possible to compare it with better-documented finds, so that it may still have a significant contribution to make to knowledge.

The circumstances in which the artefact came to be in the ground are also of central importance in interpretation. Some materials can be recycled, metals and glass amongst them, and many pieces of base-metal or precious-metal jewellery must have disappeared in the past because they were melted down to be recreated in a different form. Those that found their way into the ground did so in some instances by accident and in others through deliberate burial. Unstratified stray or surface finds and single items painstakingly excavated in a datable level on a settlement site very frequently have this in common: their original owner simply lost them and failed to recover them again. Anybody who has managed to lose a small object totally and irrevocably in a restricted indoor space will have no difficulty envisaging the ease with which an item like a coin or earring can disappear. Such casual losses are unlikely to tell us a great deal about the significance or use of the object to its owner: the fact that it was lost and not found again certainly does not imply that it was not valued.

Deliberate deposition can take place for a variety of reasons. The burial of personal ornaments with the dead was a common practice in many societies, and can be an important source of information. Cremation burials, which were the norm in the early Roman period, are useful only up to a point. Obviously grave-goods that were actually burnt with the body are generally damaged beyond recognition, but those that were placed with an urn containing cremated bone are significant because we can take them to represent valued possessions of a single individual, buried at a specific point in time, that person's death. The same is true of jewellery in inhumation burials, but these have additional potential for information: the way in which the body was laid out and the position of the jewellery in relation to the skeleton may be able to tell us how and where the items were worn. Furthermore, the sex and the approximate age of the individual can usually be established by professional examination of the bones, the presence or absence of other grave-goods may give indications of his or her material wealth and status in the community, and a fairly sound chronology for graves can often be devised, based on grave-goods such as coins and pottery.

All in all, therefore, it would appear that a Roman inhumation cemetery with grave-goods including jewellery should answer a lot of our questions. The first difficulty is simply that it was only in some periods that bodies were inhumed, and that it was not always the custom to bury jewellery with the deceased. There are other, less obvious, pitfalls in the way of straightforward interpretation. One concerns the date of personal ornaments buried with their owner: even if the date of burial can be established quite closely, for instance by the presence of coins in the total assemblage, this proves only that the jewellery was current at *or before* that date. It may have been brand-new at the time of the wearer's death, or it may have been in use for many decades – even longer if it was an inherited heirloom. This heirloom factor is comparatively unimportant with some everyday items which were buried with the dead, such as pottery, but must be taken into account with intrinsically valuable objects like precious-metal jewels.

Another potential uncertainty affects the actual types of jewellery and the way in which they seem to have been disposed upon a body. We cannot always be certain that the items were worn in exactly the same way as they were in life. The deceased person may have been dressed in his or her best clothes, with rings, necklaces, belts and the like as they would have wished to be seen on a special occasion during their lifetime, but there are other possibilities too. The body may have been wrapped in a shroud, with jewels and other possessions simply placed upon or alongside it, or there may even have been special garments for burial, decorated with ornaments that were not worn by living people. These situations could give rise to misinterpretation of excavated remains, since the textiles will have decayed and we are normally left with a skeleton into which the more robust artefacts have become intermingled.

Even assumptions about ornaments appropriate to males and females must be carefully examined when they are founded upon the interpretation of graves. Modern excavators of inhumation burials will arrange for skeletal remains to be studied by a specialist whose report will include determination of the sex of the bodies. In most cases, skeletons can be sexed with a fair degree of certainty. In the past, however, unconsciously sexist thinking sometimes led to the casual assumption that a burial accompanied by weapons must be that of a man, while one containing jewellery could only be that of a woman; sexing was done by means of the grave-goods, not the human remains themselves. We must be aware of the possible effect of this approach in the past.

Hoards

Hoards constitute the third important type of archaeological find, after site finds and burials. Groups of objects concealed for safekeeping in the Roman period were frequently, but not invariably, gold or silver in the form of coins, jewellery or plate (tableware and other utensils). Seldom found in planned excavation, treasure hoards generally used to be discovered by accident, but are now frequently located by users of metal-detectors, so the advances in archaeological techniques and recording that have been applied to finds from settlement sites and cemeteries have rarely been available to illuminate assemblages of this kind. The discovery of the late Roman hoard at Hoxne, Suffolk, in 1992, was an honourable exception, as the finder alerted the authorities in time for a controlled professional excavation to take place.

Each hoard of treasure represents an associated group of objects, and if it includes coins the date of the latest issues will normally point to the date of deposition. Patterns of association within and between hoards enable an overall dating framework to be built up and linked with finds from other sources. The heirloom factor mentioned in connection with graves must still be reckoned with in treasure caches, and it is by no means unusual for gold or silver objects buried on a single occasion to have been manufactured over a period of three generations or so.

Hoards of coins or jewellery were often deposited in a container such as a pottery jar or a metal vessel, and where a pot is included it may sometimes prove to be one of the most reliably datable objects in the group. Unfortunately, amateur finders of treasure all too often break or discard a pottery container, regarding it as unimportant compared with the precious metal items inside.

Because the burial of valuables for safekeeping and the owner's failure to recover them may be prompted by times of danger such as war or insurrection, there is a tendency for archaeologists to try to link such finds with known historical events. Treasures found in Roman Britain are regularly dated by reference to the Roman conquest in AD 43, the rebellion of the native queen Boudicca in AD 60/61, and the various upheavals of the fourth century, culminating in the final phases of the province at the beginning of the fifth century AD. While many treasures may indeed have been hidden for safety at such times of stress, we should remember that valuable possessions may be buried for purely personal reasons that do not appear in any ancient documents. The owner may have caused his wealth to be hidden simply because he was embarking on a long journey for business or family reasons, and the heavy taxation in the Roman world may have been a factor in some instances. We should also bear in mind that we know of only some of the political and military happenings of antiquity: others that are unrecorded and forgotten may have been equally compelling influences at the time.

Summary

The purpose of this chapter has been to set the scene for the discussions that follow. It may appear at times that I have strayed somewhat from the central theme of personal ornament in Roman Britain, but before we can begin to assess the evidence that will be presented and evaluated in the rest of this book, it is essential to be familiar with some of the underlying principles and limitations of archaeological research. We are entitled to ask any questions about the people of the past that our own curiosity may suggest, but we have to acknowledge that some can never be answered, and should understand why this is so. In spite of the limitations, there is still much to be learnt.

Chapter 2

The two traditions:
Celtic and Graeco-Roman

The interaction of two or more cultural traditions is one of the most fascinating phenomena that can be studied in human society, for it can lead either to intense and mindless conflict or to innovation, growth and enrichment – or indeed, both, at different phases of the relationship. It is complex and obscure even in its effects on contemporary societies and is often capable of widely differing interpretations, since few observers, being human themselves, are wholly neutral and objective in their opinions. Several references have already been made to the fact that the culture of Roman Britain combined elements from the Celtic and pre-Celtic traditions of the indigenous population and those of the Graeco-Roman world which were introduced when the country became a province of the Roman Empire. Most students of Roman Britain have fairly strong views on the extent to which Roman culture succeeded or failed in changing the underlying attitudes and behaviour of the population.

In modern times, imperialist powers have been inclined to display a patronizing arrogance towards the peoples of the countries that have come under their administration, and it would be idle to pretend that this attitude was absent in the Roman military commanders and civilian authorities in Britannia or other provinces. Roman administrators saw themselves as introducing a higher standard of civilization to those under their rule and considered it their duty to ensure that it was fully embraced and absorbed by the provincials; this view was also accepted without question by eighteenth- and nineteenth-century English scholars, who identified with the Roman conquerors rather than with the indigenous British population of antiquity. Modern scholarship may have moved too far in the opposite direction, stressing the undoubted vitality of the British Celtic tradition, and dismissing *romanitas* as a short-lived overlay that left no lasting effects. The truth lies somewhere in between these extremes, and the study of material remains can never tell us the whole story.

Personal ornament in Late Iron Age Britain

The art of the prehistoric Celts was one of the great achievements of antiquity, and metalwork was a major vehicle for its display and the principal one for its survival. This range of metalwork includes personal ornament both in gold and humbler materials. Continental and British Celtic art of the pre-Roman Iron Age is well documented in many excellent publications, so we need do no more here than make a few general points about its characteristics.[1]

Celtic art has been described by expert critics as having a "determined non-narrative quality".[2] It is not quite true to say that it is wholly abstract or non-figurative: many of the patterns have their origins in natural forms, plants and even animals, and the decorative aesthetic of the continental Celts was influenced by the Classical world and the themes that were the basis of Classical decoration. These include floral and foliate scrolls, which can easily be reduced to an abstract form in which the original naturalistic form is no longer detectable. The stylistic gulf between insular (i.e. British and Irish) Celtic art of the second and first centuries BC and Mediterranean prototypes was considerable, yet the influence of the latter was not wholly lost.

Common to Celtic art over a wide chronological and geographical span is an exquisite sense of balance in the layout and development of patterns. Curvilinear forms are set out so that positive and negative, filled areas and spaces, form a harmonious whole. Control and restraint were exercised in the use of surface texturing and relief. Very complex curvilinear patterns were designed to cover precisely the most awkward and irregularly shaped surfaces. The decoration on the terminals of some of the Snettisham torcs illustrates this very clearly.

As we shall see, the work of Greek and Hellenistic goldsmiths was technically of the highest order, but in certain respects, it would not be overstating the case to say that their designs were less sophisticated. In aiming to imitate nature closely, their principles and parameters were fairly straightforward: Celtic metalsmiths were going well beyond the concept of naturalistic art or the geometric patterns of their Bronze Age predecessors and making their own rules of form and balance, rules that produced work that still appears striking and distinctive today. Celtic tastes and sensibilities in decoration can quite easily be perceived in certain Romano-British objects, where they provide evidence of the continuing indigenous tradition in the Roman provincial environment. Apologists for the importance of the native element in Romano-British culture may have overstressed the point, but the influence is present and is fundamental to the special character of Romano-British art.

Prehistoric Celtic craftsmen were pre-eminent in metal technology as well as in artistic expression. The fashioning of gold, bronze and iron into objects of use and ornament was one of the outstanding skills of the Celts of northern Europe, and the tradition of high-quality metalworking, whether in the manufacture of jewellery or of weapons, armour, horse-trappings or domestic equipment, was extremely highly developed in pre-Roman Britain. New types of metal artefacts were introduced as part of Roman culture, but it is unlikely that the local population would have been especially impressed by their standard of workmanship, even though they might have been intrigued by the unfamiliar and exotic designs. In some respects, Celtic expertise and creativity in metalworking was more advanced than that of the Mediterranean world; for example, iron chain armour, which became standard in the armies of imperial Rome, was invented and developed in Celtic lands around 300 BC.[3]

Gold jewellery in Late Iron Age Britain was itself indirectly the heir to an even older tradition, that of the Bronze Age, the period when gold first seems to have become a significant indicator of wealth and social position. Gold ornaments of the British Bronze Age include bracelets, torcs (neck-rings) and so-called ring-money (small penannular rings) that demonstrate complete mastery of goldworking techniques and a sophisticated sense of design. Though the delicate and intricate nature of Greek and Hellenistic goldworking conveys an immediate impression of outstanding skill, we should be conscious of the high level of competence that was also exercised by northern European prehistoric goldsmiths. By the time Britain became a province of the Roman Empire in AD 43, the mastery demonstrated in the manufacture of precious-metal and base-metal ornaments was as ancient and in its own way as consummate as that of the Roman conquerors.

The outstanding characteristic of gold ornaments both of the British Late Bronze Age and Iron Age is that they appear bold and solid, often employing lavish quantities of the precious metal. Some of the elegantly simple bracelets of the Late Bronze Age can weigh more than 200 g each, while the most flamboyant of the Iron Age gold and silver alloy torcs may weigh as much as 2.5 kg. The very concept of the torc, the archetypal personal ornament of the Celtic world, is that of a large, heavy and impressive gold neck decoration.

This is not to say that devices whereby the jeweller makes the most of a given quantity of precious metal were unknown even in the earliest times. The graceful Irish Early Bronze Age neck-ornaments that are known as lunulae from their crescentic shape must have had substantial visual impact in wear, although they are made of sheet gold and in some cases used less than 2.5 g of the metal. They date to around 2000–1800 BC.

Figure 2.1 Bronze Age gold lunula from Llanllyfni, Gwynedd, Caernarfon. (Photo: British Museum)

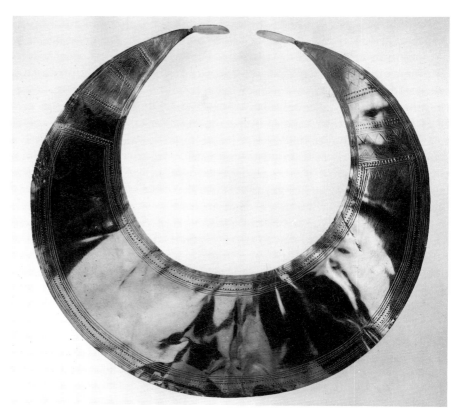

We are unable to say whether the sparing use of gold in such instances depended on actual value by weight or simply on availability at a given time, but it does demonstrate an impulse to produce the maximum visual effect. Lunulae were basically an Irish type, but examples have been found in western areas of Britain, and the influence of the deep, collar-like form may be traced in other Bronze Age jewellery, the collars made of amber in the south and jet in the north, formed of beads and spacers put together to form a crescentic ornament.

The technical expertise of the Late Bronze Age is demonstrated in the fine and extremely accurate engraving of geometric patterns on gold, the difficult and visually effective technique of flange-twisting, and the two-colour goldwork seen on some of the ring-money. Goldsmithing and design of the British Iron Age was not the direct heir of the preceding era, as gold ornaments do not feature at all in the earlier phases of the British Iron Age, but there was a continuing tradition favouring bold and bulky ornaments. Pre-eminent amongst these are the torcs with large terminals elaborately decorated in curvilinear patterns.

Torcs

A torc may be defined briefly as a decorative metal neck-ring. While some designs were less rigid than others, all are clearly distinguishable from flexible necklaces made of metal chains or beads and pendants strung on thread. The word "torc", or "torque", is derived directly from Latin (*torquis,* related to the verb *torqueo,* to twist), but while many torcs of both Bronze Age and Iron Age date indeed have a twisted appearance, this is not an invariable feature.

Classical authors alluded to torcs as characteristically Celtic ornaments, worn by fighting men in battle. The famous Pergamene statue of the Dying Gaul, dating to the third century BC (known in a Roman copy) conforms precisely to the verbal descriptions that we read in authors such as Polybius, describing the battle of Telamon in 225 BC, of a nearly naked mustachioed warrior, his hair swept up into a spiky mane and his neck adorned with a heavy, twisted gold ring.[4] The image of the golden neck-ornament as an attribute of authority and warlike power is also confirmed in the famous description by Cassius Dio of the British queen Boudicca calling her army to action against the Romans. He paints a vivid picture of a tall, loud-voiced woman with long, tawny hair and colourful garments including brooches and a "golden ornament" around her neck.[5] Although the Greek text does not specify the ornament, the general assumption that it was a torc seems plausible, even though the middle of the first century AD would be late for the wearing of such an item. Dio was writing 200 years after the event, so his words are very far from being an eyewitness account, but whether or not Boudicca actually donned a gold neck-ring to lead her troops against the Romans, the implication that a gold collar was appropriate for a Celtic leader and warlord is significant. Both literary and artistic references from the Classical world concur in attributing some special power-symbolism to torcs. Torcs formed part of the spoil if a Celtic army was defeated, and we know of a Roman, T. Manlius Torquatus, who earned his name by taking a torc from a fallen Gaulish warrior. Torcs became a recognized form of military decoration in the Roman army.[6]

Precious-metal torcs are generally found in hoard contexts, but bronze neck-rings from early pre-Roman Celtic Gaul (5th–4th century BC) are typically found in *female* graves, demonstrating that the solid metal neck-ring was not the sole preserve of the male warrior, but evidently also the mark of the adult woman. Many of these are elaborately decorated and very cunningly manufactured to form what appears to be a complete, unbroken circle. One of the most famous gold continental torcs of the fourth century BC, which has given its name to one of the phases of continental Celtic art, from Waldalgesheim in Germany, is also from a woman's grave.[7]

Figure 2.2 The Iron Age gold torc from Sedgeford, Norfolk. Although the finely twisted hoop of the neck-ring is damaged, the surviving terminal is a particularly fine example of Celtic design. (Photo: British Museum)

It has been widely accepted that the wearing of torcs was outdated on the Continent by the first century BC, although the custom was still part of the visual and literary image of the Celt, and survived well into Roman times as an attribute of gods and goddesses. Some small bronze statuettes of deities such as Venus and Mercury from Roman Gaul have added gold or silver neck-rings. However, it is worth pointing out that the change may be more apparent than real: there was a change from inhumation to cremation in the burial rite, and one of the principal contexts for finds of torcs therefore disappeared amongst the continental Celts of late pre-history.[8]

Even in the early medieval literature of the Celtic world echoes survive of the importance of torc-wearing as a symbol of authority: Olwen in the

Figure 2.3 The great torc found at Snettisham, Norfolk, in 1951, one of the finest examples of Iron Age goldworking from Britain. (Photo: British Museum)

Welsh tale *Culhwch ac Olwen* is described as wearing a gold neck-ring, obviously a token of her royal status.[9] Olwen's torc was set with jewels, and the picture in the mind of the medieval writer was probably far removed from the actuality of Iron Age gold torcs, but the existence of an ancient tradition can hardly be denied.

The Snettisham Iron Age treasures

It was in Britain in the century preceding the Roman conquest, when torcs may already have been old-fashioned on the Continent, that some of the most impressive examples of this Celtic adornment were made in gold, silver and alloys of the two metals. The extraordinary treasures discovered in a field outside a north Norfolk village, Snettisham, include some of the finest specimens known. The largest and most splendid of the torcs found in accidental discoveries in 1948, 1949 and 1950 has now been joined by numerous other examples professionally excavated in 1990 and 1991 after a metal-detector find revealed the fact that there were yet more buried caches in the area. The significance of what seems to be a vast treasury of precious metal in the tribal area of the Iceni, Boudicca's tribe, is as yet by no means fully understood.[10]

The flamboyant gold neck-rings of the first century BC did not survive in use into the Roman period, but the skills of the craftsman and the existence of the raw materials would not have evaporated; they would have been available to be turned to other purposes. Certainly they are relevant factors when we come to consider the jewellery of the post-conquest period in Britain.

British Iron Age gold and silver jewellery was, as far as we can infer in the current state of knowledge, something more akin to royal regalia than to the personal decoration of a wealthy woman or man. The coming of Roman rule must have rendered it obsolete for political reasons, and the Classical gold jewellery that was introduced into the province was not a replacement for Snettisham-type torcs and bracelets, a mere change of fashion in dress accessories, but rather the appearance of a totally new class of jewellery.

Base-metal and other jewellery

The skills of the bronzesmith, as ancient and highly developed as those of the worker in precious metals, were also greatly prized in Celtic society, and Celtic decorative motifs are most frequently preserved on bronze objects such as horse- and vehicle-trappings, arms and armour. The use of red coral, an exotic import, as an inlay or setting to provide a brilliant colour contrast gave way in due course to red glass or enamel. By the first century AD, Celtic bronzesmiths on the Continent and in Britain had achieved total mastery of enamelling on bronze in a technological tradition that was separate from that of the Classical world.

One of the most typical items of human adornment was the practical clothes-fastener known as the fibula – the safety-pin with a spring and catch-plate that can clasp a thick fold of cloth. This indispensable article of dress, safer and more sophisticated than the simple dress-pin, was in use in both Mediterranean and northern European cultures, and its development under Roman rule in Britain continued without a pause; the same is true of the bracelets, in bronze and other materials, which were common to both traditions. The great majority of Romano-British fibulae were made of bronze, and it is not difficult to perceive an unbroken Celtic tradition in the design of many of them. Iron was frequently used for this type of brooch before the Roman conquest, but gradually became less common afterwards. Dress-pins were also part of the common cultural heritage of northern and southern Europe, and although they reappear in early medieval times, they are not very common in provincial Roman society, at least in durable materials. Many of the straight pins classified as hairpins could equally well have been used to secure clothing, but the sheer abundance of fibulae makes this unlikely.

Glass beads were known, especially blue-and-white ones, which may already have had the symbolic meaning that they still retain in many cultures today as charms against the Evil Eye. Organic materials such as wood must also have been used; as always, we are hampered by the problems of survival.

Before we move on to the jewellery traditions of the Graeco-Roman world, it is worth drawing attention to the types of ornament and the techniques that were uncommon, or unknown, in the pre-Roman society of Britain. In goldworking, the absence of fine wire is noteworthy, and hence, the absence of fine and delicate chains and of decorative work based on fine wire such as filigree and filigree enamelling, a form of *cloisonné* work. The hoops of the most elaborate and flexible torcs use gold wire of fairly robust gauge to produce twisted cables rather than putting them together as links to form a chain. These gold cables can incorporate as many as sixty-four separate thick gold wires in a single object. Chains in other metals, for practical uses including the joining of pairs of bronze fibulae, were of course perfectly familiar, and their absence in the most valuable gold jewellery is undoubtedly a matter of aesthetic preference, in which weight and bold impact were more highly prized than intricacy and flexibility.

The use of neck-ornaments, bracelets and fasteners such as fibulae and pins was common to both cultural traditions, but earrings and finger-rings were apparently not customary elements in the adornment of

British Celtic women. The use of gems in the strict sense of precious and semi-precious stones was also foreign to Celtic designs, although, as we have seen, other materials (glass, coral and enamel) were used in a similar manner as inlays and studs on metal to provide a contrast of colour and texture and no doubt some symbolic meaning as well. The engraving of hardstones as seals was wholly unknown.

The Graeco-Roman tradition

A variety of influences combined in Roman jewellery, and just as there are some common factors, however tenuous, between the goldwork of the Irish and British Bronze Age and that of the last century BC in Britain, there are likewise links in the development of Classical adornment that stretch back to Mycenean and Minoan times, and even indirectly to the ancient civilization of Egypt. But the immediate forerunner of the styles of precious-metal jewellery that became familiar throughout the Roman Empire was the jewellery of the Hellenistic world, with some surviving elements of Etruscan influence.

The finest gold jewellery of the Classical world, Greek, Etruscan, Hellenistic and Roman, is well known not only because many examples survive and are displayed in museums and published in attractive and well-illustrated books, but also because it has regularly inspired jewellers of recent times, from the eighteenth century to the present day.[11] *Greek gold* by Dyfri Williams and Jack Ogden is one of the best introductions to the subject now available. Tourists in modern Greece can still purchase extremely beautiful and high-quality gold jewellery based, sometimes quite precisely, on ancient prototypes. In modern terms, it is very much more wearable than the imposing gold ornaments of the northern European Iron Age.

Hellenistic gold jewellery: fourth to first century BC

Hellenistic gold jewellery differs from the products of the Celtic north in four fundamental respects: in purpose or function; in the techniques of the craftsman; in the range of decorative motifs favoured; and in the types of object made. Such jewellery was designed for wear by any owner who could afford to possess it, unlike the gold ornaments of Celtic Britain which were probably destined mainly for ceremonial use. It is true that in certain periods and places there were legal restrictions on the possession and display of gold ornaments. Various sumptuary laws were part of the development of the Roman legal system. The fifth-century BC Law of the Twelve Tables included strict limitations on the amount of gold that

Figure 2.4 Hellenistic gold diadem of the third to second century BC from Melos: the knot of Hercules in the centre (1.6 cm wide) is set with a garnet, and the centre-piece also features beaded wire, filigree enamel and tiny filigree flower-rosettes. (Photo: British Museum)

could be buried with the dead, a provision that would have exercised some control on the circulation of the precious metal, while the Lex Oppia of the third century BC forbade various kinds of conspicuous luxury including the wearing of more than half an ounce of gold at one time. This measure was in force for only twenty years, and was doubtless often flouted. Ways were also found to circumvent the rules of the Republic and early Empire that limited the wearing of gold rings to certain classes of person and certain occasions. These attempts to control the use and ownership of gold in the developing Roman Republic have little direct relevance to our main theme, although they do serve to illustrate the importance attached to the metal as an intrinsically valuable resource.

Notwithstanding these attempts at control, in the Hellenistic world as a whole gold jewellery was made in order to display wealth and aesthetic taste, and thereby, of course, to convey implications about social status. As far as we can tell, the elaborate diadems and earrings and necklaces were ornament, pure and simple, not direct symbols of office or authority.

Goldworking techniques

A more detailed description of the techniques mentioned here will be found in Chapter 8, but a general explanation of the technical approach of the Greek and Hellenistic goldsmith is needed because it is inextricably tied up with the subjects and appearance of the ornaments produced. In marked contrast to the bold and chunky effects sought by the Celtic goldsmith, the craftsman working in the Greek tradition aimed for delicacy and intricacy – even though the final effect might by no means be restrained and austere, but rather extremely rich and opulent. These

Figure 2.5 Etruscan gold fibula from Toscanella. The elaborate pattern is carried out in fine granulation; the overall length of the brooch is 8.9 cm. Seventh century BC. (Photo: British Museum)

Figure 2.6 A seventh century BC Etruscan sheet-gold ornament with fine granulation forming naturalistic as well as abstract patterns. The overall length of the ornament is 16.5 cm: the height of the human figures seen in the enlarged detail is less than 1 cm. From Tarquinia. (Photo: British Museum)

effects were achieved using gold sheet cut and shaped in various ways, and gold wire, often of extraordinarily fine gauge. Some of the sheet-gold work consisted simply of shapes cut from the metal, for example the leaves in some of the naturalistic wreaths, but sheet could also be embossed and shaped by repoussé and other techniques, and three-dimensional sections could be soldered together to produce hollow forms. Casting could also be used for solid three-dimensional forms.

Wire can be used to make chains of a great variety of types and can also serve as relief decoration applied to a plain gold background. The result is a texturing of the gold surface. Such filigree may be further embellished with coloured enamel, glass or gems. Granulation, the attachment of minute spheres or grains of gold to the plain background, was another method of producing an interestingly textured surface; it reached its apogee in Etruria in the seventh and sixth centuries BC, and although it continued to appear in various guises throughout antiquity, the astonishing achievements of the finest Etruscan work have never been matched, let alone surpassed. Although some skilled goldsmiths in the twentieth century have managed to reproduce the methods by which this remarkable effect was produced, Etruscan granulation remains by far the finest and most accomplished demonstration of the technique in existence, as well as the most pleasing to the eye. Granulation may consist of individual gold balls as large as a pin-head, but the best Etruscan work is of dust-fine granules that to the naked eye seem merely to create a matt surface as a contrast to smooth, polished gold. Granulation was used to create patterns on a plain surface as well as being employed to cover completely some elements in a design.

Fine wire was produced by twisting and rolling techniques rather than by drawing, which did not become standard until after the period we are concerned with here. The simple chain which consists of one circular or oval link attached to the next was not normally used in Greek and Hellenistic jewellery, although it does sometimes occur in Roman work. The standard construction consisted of preformed links folded into each other and joined, the loop-in-loop chain. This method can be adapted and evolved to produce very complex chains, including flat "straps" of interlocked loop-in-loop chains that look like a narrow strip of very fine knitting in stocking-stitch.

The use of very slender wire and sheet made the most of a given quantity of gold. Just as the Irish Bronze Age craftsman produced an imposing, gleaming lunula collar out of an ounce of gold or less, the Hellenistic goldsmith could create an elaborate necklace with a flexible strap-like chain and scores of dainty, individually decorated pendants out of about the same quantity of material.

This approach was part of a long-standing Greek tradition, but a new emphasis on polychrome effects using coloured hardstones and enamelling was a Hellenistic development. Blue and turquoise enamel on gold had first been used in the Mycenean period (c. 1400 BC), but the technique seems to have been reinvented more than once, with long intervening periods in which it was unknown. Filigree enamelling, in which the enamelled area is demarcated by applied wire, is the same concept as the *cloisonné* enamelling of later eras. The gemstone most frequently found in Hellenistic work is the garnet, which is employed not only as a normal circular setting but also as a shaped inlay to emphasize the form of a gold construction such as a knot of Hercules (Fig. 2.4). Garnets were also sometimes carved in cameo. The colour contrast of the intense and brilliant yellow of high-purity gold with the blood-red of garnets is spectacular. Other hardstones were also used in rings, engraved or plain, and as beads.

Decorative motifs

At the risk of oversimplification, it is possible to state that the ultimate difference between Celtic and Classical art is that while the former is basically abstract, the latter is naturalistic and figurative. The subtly judged balance of curved lines, filled areas and voids in Celtic decoration do, of course, owe much to naturalistic forms and indeed some of them can be traced back specifically to Classical floral scrolls and palmettes, but the Celtic artist and craftsman was less concerned about reproducing the appearance of natural objects than he was with devising a pleasing pattern.

The techniques referred to above for shaping and embellishing gold in Hellenistic times were applied to creating a variety of forms that included many based on plant, animal and human motifs. Some of the most extraordinary achievements of Greek and Hellenistic craftsmen are the golden wreaths that incorporate countless delicate flowers and leaves, a permanent and precious version of an actual floral garland. These wonderful examples of the goldsmith's art, some of them embellished with coloured enamels, stand near the beginning of a jewellery tradition that has sporadically produced masterpieces throughout history, from ancient Egypt to the sixteenth and nineteenth centuries AD.[12] Gold, with its exceptional malleability, lends itself well to the imitation of plant forms. Thin sheet gold will produce convincingly delicate flower-petals and leaves, and thin wire can even reproduce the curve of slender stems. The use of enamel and coloured stones can recall, if not wholly reproduce, the colours of flowers. Unashamedly elaborate and rich, the workmanship of some of these pieces is unrivalled.

Floral and foliate motifs were part of the artistic vocabulary of Greek and Hellenistic jewellers, and so in addition to these directly representational pieces, we find floral and leafy scrolls, palmettes and stylized rosettes used in various combinations with other motifs, for example as filigree decoration on plain gold surfaces.

Animal and human or divine figures also feature frequently in Hellenistic jewellery. Some of the complex earrings in particular serve as vehicles for minute figure-sculpture in gold, with tiny cupids and Victories depending from a rosette disc (Fig. 2.8). Although small when perceived as statuettes, some are quite large as jewels: a pair of pendant earrings with Victories in the British Museum have an overall length of over 7 cm each.[13] While modest compared with some gigantic Etruscan earrings designed to cover the whole ear, these are still quite flamboyant ornaments. The taste of our own time may be uncomfortable about such pieces, although our Victorian forebears had no such reservations, but we cannot deny the exquisite workmanship that they exhibit. Such creatures as birds, dolphins and centaurs are also found as pendants to gold earrings, and necklaces, diadems and the like sometimes included human and

Figure 2.7 A Hellenistic gold necklace from Tarentum. The chain is formed of floral and foliate elements and some spherical beads, all embellished with filigree work. Three-dimensional pendants hang from the band, large female heads, small heads and pointed acorns or seed-pods. Fourth century BC. (Photo: British Museum)

animal figures as pendants and other embellishments. Animal heads appear as terminals to penannular bracelets, a design that can be traced back to earlier Persian work. These include lions and lynxes, rams and deer, as well as snakes, which will be considered in more detail below.

Inanimate objects that had special significance in the jewellery of this period leading up to the development of the Roman Empire include knots of Hercules, crescents and amphorae and spearheads. The latter forms frequently appear as series of necklace-pendants, taking on an almost non-representational aspect. The knot of Hercules – in non-Classical terms, a reef-knot – has apotropaic powers, and is a decorative motif well suited to combining with the chains, straps and other elements that occur in jewellery. Crescents, too, have symbolic meaning, and first become common in jewellery of this period. As moon-symbols, they are later found paired with the wheel, an age-old sun-symbol, in Roman jewellery from all parts of the Empire.

At the risk of repeating the obvious, we should note again the mobility and flexibility of many of the ornaments featuring the floral and other naturalistic motifs described here. Wreaths with leaves and flowers on slender gold stems, earrings with pendant figures hanging from rings and wires, necklaces with a strap of complex fine chain, supporting rows of pendants dangling from chains, they are all jewels that move with the wearer. The contrast with the solemn immobility of a heavy Celtic torc is striking.

Snake jewellery

The introduction of snakes as an important motif in jewellery belonged to the Hellenistic period, and continued as an ongoing theme in the jewellery of the Roman Empire. It therefore has an immediate relevance to our story. The fashion for serpent jewellery was carried to all parts of the Empire, and snake-rings and -bracelets were manufactured in due course by Romano-British craftsmen.

In ancient Egypt, the Egyptian cobra or uraeus (*Naja haje*), a very large, venomous and dangerous reptile, had a special symbolic role as a royal creature, but the serpent image of the Classical world is a different creature, the Asclepian snake (*Elaphe longissima*) and its relatives. Although large, these snakes are not poisonous and they are not dangerous to any creature larger than a small rodent. Their significance in Classical mythology and symbolism is wholly beneficent and is concerned with healing, the underworld, regeneration and rebirth. The principal symbol of Asclepius, the deity most specifically connected with healing in the Graeco-Roman world, is the serpent, and these reptiles also served as symbols of departed souls and ancestors. Snakes were associated with several other deities in various myths. The negative symbolism of these creatures which has survived very strongly in European culture to the present day is almost certainly closely bound up with Christian mythology.

The very long slender form of the Asclepian snake and many other related species is well suited as a basis for designs of bracelets and rings. The body can be attenuated to form several coils around the arm or finger, and it is necessary only to taper the tail end and to form a simple rendering of the head to convey the idea of the animal. In fact, many Hellenistic snake-bracelets are quite complex, and have very elegantly formed heads, sometimes with gem-set eyes and stylized scaly surfaces. One famous example combines the symbolism of snakes and of the

Hercules knot: two snakes intertwine at the tail ends in a reef-knot that is decorated with a large cabochon garnet.[14] Snake-bracelets depicting a single animal, with single or multiple coils, and very often with extra twists and turns in the neck and the slender tip of the tail, continued to be fashionable well into the first century AD, and, as we shall see, can even be found in distant provinces like Britain.

At the same time as these ornaments were becoming popular, an ancient bracelet type was adapted to snake-jewellery, the open (penannular) ring with an animal head at each terminal. In the Roman period, we can thus distinguish two fundamental snake-bracelet types, the one that is formed from a single snake, head at one end, tail at the other, and the double-headed type. Snake finger-rings, of both types, also began to appear in the Hellenistic period.

The precise way in which the heads of the snakes were modelled is relevant in the identification of the species. Snakes of the family *Colubridae*, which includes the Asclepian snake and many others such as the grass-snake common in Britain, bear a distinctive symmetrical pattern of large scales on their heads, which were clearly depicted in Hellenistic and early imperial snake jewellery. This pattern can still be traced in a highly stylized form in the snake jewellery manufactured in Roman Britain, though some of these pieces are so devolved that their meaning would be impossible to infer if it were not for their known pedigree.

Types of ornament

Of the types of gold ornament that were foreign to the Celtic lands north of the Alps, most became part of the range of jewellery familiar in the Roman Empire, but there were two that had a long history in the Greek and Hellenistic world but did not survive into the Roman period, namely gold wreaths and diadems. The finest compositions of floral and foliate motifs in Hellenistic goldwork are to be found in these crowns, which were used as funerary ornaments and also as festive decorations in life.

Earrings with elaborate sculptural pendants have been mentioned, but there were also other types current at this period. While there was little direct connection between the elaborate ear ornaments of this period and the types that eventually came into use in Roman Britain, the very concept of a jewel set in the earlobe seems to have been a Roman introduction. Certain gold ornaments of the British Bronze Age were almost certainly worn as earrings, but that tradition had long been forgotten in the final century before the Roman occupation. Some early Roman types which found their way into provincial jewellery have more than a trace of Etruscan sensibility in their plain hemispherical forms.

Figure 2.8 An exceptionally elaborate Greek gold earring of the fourth to third century BC, one of a pair found at Kyme in Aeolis. The disc features beaded wire borders, spiral patterns in filigree and a multi-petalled floral rosette. The pyramidal central pendant is flanked by two three-dimensional figures of a winged Eros, and there are three additional figures in the design. Overall length 6.5 cm. (Photo: British Museum)

Necklaces also changed, and the exceptionally fine chains and multiple rows of pendants that we find in Hellenistic pieces did not survive into early imperial work. The necklaces that were disseminated into remote provinces with the expansion of the Empire were of simpler designs, but the basic concept, a supple and mobile neck ornament based on a chain and usually incorporating beads and pendants, had not altered.

Finger-rings already had a long history in the Graeco-Roman world, both as vehicles for seals in the form of engraved stones or engraved metal bezels and as purely decorative items. Some Hellenistic designs are very elaborate, with filigree and other surface ornamentation, but there were also simple styles based on a stone set in a smoothly profiled gold hoop. The most characteristic early Roman type of finger-ring follows the latter tradition.

Base-metal and other jewellery

The contrast between north and south illustrated in the gold ornaments of the last four or three centuries BC is not repeated in practical, everyday base-metal jewellery. In Etruria, Magna Graecia further south and in the Celtic territories north of the Alps, the evolution of the fibula proceeded along parallel lines. Other base-metal fasteners and clasps were in use, as were bead necklaces and simple bracelets. These objects were part of a common culture, and there is little evidence of direct influence one way or the other once the Roman Empire unified material culture across vast areas of Europe.

Chapter 3

Finger-rings

Finger-rings were to all intents and purposes a new type of jewellery in Roman Britain. Once introduced, they rapidly became extremely popular and were manufactured in everything from gold to less expensive materials like bone and jet. Consequently they must have been available to men and women from all levels of society. While most Romano-British rings can be slotted into a known typology that is applicable to the whole of the Roman Empire, no classification is perfect, and there are always some undatable types, local variants and other oddities that defy our attempts at systematic study. Many of these are interesting in themselves, so we shall look not only at the most diagnostic types of each chronological phase, but also pick out several other interesting forms, even if they have little value for dating, or are rare and exceptional. Initially it is useful to know which sources of reference are the most helpful for the identification and study of Roman rings.

An older publication that is still of considerable value today is F. H. Marshall's 1907 catalogue of Classical rings in the British Museum.[1] The British Museum's collection of ancient rings is an extensive and important one, so the catalogue remains an excellent source of reference. However, Marshall's system of classification is idiosyncratic and far from ideal, paying too much attention to superficial decoration and too little to form, so that rings of the same type and date are often widely separated in the sections of the book. Nor is the classification readily applicable to the study of provincial Roman material. Far more relevant is the most detailed and comprehensive Roman ring typology yet attempted, that devised by Friedrich Henkel in his 1913 publication, *Römische Fingerringe der Rheinlande*.[2] Although based on finds from the Rhineland and adjacent areas, it can be applied without any adaptation to Roman Britain, and remains an indispensable work. Henkel's typology is extremely complex and it has therefore rarely been directly employed, although the use of his catalogue has exercised an almost unconscious and decidedly beneficial influence on later research. The typology recently formulated by Hélène Guiraud for the study of ancient jewellery in France is also relevant and useful for Roman Britain,[3] while the simple typology for gem-set rings set out by Martin Henig in his corpus of gems from Roman Britain is likewise of value,[4] although it is not sufficiently detailed to cover all the developments of nearly four centuries of Roman occupation in Britain. Another helpful publication is a small catalogue written originally for a temporary exhibition of rings at the Ashmolean Museum, Oxford by Gerald Taylor and Diana Scarisbrick: it covers rings of all periods, but it is a scholarly survey that repays study.[5]

First- and second-century types

Henig II and III/Guiraud 2 rings

Everyone who has some acquaintance with Roman jewellery can envisage the "typical" Roman finger-ring; a heavy metal hoop with a smoothly swelling profile tapering from the narrow back of the hoop to a broader bezel that is set with an oval gemstone engraved with some device. The gem is almost flush with the surface of the ring, fitting its setting perfectly without need of a surrounding collet or claws to retain it. Modern jewellers still refer to this type of setting as "Roman". The Henig II–III/ Guiraud 2 class of ring is found in gold, silver, bronze, and iron, with a variety of engraved and plain hardstone and glass settings, for a period of over 200 years. Non-metallic rings also echoed the shape. It can justly be regarded as the characteristic finger-ring of the early and middle Roman Empire. Countless examples survive from Britain.

These rings, types II and III in Henig's classification and likewise type 2 in Guiraud's, were derived from Hellenistic prototypes and, like their

Figure 3.1 Two typical Henig type II rings in gold (from Richborough, Kent, and Colchester). The ring from Colchester, on the right, is also illustrated in Figure 1.1. British Museum. (Photo: author)

Figure 3.2 One of the silver rings from the Snettisham jeweller's hoard, showing the faceting of the hoop in some examples of Henig type II. British Museum. (Photo: author)

forerunners, the variations that they reveal in detail are greater than is immediately obvious. One important distinction amongst the most precious rings, the gold ones, is that some are made of solid metal while others consist of sheet gold worked over a core of sulphur or other supporting material. Although the final appearance was the same, the technique of manufacture and thus the quantity of precious metal used were quite different. There was also a very perceptible development in the standard shape from the first century through the second to the early third, consisting mainly of an increasing angularity of the shoulders. By the third century, the rounded, almost circular, form had become a flattened one with a definite angle between shoulder and hoop.

Precise dating is difficult, since the type was Empire-wide and was made in so many materials: slight variations in form may be the result of manufacture in different areas and workshops, or different technological traditions as well as chronological factors. For this reason, the series of silver Henig II rings present in the Snettisham hoard is of particular importance. We know that this group was made in a single workshop in Norfolk in the second century AD, and the diversity of form that we see in the twenty-one examples in the Snettisham hoard demonstrates the range produced in one workshop during a short period of time, enabling us to judge the degree of variability possible in the products of a single source at a specific moment in time. (The Snettisham hoard is fully described in the Appendix.) We cannot necessarily apply these conclusions directly to other areas in the Empire, although it is unlikely that there were great differences. However, it tells us that in the middle of the second century in Britain, this type of ring, already a traditional and standard one, was exhibiting definite signs of the flattened, angular shape that became normal in the early third century. Another feature that appears on some of the Snettisham rings is the slight chamfering or faceting of the hoop that in a more marked form is a specific design feature of some third-century rings.

The engraved stones set in Henig II rings will be discussed in greater detail in Chapter 4. They generally have flat or slightly convex surfaces that barely stand out from the surrounding metal, so that the ring as a whole has an almost smooth profile. However, some gems were given a more prominent rounded profile, amounting to a cabochon cut, or a deep bevel and flat table that produce a truncated conical projection from the metal hoop. Gems set in type II rings were sometimes plain, without an engraved motif, and plain glass settings are also found, usually in simple bronze rings. Other glass settings were cast in moulds or impressed to produce incuse (hollowed) motifs in direct imitation of engraved hardstone, while moulded glass gems with relief decoration, glass "cameos", are also sometimes found.

These variations express the complex motivations that lay behind the wearing of the rings. Engraved gems and intaglio designs cut directly in a metal bezel were originally intended for use as seals, and that function was still important throughout the Roman period, but the tiny image of a deity or the familiar attribute of a god or goddess carried on the person would also have had a powerful apotropaic force, and this was an equally compelling reason for the wearing of rings with engraved gems in the Roman Empire. Plain stones or glass settings were likewise prized for their colour and texture, and there are many examples of quartz settings banded in different colours cut to display this feature, often without any engraving. Such rings were worn as adornment, pure and simple, although we must not forget that certain hardstones were considered to have mystic powers in themselves. Some simple rings of the type are entirely without gemstones and consist solely of fairly broad metal bands with decoration engraved directly on the bezel area. These are typically in bronze.

Snake-rings

We observed in the previous chapter that rings and bracelets in the form of serpents occupied an important place in the jewellery fashions of the Hellenistic and early Roman world. Snakes had symbolic significance in Celtic as well as Graeco-Roman religion. Serpentiform jewellery was introduced to Britain in the first century AD, and continued to be used for most of the Roman period, although datable examples tend to belong to the early and middle Empire. The majority of snake-rings found in Roman Britain were made in the province.

Figure 3.3 sets out a simple typology for snake-rings and -bracelets. The scheme follows Henkel in 1913 and Guiraud in 1975[6] in drawing a primary distinction between the jewel formed of a single snake with its head at one end and its tail at the other (type A) and the penannular ring furnished with two animal-head terminals, in this case serpents (type B). Other variants are placed in the third class, C. The type A single-snake ring is quite rare in Britain, having passed its major period of popularity by the time the island became a province of the Roman Empire. Simple spiral bronze examples are known that are probably of first-century date and are unlikely to be imports, demonstrating that the type was well known enough to be manufactured locally in non-precious metal in the first century (Fig. 1.2). Type B, with its two snake-head terminals, is known in precious and non-precious metals, and in numerous variants. A silver ring from London[7] (Fig. 3.6) belongs to a distinctive first-century type known from Pompeii; the snake heads are realistically rendered, and the hoop of the ring is so thick as to make it apparently impractical for normal wear.

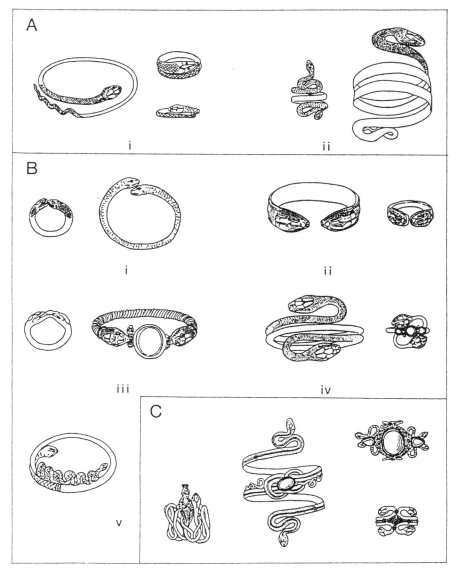

Figure 3.3 Simple typology showing the principal types of snake-rings and bracelets. Types A and B are widespread forms. Type C is a provisional classification for more complex and exceptional types, and is not directly relevant to Britain. (Drawing: author)

The more stylized version of this form, exemplified by over thirty examples in the Snettisham hoard, consists of a flat ribbon of silver with the serpent heads stamped out in low relief at the terminals. The rendering of the reptile's head is reduced to a pattern of swelling curves and lines that would be unrecognizable if the history of the type were unknown. The Snettisham series can be subdivided into the products of separate, although very similar, moulds, and the manufacture of rings such as these must have been a quick and simple process. Similar rings were made in bronze, but as yet no example of this variety has been found in gold.

Figure 3.4 The gold snake-ring of type B iv from the Backworth hoard. The same type occurs in silver in the Snettisham hoard, and bronze examples are also known. (Photo: British Museum)

Figure 3.5 Two silver snake-rings from the Snettisham jeweller's hoard, types B ii and B iv. British Museum. (Photo: author)

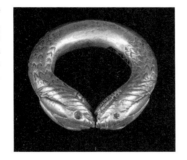

Figure 3.6 Heavy silver snake-ring (type B i), found in Great Russell Street, London. British Museum. (Photo: author).

In the same jeweller's cache from Snettisham, there are four to six examples (the exact number is uncertain because they are very fragmentary) of a somewhat more complex type of snake-ring, designated B iv in my classification, in which the two ends of the ring overlap and the heads curve back in opposite directions. The central overlap area of the hoop is ornamented with three little flattened spheres or beads of metal surrounded by beaded or milled wire. The Snettisham examples include miscast and fragmentary pieces. The type is known in silver from elsewhere in Britain, but does not appear to be current in quite this form on the Continent; examples from other provinces, for example the Rhineland, have the cross-over and recurved heads, but seem to lack the additional decoration provided by the beads and filigree that is so common, if not invariable, on the British examples. It is therefore of particular interest that the British form was also made in gold. The gold snake-ring in the

Backworth treasure is very similar indeed to the Snettisham series in silver. Since we can reasonably regard this form as a Romano-British one, the Backworth example becomes one of the pieces of evidence for the manufacture of gold jewellery in Britain. The type seems to be a first- to second-century fashion. (The Backworth treasure (a votive group found in the early nineteenth century in Northumberland) is described in the Appendix.)

Henig IV/Guiraud 4c

Another type that had already made its appearance in this period was Henig type IV (Guiraud 4c), which has a raised round or oval box-bezel set with a gem and a fairly slender hoop. Where the hoop and the bezel are attached, there are additional decorative beads or small spheres of gold. The form is quite simple and obvious, but the approach to design and manufacture is distinct from that seen in the classic Henig II type. The bezel is raised above the line of the hoop, and because the stone can be held in place by the band of gold that surrounds it, it does not need to fit precisely into a cavity in the gold. This type falls into Guiraud's type 4 (4c), but she includes a number of other variants and subtypes that have in common mainly the fact that the stone stands proud of the hoop.

Figure 3.7 One of the gold rings of Henig type IV from the Backworth treasure. (Photo: British Museum)

Henig IV/Guiraud 4c develops into a range of more highly decorated variants, including examples with filigree ornamentation that are more typical of the late Roman period than of the early Empire, but there is incontrovertible evidence of the presence of the basic type in the mid-second century, since it occurs in two closely dated hoards of this phase, the jeweller's hoard from Snettisham (already cited) and the Backworth hoard. Both hoards contain coins that give a reliable indication of the time the treasures were buried, around AD 154 in the case of the Snettisham group and a little earlier, about AD 139, for Backworth.

Wire rings: Guiraud type 6

Rings that consist of a simple metal wire encircling the finger, finished in some type of knot or cross-over pattern, are so basic that they are found not only throughout the Roman period but also in both earlier and later cultures. The form is an obvious one for bracelets as well as finger-rings, and overlapped wire bracelets are known from the British Iron Age. Overlapped wire finger-rings are more common in bronze than in silver and gold, underlining their status as simple and inexpensive pieces of jewellery. They do occur in precious metals, however, and the Snettisham hoard once again has special importance, since it includes nine examples of an unusually complex type of wire ring. Its two tapered ends are overlapped, entwined around the hoop and completed with spirals surmounted by silver globules. The area between these two terminals becomes a bezel zone that is filled in with twisted silver wire placed to form a herringbone pattern. We may refer to this distinctive type as the Snettisham overlapped wire ring.

Figure 3.8 Silver wire ring with overlapped ends from the Snettisham hoard. British Museum. (Photo: author)

The Snettisham type is known in bronze in the Rhineland, although it is not common, and there is also a single silver example from Caerleon in south Wales that must surely be a product of the Snettisham jeweller.[8] This is so far the only certainly identifiable product of the craftsman from elsewhere. Close parallels for the Snettisham type have not yet been found in gold.

Henig V

The gem-set ring type assigned by Henig to his type V has much in common with the popular type II–III, but is notable for its very wide and flattened hoop. It occurs in all metals, and was current in the second and third centuries.

Third-century rings

Keeled rings

The third and fourth centuries saw a trend towards decorative elaboration in jewellery, with an increasing interest in texture and colour.[9] There were also two developments in the morphology of rings that were characteristic of the period. In many third-century rings, the increasingly angular shoulder that was already noticeable in the previous century became an important design feature. Rings of many different types, with or without gems or inscriptions, with narrow or broad hoops, plain or decorative finishes, and in a variety of materials, take on a shape that in plan is not circular but has a sharp keel or carination, usually about half way around the hoop. Because it occurs in such a variety of forms, this shape cannot be defined as a single type in itself: within Guiraud's classification, keeled rings appear under types 2f and 2h, but also types 3e, 3f and 3g. The cross-section of the hoop in some of these rings is also distinctive. Earlier types tended to exhibit circular, oval or D-shaped sections, but many third-century keeled rings have a trapezoidal section, chamfered at each side to produce a faceted appearance.

Rings that feature a wide bezel, for example a gem-set one, and also the sharp shoulder carination described above, thereby evolve a flat, roughly triangular field at the shoulder that lends itself to decoration. Some rings of this form remain perfectly plain, but engraved lines and patterns were also popular, often based on a stylized leaf design that fits the triangular surface well. Pierced work also occurs on this shape, and piercing is a technique that increased in popularity in the late Roman period. The flattening of the upper part of the ring compared with its early Empire predecessors brings about not only increased scope for decoration of the metalwork of the hoop but also a larger potential area for the gem-setting. Keeled rings may be set with gems, or have metal bezels, engraved or worked in relief. Coin-set examples are also known. The shape is also found in non-metal rings.

Figure 3.9 An example of the keeled form; a silver ring from Winchester. British Museum. (Photo: author)

There are some third-century rings in which the angular effect is taken to extremes, so that the bezel and shoulders merge to form a wide, flat field, usually very elaborately embellished with surface decoration, but these are not as yet known from Britain. Since they occur in adjacent provinces, however, it is quite possible that examples did exist in Britain, and might one day be discovered.

Rings with hunched shoulders

Very common, on the other hand, are rings of Guiraud types 3a, 3b, 3c and 3d (Henig Xb). There are many variations and subtypes, but all may be described as having "hunched" shoulders: the shoulders are raised, ridged, cusped or otherwise emphasized by detailed shaping, and there is a clear demarcation between the shoulder and the bezel area. Two bronze rings from Chesterford, Essex and Feltwell, Norfolk, set with glass intaglios, illustrate the variant (Guiraud 3d) in which the shoulders have decorative mouldings.[10] The variants with series of ridges on the shoulders occur in bronze but not, apparently, in gold or silver.

Figure 3.10 A silver ring with hunched shoulders; from Wittering, Cambridgeshire. British Museum. (Photo: author)

Late Roman rings

Filigree and granulation

By the fourth century, the tastes of the late Antique world held sway, and in the arts generally there was an increasing enjoyment of rich colour, texture and elaborate design. In gold jewellery this took the form of a taste for textured surfaces in the metal itself, with piercing, engraving, filigree and granulation. These trends had already started to develop in the third century AD, and close dating of individual items of jewellery from the later Roman period can often be very difficult.

Gold rings featuring pierced openwork designs on the shoulders continued to be popular, and another approach to the elaboration of this feature also developed, namely the use of filigree and granulation. Filigree is wire, either applied to a solid metal surface or used on its own as an openwork pattern. Both styles were used in fourth-century jewellery, and although the technique was certainly not new, it became far more widespread in this period. Such work was executed in both plain and beaded wire, usually in the form of symmetrical curves and volutes on the shoulders of the ring, and including granulation in the form of single tiny beads of gold attached at focal points in the design. This is quite different in intention and appearance from the minutely fine granulation of earlier Classical jewellery, and also requires far less skill to create. The appearance of such rings is exemplified in some of the pieces from the Thetford treasure (Fig. 3.11), in the rings found at New Grange in Ireland[11] and in the three finger-rings from the Hoxne treasure. Bronze and even silver are far less easily worked in this manner, and it is more difficult to distinguish the characteristically intricate fourth-century designs in these metals.

The Thetford rings

The most remarkable group of rings from Britain dating to the late fourth century are those in the Thetford treasure.[12] The treasure as a whole is summarized in the Appendix, but a more detailed survey of the rings is appropriate here as a comment upon fourth-century styles. It must, however, be borne in mind that there are no known parallels for many of the rings in the group, and the assemblage must therefore be regarded as an exceptional one rather than one that is wholly representative of its period. All the evidence indicates that most of the Thetford jewellery emanates from a single source, and although many of the detailed elements in the designs can be traced back to the previous century, overall we can see the flamboyant and even ostentatious taste of the late Roman period interpreted by a highly individualistic jeweller.

One of the rings, no. 7 (the numbers refer to the catalogue entries[13]), has a bezel in the form of a vase supported by two small birds that are identifiable as woodpeckers (Fig. 3.11, 2nd row left). The cantharus-and-birds motif is a classic Bacchic device, but in this case it has a more specific relevance to the cult of Faunus: in myth, the father of Faunus was Picus, the woodpecker. The inscriptions on the silver spoons from the same treasure demonstrate the worship of Faunus in some Celtic guise. The woodpecker ring is a very impractical shape for wear, with a small D-shaped hoop and the elaborate bezel projecting a considerable distance. It is not the only piece with zoomorphic elements, since two rings (nos. 5 and 6) have shoulders in the shape of dolphins. These creatures have boar-like crests, and are very reminiscent of the dolphins that are sometimes seen in late Roman belt-buckles. Dolphins were frequently depicted in Roman decorative art at all periods, and had symbolic links with Bacchic cult. One of the dolphin-shouldered rings has an unusually large and colourful flat bezel set with gems of three colours – amethysts, garnets and emeralds (mauve, deep red and vivid green) – while the other has a relatively restrained single amethyst setting. Several of the rings are set with engraved gems, but these are re-used stones of third-century date.

Two of the rings have hoops formed of a corrugated strip of gold, a technique paralleled in the third-century Lyons hoard found in the 1840s,[14] but the use of filigree volutes is typical of fourth-century work.

Figure 3.11 The full group of 22 gold rings from the Thetford treasure. (Photo: British Museum)

One of the most remarkable Thetford rings is no. 9, which has two human faces in relief on the shoulders; it is set with a natural emerald crystal, and the two heads are of a style that is often described as Celtic, with stylized, stiff features and hair swept straight back from the forehead (Fig. 3.11, 2nd row right). A head also features as the bezel of another ring, this time a Pan-like face with horns, quite probably representing Faunus himself (no. 23).

More in the mainstream of late Antique goldwork are the rings in the treasure that are set with engraved gems and have decorative engraving on the shoulders, while there is one ring that is a well-known form, effectively a late variant of Guiraud type 4, found elsewhere in Britain and also in the Rhineland (no. 16) (Fig. 3.11, 6th row left).

No. 14 in the Thetford group has a wide bezel with three gem settings in a vertical line, flanked by complex filigree shoulders. A close parallel to this ring – the first to be recorded – came to light a few years after the discovery of the treasure. It was also found in Norfolk, but was certainly not a stray from the treasure itself. It provides a hint that the unique Thetford assemblage, which is clearly the work of a single workshop, may be of British rather than continental manufacture. Although so many of the rings cannot be closely matched elsewhere, the group as a whole is stylistically wholly in tune with the taste of the period.

The Brancaster type

One very significant form is typical of the latest Roman period in Britain and yet it is not represented in either the Thetford or Hoxne assemblages. It is exemplified by a handsome gold ring from the site of the late Roman shore-fort at Brancaster in Norfolk,[15] a jewel important not only because it is a typical example of a form that is well known in Britain and the Continent at the end of the fourth century and into the fifth, but also because it is a fine example of a Christian marriage ring. It will be discussed further under those headings, but for the moment, we are concerned mainly with its shape.

Figure 3.12 The late Roman Christian finger-ring from Brancaster, Norfolk, featuring two engraved busts and the inscription VIVAS IN DEO. (Photo: Norfolk Museums)

The characteristics of the form are that the hoop is of constant width and comparatively broad, and that the bezel is noticeably raised, usually square or rectangular in shape, and decorated in intaglio by direct engraving into

Figure 3.13 Three silver rings with engraved bezels from a hoard found at Amesbury, Wiltshire. (Photo: British Museum)

the metal. The form is found in gold, silver and bronze. Some rings with circular or polygonal bezels may be variants of the same form, for example two Christian rings from Brentwood, Essex, and from Suffolk respectively. Examples with faceted hoops, like the Senecianus ring from Silchester (which is discussed in the section on inscribed rings), may also be placed within the same class. All of these Christian rings are described more fully below.

A particularly interesting group of Brancaster-type rings in silver was found at Amesbury in Wiltshire in 1843 with a coin hoard including issues of Theodosius I; the coins point to a deposition date at the end of the fourth century or early in the fifth, that is, at the very end of the Roman period or after its formal close.[16] They have to be regarded as variants of the type, for two of them are more highly decorated than is normal, bearing engraved and cast decoration at the shoulders as well as on the bezels. The three must surely be products of a single craftsman. The motifs on the bezels are distinctive: a griffin, a bird and, on the plainest ring, a group of four very stylized objects that appear to be helmets. The latter motif appears again as a helmeted bust or head on a gold ring of the same type from Richborough, Kent,[17] while birds feature on the bezels of silver specimens from Burgate (Suffolk), Droitwich (Hereford and Worcester) and on one of the pair of Christian rings from Fifehead

Figure 3.14 A gold ring of Brancaster type with a stylized helmeted head, from Richborough, Kent. The abstract style of the engraved bezel closely resembles that of the Amesbury rings. (Photo: British Museum)

Neville (Dorset) whose whereabouts are now unknown. Another lost example was recorded from Wantage, with sea-beasts engraved on the bezel.[18] Several Brancaster-type rings have Christian motifs, including the famous gold ring of Senicianus.[19] The form was also current on the Continent, and examples in precious and base metals are illustrated in Henkel's catalogue, but the distinctive style of engraving that we see on several of the British examples argues for their local manufacture, as does the existence of the form in bronze as well as precious metals. In the Byzantine world, this type of ring continued to evolve, and raised square bezels with engraved decoration continue to feature in much later gold rings from the Mediterranean and the Byzantine East. Some of these are magnificent pieces of jewellery.

Other types of finger-rings

Guiraud type 5: ring-keys and related types

Small keys were often made in the form of finger-rings, an elegantly simple solution to the problem of security. Such rings were in use throughout the Roman period, and individual examples cannot be dated except by context. The projection from the ring hoop that forms the bit of the key evidently gave rise to decorative rings of related form that lack the practical function of the basic type.

These small keys were designed for rotary locks fitted to items such as caskets and strong-boxes. Many of them are of complex design and very sophisticated workmanship. Bronze is by far the most common material for these utilitarian objects, although iron ring-keys are also found, as are some examples that combine bronze and iron in the same way as many other utensils, for example knives, with bronze handles and iron blades. Cast or cut decoration is occasionally added to the bezel area of the ring, but the majority of rings are plain, suggesting that their decorative potential was insignificant compared with their principal function as keys.

The illustration (Fig. 3.15) shows a group of ring-keys from various British sites. The ring at the bottom left is from London, and is made of iron. It is a very delicate example of the blacksmith's craft. The other pieces are all of bronze, and they demonstrate quite a wide range from simple and fairly roughly made keys to very precise and intricate key-cutting. Another typical bronze example was found in an important grave-group from Elsenham, Essex, which is dated by coins to the middle of the second century. The Elsenham ring-key is of interest because it is from a dated find and because other bronze fittings from the box that it locked were also found in the disturbed burial. These included the lock-plate and fragments of the lock mechanism.[20]

Figure 3.15 Group of
ring-keys from various
sites in Roman Britain.
All are bronze except for
the example at the lower
left, which is of iron.
(Photo: British Museum)

Guiraud's type 5b has a symmetrical pierced lateral extension that
differs from the obvious keys of the first variant. It is represented in
Fig. 3.15 (bottom right) by a ring from Wroxeter. While it is obvious that
such rings are transitional between the true ring-keys and the wholly
decorative rings of type 5e, there are uncertainties in the classification.
We cannot be certain whether the bronze example from Wroxeter was
actually usable as a key. A gold example from Chippenham, Wiltshire,
also belongs to this transitional form, but as no actual key is known in
gold, it is more likely to be an ornamental piece.[21]

The third subgroup within this class comprises rings that are definitely
not keys, but which employ the basic form in a purely decorative manner
(Guiraud 5e). They are often in precious metals, and are known from
many Roman provinces besides Britain. A splendid example from London has a cast scene in the form of a minute shrine or *aedicula* with flanking columns, a pair of dolphins and a shell surmounting an arch, and four
cupids apparently engaged in mixing or making wine in a crater.[22] This
complex scene is on a field some 15 mm high. Its Bacchic implications are
very obvious, and the ring can in effect be regarded as a tiny portable

shrine in itself. The most common scene on rings of this nature depicts a pair of panthers or other feline animals drinking from a cantharus, often with other Bacchic motifs: there is a typical gold specimen from Corbridge that has gem-settings – now empty – on the bezel area of the hoop,[23] and a silver representative of the type from Chesterford, Essex.[24] The Chesterford ring has a small rectangular plaque (soldered to the bezel) that is decorated with a walking lion in relief and gilded. Its lateral plate is of very similar design to the Corbridge ring, with panthers flanking a pedestalled wine-vessel. Another very fine ring of this type from Kaiseraugst in Switzerland bears an inscription and an extension plate with two birds, swans or geese, and a shell; the symbolism here is of Venus rather than Bacchus.[25] The date-range for these rings would seem to be middle Empire: second to third centuries AD.

Figure 3.16 Silver ring from Chesterford, Essex, with a Bacchic motif in the bezel extension and an applied gold plaque depicting a walking lion. British Museum. (Photo: author)

Perhaps we should also mention here an extremely fine ring that must be classed along with the Guiraud 5e variants, although it has no real history, and may not in fact be a Romano-British find at all. This is the gold ring that is set with an emerald and a sapphire, the latter in the projecting secondary bezel. There is no reason to doubt that it is Roman. Although sapphires are not common in Roman jewellery, and are exceptionally rare in Romano-British finds, the nebulous tradition that attaches this elegant ring to Britain could be based on fact, and it is certainly typologically associated with the form based on the humble ring-key.[26]

Figure 3.17 An unprovenanced gold ring, possibly from Britain, set with an emerald and a cabochon sapphire. British Museum. (Photo: author)

Coin-set rings

A class of jewellery that was of minor significance in Roman Britain nevertheless deserves brief mention here, namely personal ornaments set with coins. To all intents and purposes the custom applies only to gold jewellery set with gold coins, and it appears to have been far more popular on the Continent than in Britain; there are several superb necklaces with coin-pendants from Gaulish treasure hoards. Such settings were generally in the form of pendants attached to necklace chains; coins as ring-settings were less common. There is, however, a handsome ring from Ilchester, Somerset, which is set with a gold *aureus* of Severus Alexander (AD 222–35). The coin provides a *terminus post quem* for the ring, which has a keeled form and boldly shaped and pierced shoulders. It may be of late third-century or early fourth-century date. A silver coin-set ring, which in Empire-wide terms is far more unusual, comes from a burial at Chichester; it is a heavy setting containing a denarius of Caracalla and Severus dating to AD 200.[27]

Figure 3.18 Gold ring from Ilchester, Somerset, set with a gold coin of Severus Alexander. British Museum. (Photo: author).

Rings with inscriptions

There are classes of finger-ring that have important elements in common even though they may otherwise be of different forms, and some rings with inscriptions can usefully be considered together even though they include a great diversity of form and date and therefore cut across the more generally useful classifications. Some continental rings have easily understandable inscriptions such as AMA ME, but letters and words are often more obscure than this, and may often simply be the initials or abbreviated names of owners, like the letters A.P.D. on a third-century keeled ring from London.[28] Some inscriptions appear to be specifically religious or apotropaic, both pagan and Christian, and others are evidently personal.

Rings with flat bezels on which the letters TOT are engraved, sometimes with additional linear decoration, form a Romano-British group of particular interest. Various suggestions have been made about the meaning of the word or abbreviation, but by far the most likely explanation is that it is an abbreviation for the name of a deity: rings inscribed MER, obviously for the name of Mercury, are recorded from Britain and elsewhere. The TOT rings so far known are in silver and bronze, and belong to types that suggest a middle Empire date. The example illustrated, from Lincoln, is a standard third-century shape with carinated shoulders (Fig. 3.19). If TOT is indeed a god-name, the current hypothesis is that it stands for the name Toutatis. This is the name of a Celtic god, not a Roman one: he was one of the principal Celtic deities in Gaul and Britain, and was generally identified with Mars in the Roman pantheon. The combination MARS TOUTATIS is present, for example, on one of the silver votive plaques found in the early eighteenth century at Barkway (Hertfordshire).[29]

Figure 3.19 A silver keeled ring, probably from Lincolnshire, inscribed TOT on the bezel. British Museum. (Photo: author)

These comparatively simple rings evidently employed the written name as the equivalent of a visual image of a deity engraved on a gem or directly represented in the metal. This may not be solely a reflection of the greater value of jewellery with hardstones or elaborate decoration: the written word was often perceived as possessing a special magical power in itself, and a verbal invocation to a deity may have been efficaceous in a way quite distinct from a pictorial image. In any case, we would be unwise to regard these rings as cheap substitutes for more decorative ones.

The religious inscription on one of the gold finger-rings from the Backworth treasure is a little more complex, since it is evidently votive. The ring, along with other valuables, was itself dedicated to the deity, in this case the Celtic mother-goddesses who are also mentioned on the silver vessel that contained the whole treasure. The words are inscribed on the gold bezel of a simple Henig II-type ring; they read MATR/VM.CO/COAE. The exact meaning of the second part of the dedication is uncertain, but whether it is an abbreviation of a place or person, or part of a phrase describing the goddesses (one interpretation has suggested "red

Figure 3.20 The gold ring from the Backworth treasure bearing a dedicatory inscription to the mother-goddesses. (Photo: British Museum)

mothers"), there is no doubt that the mother-goddesses were the recipients of the gift.[30] A simple silver ring with the inscription MAT/RES probably comes from Carrawburgh on the Roman Wall.[31]

Inscriptions including the word *vita*, "life", in various combinations are not uncommon, and the shades of meaning are not always easy for us to interpret. Two interesting rings from London inscribed respectively DA/MI/VITA and VITA/VOLO ("Give me life" and "I wish for life") are made in a distinctive technique, combining copper wire inlay and an iron ring.[32] The combination of two metals may well have had a symbolic significance in itself, and there is additional religious symbolism in the DA/MI/VITA ring, as the letters, picked out in niello, are on a cruciform basis of copper set in the iron, with additional copper stars in the four quadrants. There is no question of Christian meaning in this particular piece.

Written symbols and phrases were frequently used on jewellery amongst Christians though, and we shall consider them below. Apotropaic phrases such as *utere felix*, "Use (this) happily", sometimes abbreviated, may be found on jewellery and on other articles and utensils. And in the late Roman period, a person's name followed by *vivas*, "may you live!", is a very widespread invocation on personal possessions of many kinds. Although *vivas* inscriptions used to be regarded as exclusively Christian, this is not invariably so.

Hoops that were faceted in plan often formed a convenient basis for inscriptions, each small square or rectangular field bearing one letter or a divider or stop between words. A faceted bronze ring from London has the inscription VALIATIS, perhaps a corrupted form of *valetis*, "good health!"[33]

A special class of rings, represented by a few very handsome gold examples in Britain, makes use of this faceted form and bears inscriptions and other decoration entirely worked in the technique traditionally referred to as *opus interrasile*, delicate pierced work that continued to be employed in some of the finest jewellery of the Byzantine world. These rings are fairly broad bands, generally faceted, and display an openwork inscription in the central section with decorative borders above and below. Examples are known from many provinces of the Empire, but their dating is far from certain, and they could well start as early as the second century AD. One found near Bedford in the 1970s is lettered with the phrase EVSEBIO VITA, "(long) life to Eusebius"[34] (Fig. 3.21).

Two famous rings of this type from Corbridge, Northumberland raise several intriguing points. One is a very large band with sixteen facets and the other a small and dainty example with twelve fields for letters and spaces. It seems reasonable to regard them as having been made for a man and a woman respectively. The man's ring is inscribed in Greek, reminding us that there would have been many Greek-speakers in Britain during

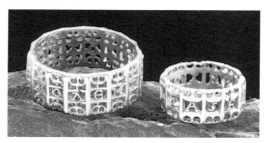

Figure 3.21 Two gold rings with pierced patterns and inscriptions: left, the Polemios ring from Corbridge, and on the right, the Eusebius ring from Bedford. (Photo: British Museum)

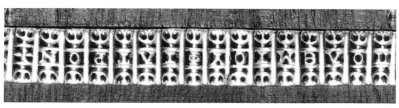

Figure 3.22 The Greek inscription on the Polemios ring shown in full in a periphery photograph. (Photo: British Museum)

Figure 3.23 The Aemilia ring from Corbridge. Museum of Antiquities, Newcastle. (Photo: University of Newcastle upon Tyne)

the Roman period. The message is POLEMIOU PHILTRON, "Polemios's love-token".[35] The woman's ring is inscribed in Latin letters AEMILIA ZESES, "may you live, Aemilia" – *zeses* is a Latinized form of a Greek word, and is the exact equivalent of *vivas*.

It is very tempting indeed to see these two distinctive and personalized rings as belonging to a couple. If so, the import of the Polemios ring is that it is a love-token to Polemios (from Aemilia?) rather than *from* him, which is our instinctive way of interpreting the message. If Polemios had given this ring to his beloved rather than receiving it, the imposing dimensions of the ring imply that the object of his affections was another man, a perfectly possible circumstance, but perhaps less likely than the Polemios and Aemilia connection put forward here.

The suggested relationship between Polemios and Aemilia is wildly speculative and could be totally mistaken, but there are other inferences that we can draw from these two rings that have a more sound basis. First, Polemios and Aemilia would have been wealthy, and they were clearly not native Britons, but would have come to the remote frontier zone of Britannia from another province. Regardless of where they are found, rings of this type display great consistency of design, and many of them have a Greek element in the inscription. This suggests that they were made in one or only a very few centres. They obviously had to be made to special order, since the inscriptions are integral to the design, unlike words that can be engraved on an existing piece of jewellery by a craftsman other than its original manufacturer.

Finally, both rings must be seen as tokens of love and affection, or even as symbols of betrothal or marriage, and they therefore belong to an important class of Roman jewellery that deserves closer examination. We can legitimately draw some conclusions from these two related pieces of jewellery found at Corbridge, even if a direct link between the two lies more in the realm of historical fiction than academic inference.

Love-tokens and marriage rings

The words on the ring of Polemios state clearly that it is a symbol of love. Equally unequivocal statements of the same sentiment are found on other inscribed rings, not necessarily impressive gold ornaments like the Corbridge example. The phrase AMA ME is engraved on a small gold ring from Carlisle, where it is combined with a stylized palm-branch, probably in its usual meaning as an emblem of victory.[36] As noted above, such mottoes also occur on a series of plain base-metal rings from the Bonn region of the Rhineland.[37]

Two bronze rings from London are also of quite simple appearance, although they required some skill to make. They take the form of thin hoops with letters incorporated so as to project above and below the line of the hoop. They read AMICA and MISCE MI.[38] The former, meaning simply "woman friend" or "sweetheart", is plain enough; the latter is a directly sexual invitation, meaning "mix with me", that is "unite with me". This use of *misceo* is not a particularly blunt sexual term but on the contrary a slightly literary euphemism. The significance of the ring is possibly further emphasized by a feature on the bezel, now damaged, which may be intended to represent a phallus. Phallic symbolism in Roman art was often not directly sexual in its meaning but concerned rather with good fortune and the avoidance of evil influences, but in combination with a phrase such as this, it would be far more specifically erotic.[39] The ring is likely to be of Romano-British manufacture. Legends such as *anima mea* ("my soul") are also to be found, and these express a romantic rather than a sensual message.

Many other rings which lack features that we can now interpret as symbols of love or commitment may nevertheless have been intended as love-tokens or betrothal/marriage rings. Without documentary evidence it is not possible to make a clear distinction between the concept of betrothal, the promise of a marriage contract, and the completion of that contract.

There are two important types of ring that we can confidently connect specifically with the formal and legally sanctioned status of betrothal or marriage rather than simply with a personal expression of an emotional or sexual relationship. They are, first, rings with a representation of two clasped right hands, and secondly, those with confronted busts of a man and a woman. Very broadly, the clasped hands tend to belong to a pagan milieu while the "portraits" of man and wife were evidently associated with Christian marriage.

The symbolism of the handshake or clasped right hands, *dextrarum iunctio*, encompassed not only the idea of friendship but also of agreement or contract. It was obviously a most appropriate image to express marriage, but it does not seem to have been in frequent use until the middle centuries of the Roman Empire. There are a few examples of the device on early rings, for example one from Chester which has the two hands incised on the gold bezel.[40] More common are later, namely third- and fourth-century, types that display the motif in relief, either as a solid casting or worked in repoussé on a metal plate mounted in the bezel. In Britain the clasped hands are comparatively rare as a device on gems, but there is one good cameo example on an onyx from Bradwell, Essex; the accompanying inscription cut in the stone is extremely difficult to read but would appear to be the Greek word OMONOIA, which means "harmony".[41]

Figure 3.24 Silver ring with clasped-hands motif on an inset thin repoussé gold setting. From Grovely Wood, Wiltshire. (Photo: British Museum)

Figure 3.25 Two late Roman gold rings with the clasped-hands device rendered in repoussé on the bezel: left, from Richborough, Kent; right, from the Thetford treasure. (Photo: British Museum)

An interesting example of the clasped-hands type is a silver ring of bold keeled form with expanded and engraved shoulders from Grovely Wood, Wiltshire.[42] It is set with a gold plate worked in relief with the *dextrarum iunctio;* the combination of the two precious metals undoubtedly had a special meaning in itself. Examples of fine filigree rings with the same motif from Richborough and the Thetford treasure are of later date.

Since most of these clasped-hands rings have the decoration rendered in relief, they were clearly not intended as seal-rings. Their decoration was complete in itself, and we can infer that they were presented and worn purely as symbols of marriage.

The other form of marriage ring is that which bears two facing heads or busts of a man and a woman. Confronted male and female profile heads were a standard device in Roman art, often used in a variety of contexts for imperial portraits, and it would therefore be mistaken to assume uncritically that any ring with two facing portraits must belong to the category of wedding or betrothal ring. Facing portrait heads need not even necessarily be husband-and-wife symbols: there is a ring from Colchester with two bearded male heads engraved on the gold bezel beneath the legend IMP that has plausibly been interpreted as depicting two emperors, probably Marcus Aurelius and Lucius Verus.[43]

Figure 3.26 Gold ring from Colchester engraved with two facing male heads and the letters IMP: possibly the Emperors Marcus Aurelius and Lucius Verus. British Museum. (Photo: author)

However, having expressed this reservation, we can say that the majority of late Roman rings with male and female portrait heads almost certainly are marriage rings. As we shall see in Chapter 5 there are some personal ornaments other than rings which combine the symbolism of the two portraits with that of the clasped hands, for example the jet pendant from Vindolanda that depicts a man and a woman kissing on the obverse and the *dextrarum iunctio* motif on the reverse.[44] This juxtaposition provides a very clear link between the two symbols and helps to support the accepted interpretation.

Most rings of the confronted-busts type are of distinctively late Roman form, and many have additional inscriptions indicating or suggesting Christian affiliations. Most are also distinguished from the clasped-hands type by being at least potentially usable as seal-rings: the busts are generally engraved into the metal bezel rather than being worked in relief.

One ring that is an exception to this rule is an example found with a fourth-century coin hoard at Whitwell, Leicestershire. With comparatively simple volutes on the shoulders, it has a repoussé bezel decorated in relief with two rather roughly executed busts. They presumably depict a man and a woman, although this is not easy to tell, and there is no inscription to clarify the function of the item. If, as it appears, this is a

Figure 3.27 Gold marriage ring from Whitwell, Leicestershire, with portraits of the husband and wife in relief. Rutland Museum. (Photo: British Museum)

marriage ring, then it is unusual in being purely decorative and symbolic, like the clasped-hands variety, rather than functioning additionally as a seal.[45]

The principal example of the confronted-busts type from Britain is the gold ring from Brancaster, Norfolk, to which we have already referred above as the exemplar for a distinctive late Roman form (Fig. 3.12).[46] Its hoop is lightly faceted and the bezel is not a perfect square. The engraved device consists of two very stylized busts with the legend VIVAS IN DEO ("may you live in God") above and below them. A noteworthy feature is that although the whole design is incuse, the inscription is intended to be read on the ring, not as an impression. An unprovenanced ring in the British Museum is of very similar form and appearance, but the portraits are surrounded by an inscription, SPERATU(S) BENERIAE, which refers to anticipated lovemaking and consequently sounds pagan and erotic rather than Christian and pious.[47]

Even more magnificent examples of such rings are known from elsewhere, for instance a specimen in the British Museum with finely engraved portraits beneath a Greek cross on a square bezel with a hoop formed of seven circular medallions, each bearing a human image inlaid in niello,[48] and one in the Dumbarton Oaks collection (Washington, DC) with finely engraved portraits and the names of the couple, Aristophanes and Vigilantia.[49] The Whitwell and Brancaster rings, which were worn in Roman Britain, and perhaps even made here, can be seen to stand at the beginning of one of the splendid traditions of Byzantine jewellery.

Rings with Christian devices or inscriptions

We have already seen that rings were frequently employed as appropriate vehicles for carrying on the person symbols of piety and good fortune. This function was not restricted to pagan usage but continued when Christianity became the favoured and official religion of the Roman Empire.

Early Christian symbolism and iconography present certain problems of interpretation. These have to be appreciated before we can comprehend the difficulties in understanding some of the devices used on small objects such as jewellery. Britain's full and formal position as a province of the Roman Empire came to an end early in the fifth century AD – the conventionally accepted date is AD 410. Throughout the fourth century, Christianity and traditional paganism had been at loggerheads: the acceptance of Christianity by the Emperor Constantine I (the Great), who reigned from AD 306 to 337, was by no means the signal that paganism had ended and Christendom had begun.

Early Christians had to create or borrow a new iconographic system, and during the many and recurrent periods of oppression they were obliged to use covert symbolism. Even by the end of the fourth century AD, when the Emperor Theodosius I (reigned AD 379–95) passed laws to outlaw pagan worship, the developing iconography of Christianity was still at an early stage: the Latin cross (†) that is now universally understood as the principal symbol of Christianity was still in the future. The most meaningful symbol at this period was still the Chi-Rho monogram, the two Greek letters that form the beginning of the Greek word *Christos* (XP). A more developed form of this was the monogram cross, a Latin cross in which the upright still retained the form of a P, the Greek letter *rho*. A more secret symbol of the early Christians was a fish, often drawn schematically in the form of two overlapping curved lines. Its basis is that the Greek word for fish, *ichthus* (ιχθυς) is an acronym of the Greek phrase that means "Jesus Christ, son of God, Saviour". The fish was an ambiguous and ambivalent symbol, as were other signs of early Christianity borrowed and reinterpreted from pagan iconography, such as doves, peacocks and palm branches. All had established pagan significance, but could be reinterpreted within a Christian iconographic system. This was a logical approach during periods of oppression and was intended to restrict understanding to those who were in the know, but the deliberate ambiguity can cause uncertainties of interpretation in modern times.

We have already referred to a gold ring from Carlisle that combines the stylized representation of a palm-branch with the words AMA ME: because Christian apologists are anxious to attribute Christian significance to every possible source, this has been classified in the past as an early Christian ring from Britain, but its third-century form and the personal nature of the inscription both argue for a pagan, or indeed an entirely non-religious, significance to the piece.

Similarly, we should be very cautious about reading Christian meanings into motifs such as fishes, peacocks, doves, dolphins, anchors, palm-branches and so on: all have respectable pagan traditions, and the most we can say is that they could have been either openly pagan symbols or covert Christian ones. It is only when we come to the Chi-Rho symbol or the monogram cross (the Greek cross – + – or the Latin cross with a "P" curve on the upright) that we are on relatively safe ground in adducing a

Christian meaning. Similarly, the exhortation *vivas*, "may you live", in combination with a personal name, is a very common Christian phrase, but it would be uncritical and misleading to imagine that it invariably indicates Christian affiliations: *vivas* inscriptions have been found in contexts such as objects in the Thetford treasure which make it clear that it is a typically late Roman style, but by no means confined to Christians. This is not the place to enter fully into the difficult arguments about early Christian iconography; we can only put forward those items of jewellery from late Roman Britain which would seem to have clear Christian connotations.[50]

Figure 3.28   Late Roman Christian gold ring from Suffolk with a carefully engraved reversed Chi-Rho monogram beneath a fruiting branch with a bird. (Photo: British Museum)

Figure 3.29   Late Roman gold ring with the Christian monogram from Brentwood, Essex. (Photo: British Museum)

Probably the finest indisputably Christian finger-ring from Roman Britain is one from Suffolk that became known in the early 1980s, but, sadly, no details are known of precisely when and where it was found.[51] It has an octagonal bezel, but is basically a late Roman Brancaster type. The engraved detail on the bezel includes a bird among vines and a Chi-Rho monogram. The vine sheltering a bird has pagan (Bacchic) antecedents but remains extremely common in Christian art, and combined with the sacred monogram makes the religious significance of this piece certain. One of the lost pair of silver rings from the villa at Fifehead Neville, Dorset, also bore the device of the monogram together with a bird,[52] and there is another fine gold ring with the monogram alone, found in the late 1940s in Brentwood, Essex.[53] With its circular bezel, the Brentwood ring is not typical of the Brancaster-type series, but it is nevertheless a classic late Roman piece. The Suffolk ring is of a size and quality that may well hint at some official function, and it may not be too far-fetched to imagine it as a bishop's ring. The Brentwood ring is more likely to be a good-quality personal item of jewellery worn by a Christian who liked to carry a symbol of his or her faith in the same way as generations of pagans had worn images of their deities.

The Brancaster marriage ring itself also belongs to the inventory of Christian jewellery in Roman Britain, as does the enigmatic Senicianus ring from Silchester.[54] The VIVAS IN DEO inscription of the Brancaster ring, combined with the stylized images of two people whom we may assume to be husband and wife; recalls Christian objects such as the great silver casket from the fourth-century hoard of silver plate found on the Esquiline Hill in Rome in the late eighteenth century; the casket is decorated with a husband-and-wife portrait amongst traditional pagan ornaments, and is inscribed SECUNDE ET PROIECTA VIVATIS IN CHRISTO, "Secundus and Projecta, may you live in Christ".[55]

The Silchester Senecianus ring is somewhat more enigmatic. It, too, is an early find from the eighteenth century, and it is a variant of the Brancaster type with a raised square bezel and engraved decoration. The hoop is faceted, however, and the inscription – reading SENICIANE VIVAS IIN DE [sic], a slightly garbled rendering of "Senicianus, may you live in God" – is engraved on the facets. The engraved device on the bezel is a male head in a bizarre, spiky style, flanked by an inscription that rather surprisingly reads VE/NVS. A lead curse tablet from the temple site at Lydney, Gloucestershire, records that one Silvianus has had a ring stolen, and he prays to the local deity Nodens to recover it from the putative thief, Senicianus. This coincidence, added to the combination of pagan and Christian sentiments and the possibility that the VIVAS inscription is secondary, has made the Senecianus ring the centre of much imaginative speculation, which, alas, can no more be proved than the equally attractive theory that Polemios and Aemilia at Corbridge were man and wife.

Several rings of Brancaster form in silver and bronze have engraved bezels with single birds of unidentifiable species: examples of these include the silver ring from Droitwich and one from a late Roman coin hoard from Burgate, Suffolk. These cannot be positively classified as Christian, but this possibility certainly exists. One ring that is somewhat intriguing because of its form was found in 1956 during the excavation of a Roman villa at Moor Park, Hertfordshire.[56] This is a bronze ring that is basically of Brancaster type with a circular bezel, but with twelve small projecting lugs. The engraved design consists of two birds flanking a branch or palm-leaf. The ring is undoubtedly a very late one, and a Christian interpretation of the device seems very plausible.

The whole question of Christian art in late Roman Britain remains a contentious one, and we must content ourselves with the likelihood that there were probably more Christians than can ever be demonstrated by material remains: small antiquities such as jewellery often constitute better evidence for the presence of the new cult than any structural remains.

Non-metallic rings

The rings that have been discussed so far are all made of metal. It is difficult to be sure just how common non-metallic finger-rings were, but there are two substances in particular of which we have interesting surviving examples, namely glass and jet. For simplicity's sake I propose to treat jet as a single material here, although in fact several glossy black substances were used, and more research is needed on the subject.[57]

Glass does not seem an especially suitable material for rings because of its fragility, but it was certainly used for this purpose, and some handsome examples of glass rings have been found in Britain and on the Continent. The full range of colours obtainable in glass was available, and shaping could be carried out by the variety of means familiar to glass-workers: twisting, pinching or moulding the glass while hot, either to imitate the forms of metal rings or to create effects that could not be achieved in metal. Some of the Rhineland examples demonstrate one way in which the flexible characteristics of glass were used in the process of manufacture: the band of glass was curved round into a hoop and at the point of joining was sealed in a mould that created a decorative bezel. At least one ring of this type is recorded from Britain, from Shakenoak, Oxfordshire. It is made of amber-coloured glass and the relief-decorated bezel depicts a full-face head, probably of a child or a cupid.[58]

Figure 3.30 A glass finger-ring from London. The hoop is a spiral twist of colourless and yellow glass, and the green glass setting is surrounded with a yellow border. (Photo: Museum of London).

Two glass rings from London belong to a well-known form, made of clear glass with spiral trails of yellow. Each has a glass bezel added in a contrasting colour, one green, one blue.[59] Clearly there is some morphological relationship with the standard type of gem-set ring (Henig II), but the characteristics of the glass have dictated the main decorative feature, namely the coloured spiral decoration of the hoop. Rings in very dark near-opaque glass that appears black (actually purple, brown or blue) may in some cases have been intended to resemble jet.

Romano-British jet jewellery was often of impressive quality, and finger-rings in this material were no exception. Jet can be intricately carved and takes a high polish, but although some necklace-pendants made of jet were complex carvings, rings of this substance tended, on the

Figure 3.31 A group of jet jewellery from South Shields, including bracelets, finger-rings and beads. Museum of Antiquities, Newcastle. (Photo: University of Newcastle upon Tyne).

whole, to be inspired by the forms of metal rings and to be decorated mainly with linear engraved ornament.

The small finds from the Roman fort at South Shields, Tyne and Wear have been well published, and in the illustrations of the jet rings from that site we can pick out several designs that belong to known and datable metal forms.[60] For example, there are third-century rings with what I have described as hunched shoulders, and others that clearly fall into the late Roman Brancaster type, with raised engraved bezels. Others still have hoops carved to imitate in a stylized form the intricate volute-patterned shoulders of the third- and fourth-century keeled rings. There are some distinctively different features as well, though; several of the South Shields rings have a bezel that is based on an elegant S-curve, evidently a characteristic design from a local workshop. A fine jet ring from London is a distant Brancaster variant, with rectangular bezel and elegant linear engraving.[61]

Quartzes such as rock-crystal and chalcedony were occasionally used to manufacture complete rings as well as stone settings. They are inclined to be very massive and flamboyant, and ill-adapted to normal wear, giving rise to the supposition that they were for funerary use, or perhaps simply for use as seals, worn suspended rather than on a finger. Specimens are known from the Rhineland, but the type is not yet known from Britain, although a smaller, plainer hardstone ring has been recorded from the important Romano-Celtic temple site at Hayling Island, Hampshire; it is carved in the form of clasped hands and is made of chalcedony.[62]

Amber occurs from time to time in Roman jewellery from Britain, but was not in common use. A fine amber ring with a head of Minerva in high relief comes from Carlisle.[63] The material, which is a fossil resin, is too soft to be very practical for wear as a finger-ring. Very elaborately carved amber finger-rings with bezels that must rank as small sculptures were made at a major manufacturing centre at Aquileia in northern Italy, and have been found elsewhere on the Continent.

Bone and antler were extensively employed for objects of use and ornament in the Roman period, and it comes as no surprise to find that finger-rings were among these objects. The simplest bone rings could be made with a minimum of shaping from a section of bone of suitable size, but more elaborate ones, with engraved or chip-carved decoration (that is, deeply cut, notched patterns), were also made. Wood could also conceivably have been used for the manufacture of finger-rings, but no certain example can be cited, and while wooden beads seem a very probable cheap form of jewellery, the material seems a less suitable choice for rings.

Enamelled rings

Rings with enamelled bezels form an interesting small group that deserves special mention. In a sense, perhaps, they belong in the next chapter, where we shall look at the coloured settings of stone and other materials placed in jewellery, especially rings. In some instances, enamelling may indeed have been used to imitate the appearance of a gem-setting, but since this could be more easily achieved with a moulded glass setting, we should suppose, rather, that coloured enamel was normally an expression of the native taste applied to a Roman type of ornament.

There is no single ring form that is found with enamelled ornament; a few examples can be placed in the classic Henig II, while more fall under Henig IV or variants of the hunched-shoulder types, often with strongly profiled shoulder forms; some are simply a wire hoop and round bezel too basic for typological attribution. Enamelling was commonplace on Romano-British brooches of many types (see Ch. 7), and rings with enamelled bezels were presumably produced by the same manufacturers. As we might expect, the patterns are often similar to those found on small disc-brooches, with concentric circles, or simple stars and rosettes. The contrasting colours of opaque enamel and the bright bronze would have made these rings, when new, rather attractive ornaments, and it is surprising that they are not more common.

Simple rings and plain rings

Before we leave the subject of finger-rings, it must be pointed out that there were many varieties in use that do not fall into any of the classifications noted above. Some of these are very basic rings that were probably home-made rather than bought as products of professional craftsmen. The very simplest forms of metal and bone rings could have been made without any special equipment or training, and it is futile to try to apply elaborate systems of classification to such fundamental items of adornment.

On most Romano-British sites, finds of base-metal jewellery will include very simple bronze rings formed of wire or of thicker flattened strips or rods of metal, with or without a bezel. Some of the hoops are decorated with regular faceted or notched patterns, resembling the bronze bracelets that were in common use throughout the Roman period in Britain. Thinner wire rings could be penannular (open circles), or made of several turns. The penannular ones could have been worn on the finger if they are of suitable size, but many earrings take exactly the same form, and it can therefore be impossible in many cases to say which type of jewellery they were. Heavier cast bronze rings with a bezel area clearly distinguished from the hoop and simple punched or engraved decoration can also be difficult to date closely or organize into a systematic typological scheme.

Some rings are completely plain, consisting of undecorated hoops or bands of metal or other material. At this level of simplicity it is not only impossible to date such items unless they are from a sound archaeological context, but it can even be difficult to identify them as finger-rings at all: perfectly plain annular hoops in bronze and even in silver cannot necessarily be assumed to be jewellery. Rings that served to attach chains to some other object are often well finished, and will be made of a metal corresponding to the rest of the item: iron, bronze and silver are all possible both for functional links and for finger-rings. For example, silver rings of the overlapped wire type (Guiraud 6) were used as suspension rings for items of silver plate such as small handled strainers in the late Roman period, and if found on their own, lacking a context, could neither be classified nor dated with confidence: rings made of simple metal wire curved round and overlapped have been used in most cultures. Bronze examples have an even wider potential range of uses.

We can usually assume that heavy plain hoops made of gold are finger-rings rather than functional fasteners or links because of the value of the metal and the consequent rarity of large, complex gold objects, but they, too, are impossible to date if they have no context. Modern examples of these forms, which we now regard as typical for wedding rings, will normally bear official hallmarks enabling us to identify the place and year of manufacture precisely, but non-European or ancient plain rings lack such marks and cannot be distinguished from one another. Analysis of the metal composition may sometimes be helpful, but it will not necessarily solve the difficulty. Even gold hoops with simple faceted ornament can belong to any era from the Roman period to the present. Gold rings made of thinner wire, either overlapped and joined or penannular, will often be earrings, or parts of earrings, rather than finger-rings.

Chapter 4

Gemstones and other settings

Engraved gems

The use of gems in Romano-British jewellery deserves to be discussed as a subject in its own right, although it cuts across the broad typological classification that forms the basis of these chapters. The point has already been made in Chapter 2 that the setting of coloured stones in jewellery, and in particular the decorative engraving of such stones for use as seals, was an ancient tradition in the Classical world but was new to the Celtic north. The mounting of coral or enamel studs on bronze was indeed an Iron Age Celtic technique, and it testifies to a similar enjoyment of the visual effect of the vivid colour contrast of a red accent against a gold-coloured background, but this is only one aspect of the appeal of stone settings as used in Classical jewellery. The widespread use of coloured stones and glass set in metal ornaments or used as beads and pendants, and the further development of enamelling in a range of colours, is one of the distinctive features that marks the classicization of jewellery in Roman Britain.

Although the craft of the gem-engraver had reached and indeed passed its apogee before Britain became part of the Roman Empire, engraved gems still constituted one of the most interesting and important innovations in the jewellery of Roman Britain. Gemstones carved with an ornamental device in intaglio, so that impressions taken from them would reveal tiny but detailed images in low relief, were sometimes set in purely decorative jewels such as pendants, but their habitual place was in rings, probably deriving directly from their original function as sealstones. A finger-ring is a convenient and secure way in which to carry a personal seal, and it was still a common practice to wear such seals in quite recent times. However, as in the eighteenth and nineteenth centuries, the decorative potential of a beautifully engraved and coloured gem often came to be more highly valued than its practical purpose as a seal, and sometimes completely superseded that function.

The study of engraved gems (glyptics) forms a specific and highly specialized area of scholarship, and it is not possible to do more than touch very superficially upon it within the scope of this book. For more detailed study, the relevant works cited in the bibliography should be consulted. Although some important new finds have been made since it was first published in 1974, Henig's *A corpus of Roman engraved gemstones from British sites* (1978) remains an essential general work of reference as well as an indispensable catalogue of British finds, while the publications of the Dutch scholar Marianne Maaskant-Kleibrink break new ground in the detailed study of techniques of gem-cutting and the light that they can shed on chronology and origins. Three vital references that post-date Martin Henig's 1978 corpus are the same author's paper on antique gems in Roman Britain, David Zienkiewicz's study of the gems from the excavations of the fortress baths at Caerleon, and Marianne Maaskant-Kleibrink's analysis of the gem-cutting styles represented in the Snettisham jeweller's hoard.[1]

Seals and sealings

In Roman Britain, as elsewhere in the Classical world, sealings made of beeswax or clay would have been used to secure letters and packages in transit and valuables in storage, and would have been necessary for the completion of legal documents such as contracts. Official customs-sealings would appear to have been made then, as now, of lead, and many of the latter have been found on military sites in Britain, although the perishable clay and wax sealings have been lost. Bronze seal-boxes, often enamelled in decorative patterns, were sometimes used to protect the fragile sealings, and their survival in some numbers in Britain testifies to the widespread use of sealings.

It is not necessary to possess a valuable engraved gemstone in order to place a distinctive mark on a blob of clay or wax: the use of sticks of sealing-wax, normally in a distinctive bright shade of red, was still commonplace in Britain in very recent times, and readers who remember using them will know that all sorts of objects were employed to impress the wax firmly over cords and knots and leave a distinctive pattern. Ordinary envelopes were also frequently sealed in this manner in the nineteenth century. The recipient of a sealed package will need to see that the sealing is unbroken and undamaged, but a known device, specific to the sender, is required to ensure that no unscrupulous person has broken the seal and simply replaced it afterwards with another. Hence, for serious use, a purpose-made sealstone is desirable.

It is impossible to say how many of the engraved gems worn in rings by inhabitants of Roman Britain were habitually used as seals by their owners, but this primary purpose was always possible. Roman society was highly bureaucratic and it is safe to assume that most men and many women would have needed to sign and perhaps seal documents from time to time.

Materials

The actual technique of gem-engraving will be discussed in Chapter 8; here we shall summarize the materials used and the iconography of the devices that were engraved on them. Most Roman engraved gems are stones that we would regard as semi-precious at best, namely several varieties of quartz. Precious stones were indeed employed in Roman jewellery: diamonds were of extremely rare occurrence, and were too hard to be engraved, and rubies were virtually unknown, probably because their main sources were beyond the reach of the Roman world, but sapphire is found fairly regularly in Roman jewellery,[2] and emerald and garnet were very popular and in frequent use. Such gems were generally left plain, the gem-engravers concentrating their efforts on the rather softer quartzes. This was not because the skills and equipment required to cut them were not available. Although emeralds were generally allowed to remain in their natural hexagonal crystalline form, garnets were frequently shaped to a conical point for setting in rings and other ornaments or indeed into complex shapes for beads and inlays, and all these gemstones, including the very hard sapphire, were drilled when necessary to enable them to be secured on a chain or in a setting by having gold wire passed into or through them.

Different types of quartz were sufficiently hard to wear well as jewellery and as sealstones, but were also easy to engrave quickly and in large numbers. Moreover, they came in a great variety of beautiful colours that provided striking contrasts with gold and other metals. The varieties used included clear rock-crystal and milky or white quartz; amethyst (mauve to violet) and citrine (yellow); chalcedony, a term applied to translucent or near-opaque quartzes in a range of mostly pale colours; carnelian and sard (translucent, in colours from orange-red to brown); prase, chrysoprase and plasma (shades of green); and jasper, a glossy opaque stone that occurs in many colours, but was particularly favoured in a rich terracotta or sealing-wax red. Various agates, especially banded agates with layers of different colours, were also important, and onyx or nicolo gems with alternating layers contrasting grey or white with black, brown or dark blue were used with great skill to emphasize the figures engraved upon them.[3]

The fashions in the choice of gemstone and its form changed and developed, just as the shapes of the rings themselves did, although fine engraved stones were often re-used in new settings, leading to an apparent discrepancy between the stylistic date of the ring and its setting. In general, there appears to have been a tendency for the more transparent stones to be most favoured in the early Empire and it was also in the earlier centuries that gems with a high, convex upper surface were most common.[4] A comparatively clear stone such as rock-crystal or citrine, shaped so that the engraved surface is convex, is very difficult to "read" in intaglio; the engraved ornament is clearly seen only in impression. By the middle Empire, the late second and third centuries, translucent to opaque stones, often with a flat surface, were more common. On these, typically red jasper or carnelian, the detail of the engraved ornament can more easily be seen on the stone itself. In the case of nicolo, the banded onyx is cut so that the layers are horizontal, and the engraved motif then shows up as a dark shape against the flat background of the upper, pale band.

This trend was obviously connected with the increasing importance of gems as pure decoration and possibly with a corresponding reduction of their functional role as sealstones. Gems that bear no engraved ornament at all, but which were cut and shaped to exploit the beauty and colour of the stone, may be found even in quite early rings. A superb third-century example is a ring from Gainsborough, Lincolnshire, with pierced shoulders and a projecting banded agate of tapered, flat-topped form.[5] Another significant factor in the choice of a particular stone would have been the apotropaic powers or characteristics attributed to certain crystals. It has already been noted that amethysts were held to provide some protection against drunkenness, and it is common for them to bear devices that also refer to the worship of Bacchus, the wine-god.

The great majority of carved gemstones were engraved in intaglio, so that the impression would display the design in relief. Cameos were also cut, however, and these were clearly intended solely for decoration. Although the larger examples were often set in pendants, many cameo-set rings are known as well. The range of subjects was rather narrower, and the use of banded stones to emphasize the form, sometimes in a very elaborate way, was common.

Cheaper imitations of hardstones were made in Roman times, as at all other periods, from glass (often termed paste in this context). Some glass gems from the Classical world are of extremely high quality in artistic terms, and they could be engraved using wheels and drills, exactly like quartz. The fine "nicolo" depicting Bellerophon spearing the Chimaera, set in a late Roman ring from Essex, is an example of a glass paste reproducing the appearance of a stone and worked in the same way.[6] However, an intaglio (or cameo) motif on glass can also be produced by the much simpler process of moulding, and the many humble glass settings in simple bronze rings from Roman Britain were made by this means. The

Figure 4.1 A bronze keeled ring with moulded green-glass setting, from Littlebury, Essex: a modest version of more expensive gold-and-gem rings. British Museum. (Photo: author)

Figure 4.2 A late Roman finger-ring found at Havering, Essex, with an engraved glass setting imitating nicolo. The device, which is very well executed, depicts Bellerophon, mounted on Pegasus, slaying the Chimaera. (Photo: British Museum).

definition of the design cannot be as clear and precise as in the case of a cut intaglio, but with such small objects, quite close scrutiny is sometimes needed to perceive that fact. The colours of natural stones and their varying degrees of transparency or opacity, including the contrasting layers and stripes of banded agates, could be imitated closely and most effectively in glass. Nevertheless, Romano-British glass intaglios tend in most cases to employ the easily available colours of glass, a natural light blue-green and light or dark opaque blue. Two examples in the British Museum collection, from Feltwell, Norfolk and Chesterford, Essex, are typical.[7] They also demonstrate the extremely simple and stylized stick-figures that are usually found on these modest moulded paste "gems".

I have already referred in the previous chapter to other materials used for ring-settings, and should perhaps repeat here that organic substances such as amber, ivory and bone, coral and jet could all be carved to create elements of jewellery as well as other decorative items including plain or fancy beads for use in necklaces and pendants.

Iconography

The range of motifs used on Roman engraved gems has already been briefly noted, but we can now look at the subject in rather more detail. Representations of Graeco-Roman gods and goddesses and personifications, the attributes (animal or inanimate) of these figures, and the symbolism of some other objects can be understood comparatively easily today because the iconographic traditions of Classical paganism have never been wholly lost in Europe. We are able to recognize a representation of a deity such as Apollo or Venus even when it is depicted in a stylized manner on an oval field less than 1 cm high. The poses and accompanying details of such figures were reproduced throughout the Classical world in life-size statues, small statuettes, paintings and coin-types and carvings of all kinds.

Whether an engraved gem was perceived and valued primarily as a sealstone or as part of an article of adornment, it is safe to assume that the owner chose the subject of the device with conscious deliberation, selecting an image that was fortunate or protective, or one that had some personal meaning for him or her. In later eras, coats-of-arms or elements from them, such as the crest or motto, were a common, indeed a standard, choice for signet rings, and although heraldry as such had not evolved in antiquity, devices that refer in the same way to elements in the owner's life, name, interests or occupation are known to have been favoured. Symbols of prosperity and fertility were thus especially common on gems. These can take the form of objects such as ears of corn, corn-measures and cornucopiae (horns of plenty) or of personifications and deities like Bonus Eventus, Ceres and Fortuna. The two most common subjects on the series of over one hundred carnelians from the Snettisham Roman jeweller's hoard are Bonus Eventus and Ceres. These stones were cut in Roman Britain, but the figures, simple and stylized as they are, are unmistakable and entirely Classical in their pedigree. General good-luck subjects are also prominent in another important group of gems from Britain, those from the fortress baths at Caerleon.[8] Almost anyone could find personal relevance in a motif that was devoted to the promotion of health, wealth and good luck.

It comes as no surprise to find that on military sites, images of Mars, Minerva and Victory are common subjects on the gemstones lost from the rings of soldiers, as are eagles, with or without military standards. All these are connected with war and victory, with the protection of "us" and the defeat of "them". Representations of the standard pantheon of Roman deities, such as Jupiter, Mercury, Venus, and so forth, are all common,

Figure 4.3 The 110 unmounted engraved carnelians from the Snettisham jeweller's hoard. (Photo: British Museum)

and reflect the widespread acceptance and integration into daily life of Graeco-Roman paganism that is amply demonstrated in other evidence from the province.

We also find images that refer to more exotic cults: from York, there is a very fine carnelian expertly cut with a head of the horned Jupiter Ammon in high relief,[9] and from Warlingham in Surrey there is an iron ring with a head of Helioserapis engraved on red jasper: the same subject is repeated on a gem from Vindolanda, Chesterholm, using the same material, jasper.[10] That fine gems were often set in iron rings is further underlined by the beautiful Hercules head on jasper in an iron ring from Malton, Yorkshire:[11] many of the stone ring-settings that are found on archaeological sites probably came from iron rings that have corroded away completely. Another red jasper with the image of an exotic deity was found in the nineteenth century at the Roman site of Wroxeter (Shropshire); it has a fairly simple engraving of Isis or a priestess of her cult. The gem is of middle Empire date, but the ring in which it was set has not survived.[12] Another unusual subject appears in one of the Thetford rings, a small, dark chalcedony gem in first-century style bearing an image of the Tyche (city-goddess) of Antioch, set in a fourth-century ring.

Figure 4.4 Two iron finger-rings set with fine-quality engraved jasper stones. On the left, from Malton, North Yorkshire, is a head of Hercules; on the right, from Warlingham, Surrey, a head of Helioserapis. (Photo: British Museum)

It is from the Thetford treasure, too, that we find a good example of a gnostic gem, a late Antique type pertaining to one of the more obscure and mystical religious cults of that period. On the front of the stone, which is a dull brownish jasper, is an engraving of a cockerel-headed, snake-legged monster, and on the reverse, where it would not be seen but would still have been efficacious as a charm, is a Greek inscription listing the magical names Abrasax and Sabaoth.[13] There are a few other gems of this type from Britain.

By the time that Christian iconography began to appear openly on jewellery, namely in the fourth century AD, the craft of gem-engraving was in decline and, as we have already seen in the previous chapter, the form taken by these symbols on rings is generally direct engraving on to the metal bezel. The picture is complicated, however, by the borrowing of pagan images and their reinterpretation in Christian terms, so that some engraved gems used or re-used in late rings, such as the handsome nicolo paste from Havering with the scene of Bellerophon mounted on his winged horse Pegasus and slaughtering the Chimaera, could have a Christian significance (Fig 4.1).[14] The scene is straight from pagan mythology, but as an allegory of the conquest of evil, it was used in Christian contexts, as for example on the famous mosaic floor with the head of Christ from Hinton St Mary, Dorset. We cannot say what interpretation was placed on the decoration of the Havering ring by its wearer. Pegasus without Bellerophon is found in a beautiful mid-first-century banded black-and-white agate from Eastcheap, London, one of a group of four gems that may be products of a London gem-cutter's workshop at this early date.[15]

Representations of animals and objects that may seem quite whimsical and arbitrary to us may have conveyed symbolic messages to their wearers. For example the Indian ring-necked parrots that are quite common gem-devices are connected with the cult of Bacchus, while doves were birds of Venus, and later had Christian connotations. Other Bacchic emblems included panthers, bunches of grapes, wine-cups, and amphorae (wine-jars) as well as representations of the god himself and his associates, Silenus, satyrs and maenads. Another intriguing type of device was the "combination" image comprising two or more heads or other motifs; these were probably regarded as charms against evil.[16] The iconography of gems found in Roman Britain is dealt with at length in Henig (1978).

One feature about the range of imagery on Roman gems must by now have become obvious to the reader even in this extremely brief survey: the iconography appears to be totally and uncompromisingly Classical. We do not find Celtic deities depicted on gems, such as the three mother-goddesses, the warrior god on horseback who is well attested in Roman Britain, or even the Celtic horse-goddess Epona who was widely adopted by cavalry soldiers of many nationalities and consequently worshipped throughout the Empire. There is a significant parallel in the iconography of Roman mosaic floors in Britain; as in the case of engraved gems, the craft was learnt and practised by local artists, but as the idea itself and the techniques were imported, the traditional motifs, all Classical, were firmly adhered to, and no visual element of Celtic art intruded. The only possible exceptions may be amongst the moulded glass intaglios found in some bronze rings, decorated with very simple standing figures that could conceivably be of Celtic deities.

This is not to say that some individuals might not have attributed non-Roman interpretations to the gems they wore. Perhaps if we were to ask a Roman Briton the name of the god represented with helmet, shield and spear on the carnelian in his ring, he would have said, not "Mars", but "Toutatis". It is an interesting speculation, but wholly incapable of proof. As we have already seen, the god-names that appear in abbreviated form on some inscribed rings include Celtic as well as Latin names.

It is possible to draw other inferences from the virtual absence of native religious iconography on gems. Precious-metal rings set with engraved gems would have been beyond the resources of the poorer members of Romano-British society, and it is precisely amongst these people that the traditional native religions might have been most faithfully observed. Some confirmation for this interpretation may be seen in the comparative frequency of gems depicting symbols of the mystery cults originating in the eastern Empire. Many, or most, adherents of these exotic faiths would probably have been foreign immigrants in fairly lucrative occupations, able to acquire high-quality jewellery.

There may be some truth in this interpretation of the subjects found on gems in terms of the social stratification of Romano-British society, but considerable caution is required. Successful, well-to-do members of the middle classes undoubtedly saw themselves as Romans, however purely British their pedigrees may have been, and in acquiring the material trappings of an inhabitant of the Roman Empire, the last thing they would have wished to do would have been to dilute or undermine these symbols by visibly adapting them to Celtic taste. An engraved quartz sealstone set in a ring was a Roman object; an owner who prized it would have valued that very quality. Roman tradition and symbolism were native to Roman objects such as mosaics and gems, but the enjoyment of such marks of cosmopolitan sensibility would not in itself necessarily have prevented a Roman of native race from continuing to venerate the ancient Celtic deities in other contexts, in the ways and places appropriate and traditional to them.

Cameos

Cameo-cut gems were not at all common in Roman Britain. The range of subjects found upon them reflects those popular on cameos throughout the Empire, and these subjects are notably more restricted than the vast repertoire found on intaglios. Martin Henig's catalogue of a splendid private collection of Roman cameos, that of Derek Content and his family, provides the best survey of this class of gem.[17]

One of the universal subjects for cameos was the head of Medusa, the gorgon whose glance could turn into stone the enemy who confronted her. Rings from an early fourth-century hoard found near Cardiff and one from Vindolanda (Chesterholm) both contain small onyx cameos

Figure 4.5 A cameo of Medusa set in a gold ring from the hoard found at Sully Moors, near Cardiff. (Photo: British Museum)

with Medusa-heads: both could have been found anywhere in the Roman Empire.[18] There are several other Medusa-head cameos from Britain including some superb pendants carved in jet which will be described in Chapter 5.

There are two examples on cameo-cut stone of the *dextrarum iunctio*, the clasped right hands of concord that have already been discussed as motifs on marriage rings. The finest is a layered onyx from North Wraxall, near Chippenham, Wiltshire, which in addition to the hands bears an inscription in Greek invoking good fortune and harmony.[19] A similar Greek inscription on its own – representing a well-known class of cameo – is seen on a third-century ring from Keynsham.[20]

Two handsome animal cameos should be mentioned. First, the large and splendid sardonyx from South Shields, Tyne and Wear, which has regularly featured for generations in books on Roman Britain. It depicts a bear and its prey, probably a goat, in white against a brown background.[21] The lion pendant from the Thetford treasure is quite small, but it is an interesting object. Made of onyx layered in dark blue and pale

Figure 4.6 One of the pendants from the Thetford treasure, set with an onyx (nicolo) cameo of a walking lion. The gem is well worn and has been reset on more than one occasion. Length 2 cm. (Photo: British Museum)

Figure 4.7 A large sardonyx cameo of a bear found at South Shields. Length 4.7 cm. (Photo: University of Newcastle upon Tyne)

blue-grey (nicolo), it is set as a pendant in gold, but had been cut down and reset not once but twice in its history before it was finally buried at the end of the fourth century. It is not surprising that it is very worn, and we can safely assume that it had been greatly valued by successive owners.[22]

The hero Hercules is the subject of several fine cameos. One, found in 1883 at the site of the legionary fortress of Legion II Augusta at Caerleon in south Wales, is cut on red-and-white sardonyx that, although sadly damaged by heat, still reveals a striking image of the young Hercules wearing the skin of the Nemean lion, one of his victims, as a headdress.[23] Another Hercules-head cameo could be classed as even finer, and it is in superb condition: found at Wiveliscombe, Somerset, it is probably a Roman-period import, but there is just a chance that it was brought into the country in more recent times from another Roman province.[24] Unlike these rather beautiful, idealized heads, another example, from South Shields, has much coarser features, which may represent the Emperor Caracalla in the guise of Hercules.[25]

Figure 4.8 A very fine Roman cameo depicting the head of Hercules, from Wiveliscombe, Somerset. In private ownership. Height 3.2 cm. (Photo: British Museum)

Plain gems and pearls

The use of plain gemstones or pastes in rings has already been noted. In later Roman jewellery especially this can be attributed both to changing fashions and to the decreasing availability of engraved stones. The settings in the Thetford rings, for example, are a mixture of re-used intaglios and undecorated stones, presumably new, such as emeralds, garnets and amethysts, plus some glass settings. There are also two intricately worked glass pastes with inlaid patterns in gold wire. These complex little settings clearly demonstrate that intaglios were no longer functionally important, since moulded glass gems with incuse motifs would have been far simpler to make. The preference for multi-coloured jewellery was an aspect of late Roman taste, and this bold polychrome effect took precedence over the skilful carving of single gems.

Stones used as beads or pendant drops in necklaces and earrings were not normally engraved, although they were often carefully shaped and had to be accurately drilled so that they could be secured or threaded on wire. Emeralds were left in their natural crystalline form, a hexagonal prism, and indeed green glass beads in this shape, obviously intended to imitate the precious stone, are quite common. There are green glass "emerald" beads in the Thetford assemblage that are in fact octagonal in section, but which still present an emerald-like appearance. Another popular form for beads of various materials was a flattened lentoid disc or oval. Requiring careful cutting, polishing and piercing, these beads demonstrate skilled craftsmanship.

Pearls were greatly admired and could be very costly. They were used far more extensively than is now apparent when we look at surviving pieces of jewellery, because they have often disappeared from their settings: like many other organic objects, they are often badly damaged or destroyed by being buried for a long period. Many of the pearls used in Roman jewellery were traded from as far afield as India and the Persian Gulf by way of Egypt, but there must have been many minor sources of true and freshwater pearls, and Britain itself was one. The first-century writer Cornelius Tacitus listed pearls amongst the natural resources of Britannia, and although his description of them as "cloudy and leaden-hued" sounds unenthusiastic, it is likely that pearls in colours other than white had their appeal in antiquity as they still do today.[26] Their naturally spheroid shapes make them particularly suitable as beads in necklaces and drops depending from earrings. The Romano-Egyptian mummy-portraits give some idea of the popularity of pearl settings on their own and combined with coloured gems, and there is no reason to doubt that they were as sought-after in Britain as elsewhere in the Empire.

Chapter 5

Necklaces and bracelets

Necklaces and bracelets were part of feminine costume in the Roman world, and were intended purely for adornment, having no utilitarian function. Gold bracelets in particular would have been valuable possessions, as they use substantial quantities of metal. While finger-rings and earrings can quite easily be lost, larger objects such as chains and bracelets made of gold and silver rarely found their way into the ground by accident, and we must rely on graves and treasure hoards for the actual examples on which to base our survey of the types worn in Roman Britain. The number of surviving gold ornaments of these types is therefore fairly small. But new finds can come to light at any time and can demonstrate the presence of types that were formerly thought to be absent from Britain: this point was well illustrated by the discovery of the extraordinary Hoxne hoard in November 1992. While the Hoxne and Thetford treasures prove that some very opulent gold jewellery was extant in late fourth-century Britain, there is little evidence from the previous century for material of the same quality. The adjacent provinces of Gaul, however, have produced several important assemblages of that date, and it is reasonable to infer that similar jewellery would have been in use amongst the most affluent inhabitants of Britain. By contrast, necklaces and bracelets of non-precious materials are found both in graves and on settlement sites.

Gold jewellery worn around the neck has already been discussed at some length in Chapter 2, where the contrast between the Celtic Iron Age tradition and that of the Classical world was noted. The precious-metal necklaces worn in Roman Britain seem to have conformed completely to the fashions of the Roman world, and it is not difficult to find parallels from far-distant parts of the Empire for necklaces discovered in Britain. The same is true of gold bracelets.

The survival of painted mummy-portraits from Roman Egypt depicting the deceased woman wearing her finery – necklaces, earrings, bracelets, rings and sometimes hair-ornaments – has proved invaluable for scholars

Figure 5.1 A beautifully painted Egyptian mummy-portrait from er-Rubayat, in the Fayum, dating to the late second century. The young woman's earrings are square emeralds with pendant pearls, and her opulent gem-set necklace is a type that has not yet been found in Britain. (Photo: British Museum)

studying the jewellery of other provinces of the Roman Empire. Naturally some caution needs to be exercised, since Egypt was a land with its own highly distinctive and ancient cultural tradition, and it would be rash to assume uncritically that the ornaments worn there in the Roman period were exactly like those fashionable in Italy, Greece or the Celtic provinces north of the Alps. It is perhaps something of a surprise to find that the precious-metal ornaments faithfully illustrated in the paintings do indeed closely resemble actual examples of jewellery found in many different areas of the Empire. It is possible to use Romano-Egyptian paintings as a source of information on certain aspects of Romano-British jewellery. This is in itself a remarkable testimony to the homogeneity of Roman culture amongst the wealthier sections of society. Fashions current within court circles and the aristocracy in Rome itself would have been known to leaders of society in other areas, and they would not have

Figure 5.2 Romano-Egyptian mummy-portrait of the second century, from Hawara in the Fayum. The woman wears a single gold pin in her hair, hoop earrings with pearls and other stones, and two necklaces (a chain with a pendant and a string of beads). (Photo: British Museum)

wished to appear "provincial" by failing to conform to these standards. Parallels with more recent imperialist regimes are obvious.

It is only from Egypt that these fine funerary paintings survive, but sculpture, especially in the form of gravestones, sometimes shows jewellery in use as well. The splendid series of carved funerary reliefs from the great city of Palmyra (Syria) represent richly bejewelled women of the Roman period, but Palmyrene fashions did have more distinctively local features. Carved tombstones depicting personal ornament also exist in Roman Britain, but unfortunately the style of Romano-British sculpture is more impressionistic than that of some other provinces, and is thus less informative than we might wish. Nevertheless, the archaeologist dealing with the Roman period must be grateful for all evidence of this kind, although it is far sparser than the comparable evidence from recent periods.

Figure 5.3 A funerary relief of the second century AD from Palmyra, Syria. The deceased woman, whose name is given as Tamm, daughter of Shamshigeram, is depicted wearing earrings, necklaces, bracelets and a round brooch. Her garments are decorated with panels of intricate embroidery or woven patterns. She holds a distaff and spindle in her left hand. (Photo: British Museum)

Necklaces

One observation that emerges from the pictorial and sculptural evidence is that necklaces were frequently worn more than one at a time. A short choker-style necklace could be combined with one or several longer chains, and gold jewellery was also mixed with strings of beads. Many gold necklaces consisted only of a chain with a decorative clasp and a pendant of some kind, while others included beads of glass or semi-precious stones. The intricacy of the chain varied, and from the Continent there are some fine examples of flexible chains made of complex decorative units stamped out in gold sheet in the form of stylized leaves or volutes; these are known in German as *Gliederhalsbänder*. Ornamental gold elements of this kind and actual gold beads were sometimes used in combination with glass or hardstone beads.

Gold chains were occasionally constructed from single circular or oval links, but they are not typical of Roman jewellery; when these basic links were employed, they were often of flattened, ribbon-like strips which create an effect like a paper chain. Far more common were wire links folded double and then twisted half-way through 90° to form a double link in

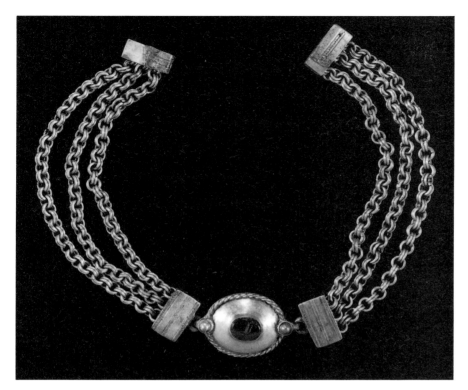

Figure 5.4 The silver necklace from the Aesica hoard, a triple-strand chain with spacers and a central element set with a carnelian. Museum of Antiquities, Newcastle. (Photo: University of Newcastle upon Tyne)

two planes, or links flattened and compressed in the centre into a figure-eight form. A more elaborate variant of the latter is a knot of Hercules (a reef-knot), which may be an actual interlocked pair of links or often simply a flat, two-dimensional representation of the shape. Either way, Hercules-knot links were both decorative and apotropaic.

Loop-in-loop chains were very characteristic of Roman jewellery and belong to an unbroken Classical tradition going back to Hellenistic and earlier jewellery. They consist of links that are doubled and have one or more folded links passing through them in series. There are simple single loop-in-loop chains but very complex examples were made that give the appearance of a smooth round-sectioned cord with a knitted or plaited surface. Modern jewellers describe this construction as a foxtail chain, and I shall use this term here rather than the more cumbersome "loop-in-loop" or the misleading description "plaited". The methods of construction are more fully described in Chapter 8.

Clasps were functionally very simple hook-and-eye devices, although they could incorporate quite intricate decorative elements. Where beads formed part of a chain, they were threaded on fine wire, often between ornamental gold links. Necklaces consisting of gold chain alone were sometimes worn, not only the decorative *Gliederhalsbänder* already

91

mentioned, but quite plain chains, for instance a superb triple-band choker found near Carlisle that fits high on the neck, allowing other, longer necklaces to be worn with it. The three chains of which it is composed are simple folded 90° links, but the clasp and a central movable spacer keep the three chains parallel in wear, and although the ornament is comparatively simple in construction, it would have appeared elegant and sophisticated.[1] This necklace was apparently found with coins that date its deposition to the second half of the second century.

More often, a chain would include an ornamented clasp and a pendant of some kind. The unusual silver necklace from the "Aesica" (Great Chesters) hoard has a triple chain like that of the Carlisle gold choker, likewise kept in parallel by terminals and spacers, but also including a brooch-like oval element set with a carnelian: the object is obviously Romano-British but is Classical in tradition.[2]

Chains with wheels and crescents

Romano-Egyptian paintings and archaeological finds from Italy and the northern provinces, including Britain, all testify to the popularity of necklaces that had a circular, spoked wheel-like element decorating the clasp and a crescentic pendant attached to the chain. An openwork circular decoration attached to the fastener of a neck chain continued to be a common feature in Byzantine jewellery, and indeed often became extremely florid in late Antique pieces. There are wheel-and-crescent necklaces from Roman Britain in gold and silver but the precise form seen in precious metal does not, so far as we know, appear in bronze. Gold examples such as those from Dolaucothi and the Backworth treasure were probably made in Britain, but this cannot be inferred from their design, which would be at home almost anywhere in the Roman Empire. The silver examples from the Snettisham hoard are certainly of Romano-British manufacture, as is a very similar chain from the Roman site at Newstead in Scotland.[3] In addition to the conventional wheel motifs, the Snettisham chains include clasps in the form of domed discs surrounded with decorative beaded wire. These are surely a rarer variant of the wheel, with the same symbolism, and have also been found on gold necklaces from as far afield as Italy and Egypt.

The wheels and crescents had symbolic meaning. Wheels were an age-old solar sign, while the crescent, obviously enough, indicated the moon. In the Roman period, such celestial symbolism was very generalized. Wheels were also significant in Celtic religious iconography, as an attribute of the god Taranis, often conflated with Jupiter; the history of the symbolism is effectively the same as it was in the Mediterranean. It would be wrong to assert, as has sometimes been done, that the wheel

Figure 5.5 Necklaces and bracelet from the Backworth hoard, incorporating wheel-and-crescent ornaments. (Photo: British Museum)

Figure 5.6 Three silver wheels and three crescent pendants from necklaces, part of the Snettisham Roman jeweller's hoard. British Museum. Diameter of centre wheel 2.1 cm. (Photo: author)

elements in Romano-British jewellery were derived directly from Celtic religious iconography. It is probably true, however, that the significance of wheels in Celtic sky-symbolism might have made these Classical motifs especially appealing and acceptable to Romano-British wearers.

Gold and silver chains with pendants

Comparatively plain chains designed to be worn with a pendant appear in some of the late Roman treasure hoards from Britain, notably those from Thetford and Hoxne. In the Thetford treasure, the pendants themselves are present, although it is not possible to say which one belonged to

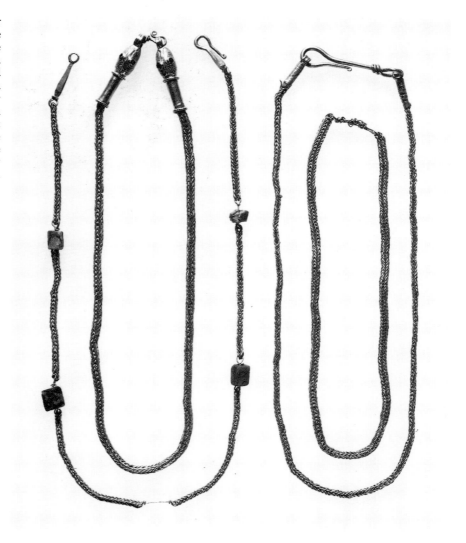

Figure 5.7 Four necklace chains from the Thetford treasure. The chain on the left with beads has one emerald and three glass beads in a green-and-yellow mixture. The foxtail chain is competently made, but not as high quality as the examples in the Hoxne treasure. Fourth century AD. (Photo: British Museum)

which chain – if indeed they were intended to match in this way. There are six gold chains in the Hoxne treasure that would almost certainly have been used with pendants rather than alone, but none of the pendants was buried with the hoard. Possibly one of the owners of the Hoxne gold took favourite gem-set or other pendants away with her while other material was hidden away for safekeeping.

The necklace-clasp was still an important feature in these late Antique jewels and remained an area to be embellished; one of the Hoxne chains has a tiny openwork circle attached to the fastener, but instead of a pagan wheel symbol, it contains a monogram cross, one of many Christian emblems in the hoard. Long slender pyramidal or conical terminals, some with added filigree embellishment, or decorative volutes in thick gold wire, were used to make the clasp area more elaborate and ornamental, as were zoomorphic terminals. In the latter, the ends of the chain were inserted into sleeves worked into the shape of an animal head. One of the Thetford chains has snake-head terminals, harking back to the frequent use of this animal in earlier jewellery, while the Hoxne examples include the equally traditional lion heads and also dolphins, creatures that were likewise common in Roman iconography, both pagan and Christian. Most of the chains themselves in these two important late hoards are heavy, complex foxtail chains, but there are some simpler links and one quite different type: one of the Thetford necklaces is formed of little gold beads, probably originally interspersed with hardstone or glass beads.

Although silver was used quite extensively in Roman Britain for finger-rings and bracelets, it was evidently rather less common in the form of chains for necklaces; the Aesica and Snettisham necklaces are therefore of special interest. The manufacture of the more intricate foxtail chains would have been even more difficult in silver than in gold, and surviving examples are not common, although there are some exceptionally hand-

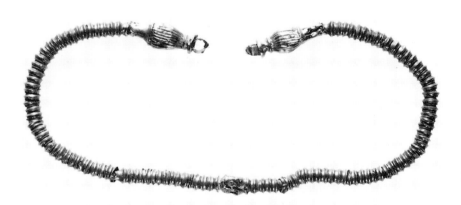

Figure 5.8 Part of a necklace from the Thetford treasure composed of small interlocking gold beads. These may have been interspersed with beads or other gold elements: many small objects were probably overlooked when the Thetford material was removed from the ground. (Photo: British Museum)

some examples from Roman jewellery hoards found in Germany; one fine specimen known from Britain is the silver chain which joins the pair of silver trumpet-brooches from Chorley, Lancashire, which are discussed in Chapter 7 (Fig. 7.7), although this is not a necklace as such.

The Hoxne body-chain

One wholly exceptional gold chain from Britain is the elaborate body-chain from the Hoxne treasure. It consists of a kind of gold harness constructed of flat straps of loop-in-loop chain, two of which were worn passed over the shoulders, and two under the arms, joining at strap-unions on the chest and back of the wearer. One of these joining pieces is an oval jewelled element containing a large plain amethyst surrounded by four almond-shaped garnets alternating with four circular settings that are now empty. They may well have contained pearls that have decayed. The other clasp is a gold coin set in an ornamental octagonal mount with a foliate scroll pattern. The coin is a solidus of the Emperor Gratian (AD 367–83). This chain can scarcely be described as a necklace although it has elements in common with necklaces. The type, although rare, is known to have existed centuries earlier in Hellenistic times and still to have been current in the Byzantine world as late as the sixth century AD. Representations of body-chains in wear are well known in Roman art, from mosaics and decorated silver to terracotta figurines, but the wearers generally appear to be goddesses – even Venus herself, as on the mosaic from Low Ham – or nymphs, rather than mortals.[4] The type was apparently a long-lived and traditional one, but in all probability its use was very restricted, perhaps to women of exceptionally high rank, or to specific formal occasions.

Base-metal chains

Bronze chains of many types were made for a great variety of practical purposes, and it is often quite difficult to establish which of them were intended for wear as personal ornament. Unless they include beads or pendants or are of complex loop-in-loop construction, it is often more sensible to avoid definite identification as jewellery, but plain bronze chain necklaces must have existed in considerable numbers. One interesting example from the important site of Richborough, Kent, has a simple medallion-like bronze pendant and links which are closed S-shapes, recalling the figure-eight links which are often found in gold chains.[5]

Metal chains with beads

Some of the most spectacular Roman gold necklaces are those that incorporate coloured beads, generally made of semi-precious stones. Emerald

Figure 5.9 The body-chain from the Hoxne treasure. In wear, the two hooks would have been attached to two rings behind the coin-set clasp. The coin, a *solidus* of the Emperor Gratian (AD 367–83) establishes the date after which the ornament was made. The gem-set clasp, very similar in style to some of the Thetford ring-bezels, contains an amethyst and four garnets: the lost settings were probably pearls. (Photo: British Museum)

crystals from Egypt – cloudy and opaque compared with modern gem-quality emeralds, but of an intense and vivid shade of green – were typically used as beads forming part of neck ornaments. Gold chains in which

Figure 5.10 A terracotta figure from Egypt of Roman date showing a woman wearing a body-chain. (Photo: British Museum)

emeralds in their natural hexagonal form alternate with decorative gold links were made throughout the Roman period and come from all parts of the Empire. Britain is no exception. A small fragment from a high-quality emerald necklace with figure-of-eight gold links was found in a second-century context in London while later examples using slender foxtail chain between the beads have come from Canterbury and the Thetford treasure. The Thetford example also illustrates the way in which green glass beads were sometimes used as substitutes for real emeralds. Garnets, amethysts, sapphires, carnelian and pearls were also used in gold-and-gem necklaces, often colourfully combined and having their different colours emphasized by different shaping of the beads. While emeralds were nearly always allowed to retain their naturally decorative crystalline form, other stones were shaped into discs of flattened lentoid form or into cylindrical, spherical or faceted beads. The gold elements between the beads were sometimes intricate links or beads that form an effective foil to the colours and shapes of the gems.

Roman Britain has not yet revealed much evidence for gold necklaces of this type, but there is no reason to doubt that they existed there. A dainty and colourful chain from London employs glass beads in green, purple and opaque white to simulate emerald, amethyst and pearl respectively; they are on links of fine gold wire.[6] Translucent blue glass beads may sometimes be intended to imitate sapphire. Where these slightly less opulent versions exist, it is reasonable to infer that more splendid gem necklaces were also known.

There were other types of gem necklace in which hardstones were incorporated as settings rather than being perforated to make beads. Some of these are amongst the most beautiful Roman necklaces to survive but, once more, fine examples have yet to be found in Britain. From Pompeii and elsewhere there are wide collars of multiple chains that support box-settings containing large stones. Necklaces of this type may be seen on many of the Egyptian mummy-portraits. Gem-settings alternating with gold links, or decorative elements in sheet gold such as discs or pelta shapes, sometimes further embellished with a series of gem-pendants, are known from many assemblages of Roman jewellery from the northern provinces of the Empire, for example the famous group of third-century jewellery found in 1841 in Lyons.[7] The series of gem-set gold plaques from the small Rhayader hoard (described below in the section on bracelets) could be a jewelled collar, but whatever its function, it is an unusual ornament.

Elaboration of a different kind is seen in the superb bead necklaces from another French find, the rich hoard from Eauze in south-western France, which came to light in 1985. These are designed in the form of short multiple strands of tiny beads separated from the next series by complex gold links or beads. Although based on gold wire and chain, these showy necklaces come closer in appearance to strings of beads threaded on a non-metallic support.[8]

Base-metal chains with beads were worn as less expensive alternatives to the gold versions that have been described, but they are fragile objects, and those that survive probably convey little idea of their range or ubiquity. One grave from the late Roman cemetery at Lankhills near Winchester contained a bronze chain with glass beads of different shapes and colours and at least one coral bead, and there are many examples from published late Roman cemeteries in Hungary.[9] Such ornaments will have survived better in graves than on settlement sites, and where cemeteries have been skillfully excavated and carefully published, the objects will be recorded; their apparent absence or rarity from other areas may be attributable only to lack of excavation and publication.

Strings of beads

Necklaces made of beads strung on thread rather than metal wire are seldom found and retrieved in a form that enables their original appearance to be accurately and confidently reconstructed. Beads found out of context can be impossible to date; the same materials and shapes were used in widely differing periods and places. Sophisticated glass beads were used and probably made in Britain in the Iron Age, and coloured beads in a variety of materials must have been traditional ornaments in Roman Britain, but their sporadic survival warns us that those that do exist may not be fully representative of the types that were in fashion. A very long string of minute blue glass beads found in London was recovered only because it was deposited in a grave that was excavated by skilled professional archaeologists.[10] The beads are around 3 mm in diameter, and once scattered by the decay of the thread that held them together, it is unlikely that they would have been recovered in casual digging. Rather larger blue glass beads of biconical form have been found in many Roman contexts, and were obviously a widespread, popular and ancient type: such beads have been found in Iron Age Europe. The same shape was sometimes used for hollow gold beads. The remains of another bead necklace from London is in the form of clear glass beads containing gold foil, an exotic type that has been found on a number of Romano-British sites.[11] Amber was also used for bead necklaces; an example survives from London.[12]

A small necklace found in 1833 at Felixstowe, Suffolk, apparently inside an elegantly shaped little flanged green glass bowl that is also still extant, is probably typical of many such ornaments that have been

Figure 5.11 A long string of tiny blue glass beads from a Roman burial outside the London city wall. The individual beads are between 2.5 and 3 mm in diameter. Museum of London (Photo: Museum of London)

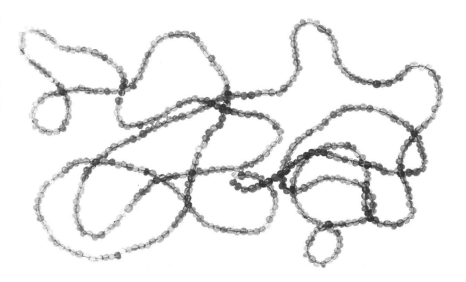

dispersed and lost. Although the early date of the discovery means that the details are sparse, we can infer that the objects are from a late Roman grave, very probably of the fourth century. The beads are tiny dark-blue glass ones that appear black, interspersed with irregular cylindrical beads of coral, now white-to-buff in colour, but originally pink or orange. Several examples of coral beads occur in the Lankhills cemetery, and of course this exotic material had been known and prized in Britain long before the Roman period. The present arrangement of the beads on a thread is modern, and we cannot tell whether the larger and smaller coral beads were systematically graduated or whether all the beads were threaded fairly haphazardly.

While small glass and hardstone beads can easily be overlooked during excavation, the typical Roman "melon" beads are frequently seen in museum collections because they are very large and robust. Their distinctive spheroid shape with raised ribs accounts for the name. Melon beads were often made of faience or frit, a glass-like material with a light-blue or turquoise glazed surface. The manufacture and use of faience was particularly associated with Egypt in dynastic and later times, but faience melon beads must have been made in many areas in the Roman period. The form is also frequently found in glass of various colours, including deep cobalt blue, and in jet. Glass melon beads were made in London and probably elsewhere in Britain, but they are an Empire-wide type.[13] Occasionally gold or hardstone beads of ribbed melon form occur in necklaces.

Beads made of jet and related black materials were widespread in Roman Britain, as we might expect from the general popularity of these

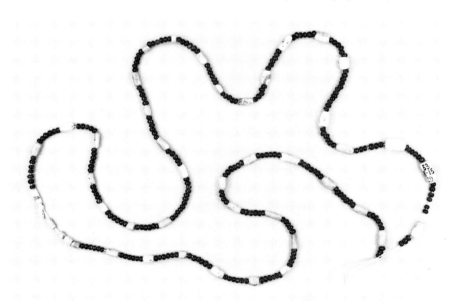

Figure 5.12 A string of glass and coral beads from a late Roman grave at Felixstowe. The coral is now faded to white or cream, but would originally have been a bright pink or orange contrast to the near-black glass beads. British Museum. (Photo: author)

Figure 5.13 Part of a necklace combining jet and glass beads of different shapes and a series of bronze pendants which originally carried green glass beads. The large jet bead in the centre is a type which was designed not as a necklace-pendant but as an element for making up segmented jet bracelets. From Exning, Suffolk. British Museum. (Photo: author)

Figure 5.14 Examples of melon beads. These are all made of the most typical material, turquoise-coloured glass fruit. They also occur in green and blue glass, and sometimes in other substances. Diameter of largest bead *c.* 2 cm. British Museum (Photo: author)

substances in jewellery. The beads occur in a great variety of forms, and would seem to have been used alone as well as in combination with other materials. One particularly intriguing type is an interlocking cylindrical jet bead with a raised zig-zag pattern on the outside and zig-zag ends that engage with the adjacent bead: a string of such beads looks exactly like a jet version of a metal foxtail chain.[14] Another type of bead necklace that looks like a flexible cord was made of flat disc beads of jet perforated in the centre. The same type occurred in stone, fossil materials and bone. Large jet beads of plano-convex section, often with two perforations and bearing ribbed or other relief decoration, may have been elements for necklaces (or bracelets) formed entirely of such segments, but could also have served as central pendants on their own. All these types of jet jewellery were also in use in the Rhineland.

An extensive range of Romano-British beads is illustrated and discussed in Crummy's 1983 catalogue of small finds from Colchester, while Guido (1978) is still the standard work on glass beads from the Roman period and late prehistory in Britain. There are two problems that still remain. The great appeal of beads as elements of jewellery was, and is, their capacity for combining in countless different ways to form ornaments of various kinds, and even though we can distinguish many bead types, rare and common, there are far too few instances where we can see exactly how contrasting types were assembled and strung together for wear. Even careful excavation cannot always reveal the order in which beads were arranged, and many of the reconstructed necklaces in museums, like the glass-and-coral one from Felixstowe, have simply been restrung in a way that seemed feasible to a nineteenth- or twentieth-century curator.

Another problem concerns beads made of perishable organic materials such as wood and seeds. Wood must have been used, and it is more than likely that natural objects such as dried lentils, shells and even animal teeth may also have been employed. Such objects are still commonly used in personal ornament today. Wooden and bone beads could have been coloured to resemble glass or stone, and such colour seldom survives even if the bead itself is made of a robust material.

Overall, in spite of the limited numbers of gold and silver necklaces that survive, we probably know more about these valuable ornaments, worn by the wealthier elements in Romano-British society, than we do about the more modest ornaments favoured by a far larger proportion of the female population. As I have emphasized, the gold and silver necklaces, with or without semi-precious stones, were in general similar in style to those found throughout the Empire, but there might have been distinctive local patterns amongst the inexpensive bead necklaces, possibly embodying echoes of pre-Roman jewellery traditions. The limitations of archaeological survival make it impossible for us to judge. Speculation is fruitless, but it is important to reflect that what we see in treasure hoards and in the funerary illustrations of Roman international fashion may represent only a small part of the costume that would have been worn in the towns and countryside of the Roman province.

Pendants

Because many types of necklace incorporated single or multiple pendent elements as an integral part of the design, it is not always possible to speak of pendants as a specific form of jewellery. However, some forms of pendant were undoubtedly separate items and might have had greater significance and value to the owner than the chain or ribbon from which they were suspended. They were made in a variety of materials and forms, and some clearly had amuletic functions in addition to their decorative aspects.

The pendants most often associated with gold chains of high value were themselves made of gold, with or without gems or other additional features such as gold coins. Mounts for coins and gems could be simple gold collets or very elaborate frames with pierced work or filigree. The splendid gold-coin pendants that became very popular in high-quality jewellery in the third century are not yet represented in finds from Britain, although there is no reason to doubt that such pieces were worn by the wealthy in this province: it has already been noted that third-century hoards such as those from Beaurains (Arras) and Eauze in Gaul have not yet been discovered in Britain.[15] These all include magnificent necklaces with several coin pendants in intricate mounts, separated by decorated tubular gold spacers.

The jewellery in the Thetford treasure constitutes one of the finest groups of high-quality goldwork found together in Roman Britain, and although it was buried at the end of the fourth century or the beginning of the fifth, the taste and style that it embodies is in a direct line of development from trends that had already come into fashion more than a century earlier.[16] There are two good examples of gem pendants in the group,

Figure 5.15 The unmounted carnelian from the Thetford treasure engraved with Venus and Cupid with the armour of Mars. The stone, now 2.2 cm high, was originally designed as an oval, but has been cut down for resetting in a rectangular mount. (Photo: British Museum)

one a nicolo cameo of a walking lion in a very simple gold frame (Fig. 4.6), the other an intaglio Diana on an oval milky-white chalcedony in a slightly more decorative mount. Both gems are substantially earlier than the hoard's date of deposition, and it has already been noted that the lion cameo had been set twice before in different mounts. The stone obviously had its own value as an heirloom. The large unmounted carnelian of Venus and Cupid in the same treasure, its original oval form trimmed down to a sub-rectangular one, may also have been destined for use as a pendant, although it could equally well have been set in a large finger-ring.

It is also in the Thetford assemblage that two other interesting classes of pendant appear. One is a very ancient and widespread form of amulet-case pendant, a gold cylinder with two suspension rings worn horizontally on a chain. Forerunners of such amulets were known in ancient Egypt, and their descendants continued into post-medieval times. The Thetford amulet-case is hexagonal in section and has simple flat terminals; Roman examples are known that are more decorative, with applied filigree and animal-head terminals. Some have been found to contain thin leaves of gold foil with magical inscriptions, but the Thetford amulet contained only a quantity of sulphur.

Figure 5.16 A gold necklace-pendant in the form of an amulet-case. From the Thetford treasure. Length 3.9 cm. (Photo: British Museum)

Figure 5.17 (a) One of the two stylized Hercules-club pendants from the Thetford treasure. This example has dark-blue glass with an inlaid pattern in gold set in the base. Length 3.6 cm. (b) Base of pendant. (Photo: British Museum)

The other Thetford pendants are two unusually large and heavy examples of the stylized clubs of Hercules that had been worn as earrings since the first century; it is impossible to know whether the Thetford clubs of Hercules were intended as necklace-pendants or earrings, but the former use seems more likely. They are not a matching pair. The club of the mythical hero Hercules was his most characteristic attribute, and was widely used in Roman decorative art, reduced to an elongated conical shape with regular round or oval protuberances to represent the rough knots of the original weapon.[17]

Actual representations of deities in pendants are usually confined to gems, although there are some Romano-Egyptian gold plaques featuring Isis and Serapis. The son of Isis, Harpocrates (Horus), was represented in a series of miniature precious-metal statuettes that have been found in many provinces, including Britain, and are thought to be items of jewellery rather than statuettes intended for display in a household or temple shrine. Small suspendable statuettes of Isis and Serapis are also known. There is a fine silver Harpocrates from London that was found in the Thames in the early nineteenth century, and gold specimens are also extant, although not from Britain. The Thames Harpocrates wears a gold body-chain, and has a large gold ring at his back that may have been used for suspension.[18]

Figure 5.18 Small silver statuette of a pantheistic Harpocrates, from the Thames at London. The romanized Egyptian god wears a gold body-chain and has a gold suspension ring at the back; he would have been worn as an amulet. Height 6.8 cm. (Photo: British Museum)

The head of Medusa was a common subject for a hardstone cameo pendant. The gorgon whose gaze could turn to stone those who confronted her was a powerful protector, and the strong female face with intently staring eyes and with wings and writhing snakes in her tangled locks was a wonderful subject fully appreciated by Roman artists in all media. The face of Medusa is found in several superb jet pendants made in Britain; similar examples found in the Rhineland may be exports from Britain, although there is much still to be learnt about the manufacture of provincial Roman jewellery in jet.[19] York was definitely one centre of

Figure 5.19 A jet pendant carved in cameo with the head of Medusa, from London. Width 4.3 cm. Museum of London. (Photo: Museum of London)

manufacture, but it is possible that the craft was also practised in other major towns.

The larger London Medusa-head pendant is one of the finest examples of the type, a powerful and effective image that is wholly Classical, yet executed in a local material. Other impressive jet cameo pendants include several from York with a variety of designs and one from Vindolanda that depicts a kissing couple on one side and clasped hands on the other, very obviously a betrothal/marriage symbol; from Colchester there is a superbly carved oval pendant depicting two cupids engaged in some craft activity, possibly pottery manufacture.[20] Cupids as artisans are almost a

Figure 5.20 Two cupids working, probably making a pot. This jet pendant from Colchester is another example of Roman taste expressed in a native material. Width 5.5 cm. (Photo: British Museum)

cliché of Roman art. The special interest of such pieces is that they are exceptionally integrated examples of combined native and Roman craftsmanship and iconography. Jet pendants and probably others made of glass or bone might well have been worn on ribbon, soft leather thongs or lengths of textile thread rather than metal chains, or they may have been combined with small jet or other beads. Some of the Romano-Egyptian paintings clearly show pendants suspended on black ribbons.

Decorative objects of base metal and other materials such as glass, bone and antler are familiar as archaeological "small finds", but unfortunately it can be hard to say whether they were intended for human adornment or for other purposes, for example as decorative elements of horse-harness. Bronze and antler pendants with phallic decoration are normally assigned to the latter category, but small gold or coral pendants of phallic form or with phallic ornament are known from Roman Italy and other provinces, and are interpreted, following literary references, as apotropaic pendants worn by boys. It remains unlikely that the comparatively large bronze phalli which are more widespread than the precious-metal examples have anything to do with feminine jewellery. Amulets, of course, do not have to be worn around the neck, but can be attached to the person or to clothing in a variety of ways.

Bracelets

Bracelets of many different designs and materials evolved within the extensive geographical and chronological range of the Roman Empire. They were far from being a new introduction in Britain; jewellery worn on the arm had an extremely ancient history in the Iron Age and Bronze Age of Britain and Europe, although they were apparently not very often worn in the Late Iron Age. The same kind of evidence is available as for necklaces, and although precious-metal bracelets do not survive in very large numbers, they are illustrated in paintings and sculpture from various Roman provinces.

I should first set out the terminology I propose to use here, since the terms bracelet, bangle and armlet have not always been defined in the same way. There is general consensus that the word "armlet" best denotes an ornament worn pushed up on the upper arm, and I shall follow this usage. "Bangle" is a word of Anglo-Indian derivation, and it implies an arm-ornament that is a rigid ring, most typically one of glass, bone or other non-metallic material. "Bracelet", traditionally and etymologically a generic term used for any arm-ornament, rigid or flexible, worn on the wrist or the upper arm, loose or tight, has recently been more narrowly defined by some authorities[21] to create a neat contrast with bangle, namely to indicate a flexible arm-ornament, while bangle indicates a rigid one. This distinction has been taken up by many jewellery traders, but it is not justified by usage or tradition, and will not be observed here: all arm-ornaments are bracelets, but some of them, in the form of solid complete rings, may be more precisely defined as bangles. There are hinged and segmented forms that are made up of rigid elements, and cannot be slotted comfortably into a neatly contrasting classification. Bracelet encompasses all of them.

The bracelets worn in Roman Britain span the range we have now come to expect, from sumptuous gold examples that would be familiar amongst the wealthier sections of the population anywhere in the Empire to very modest specimens. Many types were evidently designed to be worn in pairs, one on each arm, a usage confirmed by mummy-portraits and funerary sculptures. As noted above at the beginning of this chapter, a single new discovery of a treasure hoard can make a vast difference to the range of gold forms represented in Britain, and because the Hoxne bracelets have at one stroke enormously increased the variety of gold bracelets known from Roman Britain, they will be discussed in some detail below. Bronze bracelets, as well as those of non-metallic materials, survive in large numbers from settlement sites and from inhumation graves.

Snake bracelets

The typology for snake jewellery illustrated in Chapter 3 applies equally to rings and bracelets, and examples of several bracelet variants made of gold, silver and bronze have been found in Britain. The fine spiral bracelets of type A are early, as we might expect from their Hellenistic antecedents, but the type is represented in Britain by a damaged, yet still elegant, example from a small hoard found at Llandovery.[22] This ornament has been pulled out of its original spiral form, but the careful and detailed goldsmith's work that has gone into representing the reptile's head, scales and the inset glass eyes can still be appreciated. In the same hoard was a broken snake-bracelet of type B iii; in its flattened form and stylized rendering of the head we see the trend away from naturalism that is typical of this type of jewellery in later centuries.

The type of snake-bracelet that became common in Roman Britain was a very stylized version of the flattened penannular form with two snake-head terminals, B ii. An example in gold comes from Newport Pagnell (Buckinghamshire), but it is not wholly typical, partly because the details of the terminals are worked directly in the metal, not cast as they are in the more usual silver or bronze examples.[23] In general, casting is used far less in goldworking than it is in the more hard and brittle copper alloys. A

Figure 5.21 Gold snake-bracelet of type B ii from Newport Pagnell, Buckinghamshire. (Photo: British Museum)

pair of very small, slender and simplified penannular gold snake-bracelets also form part of a suite of jewellery from a child's burial at Southfleet, Kent.[24]

Five silver serpent-bracelets of the classic Romano-British type B ii were found in the Snettisham jeweller's hoard, forming an exact counterpart to the much larger series of type B ii snake-rings. As in the case of the rings, the stylization of the flattened heads is so extreme that it is necessary to know the history of the type in order to recognize them at all. An interesting development that was not matched on the rings was the elaboration of the engraved decoration on the hoop of the bracelet. Simple lattice-decoration obviously developed from an attempt to indicate the scales of the snake fairly realistically, but the engraving evolved into purely ornamental patterns. The Snettisham silver bracelets have panels of abstract motifs, and in one case, a vine-scroll that has no connection at all to the serpent which forms the basis of the design. A beautiful silver pair from Castlethorpe, Buckinghamshire also exhibit irrelevant hoop decoration with engraved lines, dots and lozenges. In addition, they bear the personal name VERNICO scratched on the inside surface.[25] The Snettisham hoard was buried in the mid-second century, and this gives us clear information about one period in which bracelets of this characteris-

Figure 5.22 A set of gold jewellery belonging to a little girl: the pair of snake-bracelets and the small ring set with a conical garnet are from a child's burial found at Southfleet, Kent. (Photo: British Museum)

Figure 5.23 Three silver snake-bracelets from the Snettisham jeweller's hoard; they were bent in order to insert them through the narrow mouth of the pottery container which held the whole treasure. British Museum. (Photo: author)

tic type were in use; the type would seem to have been in fashion from the first century to the early third century, if not longer.

Bronze examples of the flattened, penannular serpent are quite common, some of them closely resembling the finer silver ones, with broad hoops and detailed cast and engraved ornament, while others are little more than narrow bronze bands with slightly expanded flattened oval terminals. In all probability the owner of such a bracelet would have been well aware of its snake form, however simplified, and would have regarded the design as one that had specific apotropaic or healing properties.

Other gold and silver bracelets

The Backworth treasure was buried in the middle of the second century, like the Snettisham cache (see the Appendix). It includes one gold bracelet of a distinctive early Roman type that is not otherwise recorded from Britain, consisting of a flexible chain carrying a series of spherical hollow gold beads. Somewhat similar bracelets with double gold beads were found at Pompeii. The Backworth bracelet also has a wheel clasp that closely matches those on the two necklaces in the same treasure. Such jewellery belongs firmly in the mainstream of metropolitan Roman fashion, and it was probably more common amongst the wealthier women of early Roman Britain than the number of surviving examples suggests.

Much rarer types are represented in a small hoard found in 1899 at Rhayader in mid-Wales. One is undoubtedly a bracelet, while the other is an incomplete ornament of uncertain use: it has been variously described as being from a bracelet or a diadem or other head-ornament, but could also in fact be part of a choker or collar-type necklace.[26]

The Rhayader piece that is certainly a bracelet is broken into pieces and flattened out, but is a delicately made ornament which would originally have been very attractive in appearance. It consists of a broad ribbon of gold with applied filigree decoration in plain and beaded wire. The filigree features plain wire forming a plait or guilloche, not the series of interlocked links that form "plaited" (foxtail) chain, but the normal over-and-under pattern used to form plaits in textile. Plaited wire of this kind has been found on gold ornaments from distant parts of the Empire, for example on an elaborate gold brooch from Dura Europos in Syria.[27] Part of a hinge mechanism survives, which indicates that the bracelet was formed of two semicircular hoops with a hinge and fastener. Perhaps its most intriguing aspect is that there are small cells of enamelling in blue and green within areas demarcated by applied gold wire. Such enamelling on gold was known in earlier Classical gold jewellery, but it is not part of

Figure 5.26 A gem-set ornament (bracelet or collar) from Rhayader, Powys, consisting of plaques with filigree and claw-set dark blue glass and carnelian. Length of plaques c. 3 cm. (Photo: British Museum)

the Celtic or provincial Roman tradition, and this bracelet remains an exceptional and important item.

The other article from the same group consists of a series of rectangular gold plaques attached to each other by fairly crude hooks and eyes soldered to the backs of the elements. Each plaque is set with a large plain stone, the terracotta colour of carnelian alternating with dark blue glass. The collets have very sharp triangular claws rubbed over to hold the settings in place, and raised filigree in the surrounding border. The links between the plaques are covered with narrow plaques of sheet gold ornamented in repoussé with pelta shapes. The ornament is complex and elaborate, but the overall effect is gaudy and almost barbaric, and the treatment of the reverse side in particular is quite rough, wholly unlike the enamelled bracelet with which it was found. The function of the piece remains enigmatic. It could be a bracelet or armlet, but would also have worked, albeit uncomfortably, as a collar-type necklace. The plaques are attached to each other to form a straight band rather than the curved one that would be needed for a longer necklace. It has also been suggested that the object is a diadem, a tiara-like head-ornament: somewhat similar jewelled plaques of Byzantine date are thought to have served this function. The claw-set large plain carnelian also occurs in a gold bracelet now in the Römisch-Germanisches Museum in Cologne. The Rhayader hoard contained a gold finger-ring which indicates a second-century date for the group.

A single gold plaque that may well be from an ornament of similar construction to the Rhayader bracelet/choker comes from Colchester.[28] Its decoration demonstrates several goldworking techniques, with applied

Figure 5.27 Gold plaque from a larger ornament, perhaps a bracelet, featuring a portrait of the Empress Faustina, worked in repoussé surrounded with decorative borders in filigree. Length 3.8 cm. From Colchester. (Photo: British Museum)

wire and repoussé sheet, but it is unusual in that the decoration itself reveals the date. The plaque features a portrait bust of an empress, easily identifiable by her hairstyle and profile as Faustina the Elder, who died in AD 141.

Gold bangles of completely annular form, usually of solid or hollow circular cross-section with decoration in relief, gem-set bangles, and flexible or segmented bracelets are all known from other provinces, and in due course examples will surely come to light in Britain. Certain types, such as the twisted or overlapped wire bracelets described below, were made in all metals. From the present evidence, we cannot positively define types that were characteristic of silver rather than gold or bronze. Some broad silver bangles incorporating gem-settings are known from middle Empire hoards in Britain, and can be assumed to be locally made. A third-century coin-hoard from Cadeby (Lincolnshire) contained a matching pair of fine silver penannular snake-bracelets of type B ii and also a pair of broad silver bangles with simple engraved decoration and applied carnelian settings. There is a similar bracelet in the Aesica hoard.

Late Roman gold bracelets: the Thetford and Hoxne treasures

Although the beginning of late Roman fashions in gold bracelets is scarcely represented in Britain because of the lack of third-century hoards, two major hoards from the closing years of the province, Thetford and Hoxne, both contain pieces of outstanding importance.

There are four gold bracelets in the Thetford hoard and no fewer than nineteen from Hoxne. The Thetford group includes an exceptionally thick and heavy specimen of the twisted-wire form (discussed more fully below) with a carefully shaped and decorated hook-and-eye fastening. It weighs over 100 g. The other single bracelet belongs to a type that is found sporadically in hoards and graves from the third century onwards, that is, a bangle with gem-settings around the entire circumference. The Thetford example has alternating circular and diamond-shaped cells, only four of which still retain their blue-green glass settings. All belong to the lozenge-shaped compartments, and the circular settings would probably have contained stones or pastes of a contrasting colour, perhaps garnets. One of the best parallels for this gem-set type in gold comes from the Ténès treasure (Algeria), which is of early fifth-century date.[29]

The other two bracelets in the Thetford find are a perfectly matching pair in pristine condition belonging to a rare and distinctive type. They are made of a broad ribbon of gold sheet that has been finely ridged or crimped both horizontally and transversely to produce an overall effect that looks a little like basket-work. The edges of the hoop are bordered with rims of rectangular-sectioned gold bar.

Figure 5.28 Heavy twisted wire bracelet with a hook-and-eye fastening from the Thetford treasure. (Photo: British Museum)

Figure 5.29 A bracelet from the Thetford treasure which consists of a series of gem-settings. Only four of the stones survive, blue-green glass settings occupying lozenge-shaped cells. There would have been contrasting stones (garnets or pearls, perhaps?) in the circular cells. (Photo: British Museum)

The Thetford "crimped-ribbon" or corrugated bracelets closely resemble a pair from the hoard of jewellery discovered at Lyons in 1841.[30] The Lyons assemblage is of third-century date, yet the deposition of the Thetford treasure took place within the last couple of decades of Roman rule in Britain, at the end of the fourth century or the beginning of the fifth, a fact clearly demonstrated by the late forms of the silver spoons in the hoard. Late Roman fashion in jewellery, with its more flamboyant

Figure 5.30 A matching pair of corrugated gold bracelets in the Thetford treasure. (Photo: British Museum)

colour and texture, developed in the third century and continued in an unbroken evolution into Byzantine times. It can be difficult to date individual pieces closely, and coin-dated hoards are therefore of great importance in furthering research.

The Hoxne treasure, in which the associated coins (around 15,000 of them in all) establish a date of deposition after AD 407, provides important additional evidence for the continuing presence and use of Thetford/Lyons type corrugated bracelets in the fourth century. All the Hoxne bracelets are of bangle type, complete circles of rigid construction that have no clasp but were simply slipped on over the hand. Four of them belong to the same type as the Thetford pair. The ridging of the gold sheet is finer and closer, producing a more solid appearance, but the ornaments were worked and put together in exactly the same way. The set of four consists of two broad bangles just over 1 cm wide, like the Thetford ones, and two matching narrow ones, each weighing half as much as a broad bangle.

There are other pairs and one other set of four matching bracelets in the Hoxne group. One pair of broad bangles is superbly decorated in repoussé relief with animals and a huntsman. One of the pair also features a tiny figure of a nereid (sea-nymph). Three other bracelets have a related hunting theme, but they are not a matching set, and the technique consists of engraved figures and some piercing of the background. This pierced work is fairly simple, as it is on a set of four bracelets with a geometric pattern of repeating circles and lozenges, likewise embellished with incised details. However, the Hoxne bracelets also include four individual examples of fine pierced work (*opus interrasile*) of outstanding quality. One of these is a large armlet with a diameter of around 10 cm and a weight of nearly 140 g. The upper and lower borders of this ornament are hollow rolls of thick gold sheet with repoussé ornament; such elements are also known as separate bangles in their own right in third- and fourth-century hoards from various provinces. Between them a deep zone of pierced

Figure 5.31 Six of the bracelets from the Hoxne treasure, including the large pierced-work armlet and two of the other *opus interrasile* examples as well as the matching repoussé pair. (Photo: British Museum)

work includes panels of foliate ornament, some with leaf patterns left solid against a lace-like background of openwork.

One of the smaller pierced bracelets is of even finer work, a geometric diaper pattern of rectangles and lozenges with minute leafy scroll designs filling the framework. But perhaps the most remarkable of all the nineteen bracelets in this amazing assemblage is the one that was custom-made for its owner and gives her name. Incorporated in the lacy patterns are the words VTERE FELIX DOMINA JULIANE: "use (this) happily, Lady Juliana". The quantity and quality of the gold jewellery in the Hoxne hoard, and of the silver tableware, indicates that it belonged to a family of very great wealth who may well have had estates in many different provinces of the Empire. We cannot say where bracelets like these were made; they are of international late Roman style. What is important is that they were buried, and therefore presumably sometimes worn and used, in Britain. The very finest class of jewellery available was thus to be found in Britain in the late Roman period just as it was in the first century when the province had recently become part of the Empire.

Figure 5.32 Juliana's bracelet from the Hoxne treasure. The inscription wishing good luck to the owner, Juliana, is worked into the pierced design. (Photo: British Museum)

117

Wire bracelets

Like the simplest finger-rings and earrings, many bracelets are of absolutely basic annular or penannular forms that develop naturally from the nature of metal wire or rod, and were consequently in widespread use at different times and places in history. Coloured glass beads and other beads or pendants were quite often attached to simple metal bracelets in the pre-Roman Iron Age, and this custom apparently continued in use in the Roman period. Beads and other separate "charms" may have been regarded as amuletic as well as ornamental. A small twisted-wire bronze bracelet from Colchester is provided not only with a blue glass bead but a bronze bell.[31]

Bangles of overlapped wire, constructed like finger-rings of Guiraud's type 6, were also already known in Iron Age Britain. They were common in the Roman period and were made in all possible metals – gold, silver, bronze and iron. (They are classified as type 8 in Allason-Jones & Miket 1984.) Some are large enough to have been worn as armlets or indeed anklets. Iron examples seldom survive because thin iron wire can be virtually destroyed by corrosion, but the form is common in bronze and is known in silver and in gold. Some bracelets of this form may have been purposely designed so that the overlapped ends form an expandable sliding clasp, enabling the ornament to be enlarged a little while being slipped on over the hand. This is probably not the primary function of the construction, however; finger-rings and earrings were also made in this way and were not supposed to be movable.

Even more common, especially in bronze, are wire bracelets that consist of two or more wires twisted together into a rope or cable and terminating in a catch that is either a hook-and-eye arrangement or a pair of hooks. The simplest version is made from a single wire folded in half and twisted so that one end forms the loop for the clasp and the two free ends can form the hook, but there are many variations. Some cable bracelets are slender and loosely twisted, while others consist of several thick, tightly twisted wires: the wire can either be tapered towards the ends, or the cable can be of constant section, its ends bound by neat collars to which the elements of the clasp are attached. Some bronze examples appear to have made use of different alloys, or indeed a combination of bronze and iron wires, to create a multicoloured effect, a device that is still popular in gold jewellery today.

The gold examples of the simplest twisted cable type have hook-and-eye clasps that have been carefully shaped and given some additional decoration. A pair, said to be from Sussex, that came to the British Museum as part of the Payne Knight bequest in 1824 are typical,[32] and they are very similar to a pair from an important small hoard of late Roman jewellery found at the sacred prehistoric site of New Grange in

Ireland.[33] A fourth-century date is also supported by the superb bracelet of this type in the Thetford treasure, although it is a thicker and heavier piece than the others. Another example was present in the hoard from Ténès, Algeria, buried early in the fifth century.[34] In spite of these late associations, however, it would be unwise to state dogmatically that such ornaments were current only in the late Roman world; the design is too obvious and the sample too small.

There were some variations of the twisted cable form in gold, principally one in which the fastening incorporates a large additional decorative element, often a gem-setting. Some snake-bracelets and other types with decorated terminals were also made with a hoop of twisted wires, and the effect of a thick cable was sometimes imitated in hollow sheet gold shaped over a core. In fact, the appearance of a twisted band around the arm, achieved in a variety of techniques and materials, was generally popular.

Other bronze bracelets

In addition to the ubiquitous twisted-wire bronze bracelets there were other common types that have been found in considerable numbers on Roman settlement sites and in graves. Various general typologies have been attempted,[35] and most have some merit in helping to describe the objects succinctly, but a comprehensive typology would need to have an excessively large number of types and subtypes to encompass what is really simply a continuum of obvious shapes for an arm-ring – complete rings and open or spiral ones, some broad, some narrow, with butted, overlapped or clasped ends. There is an equally wide but simple variety of decoration executed by engraving, punching, casting and possibly filing. One decorative technique that is notable by its absence is enamelling. It might be thought that a cast bronze bangle would be an ideal subject for colourful enamelled decoration, and such an item would not have presented the slightest difficulty to the highly skilled bronzeworkers and enamellers working in Roman Britain, yet bronze bracelets were apparently never treated in this way. It is idle to speculate on the reasons, but the point is worth noting.

The geometric patterns found on both silver and bronze examples of the Romano-British penannular snake-bracelets were also used on plain broad bangles without serpent-head terminals, and in later Roman Britain especially, quite narrow bronze hoops with geometric designs sharply engraved or cut in the so-called "chip-carved" style were abundant. Scores of patterns have been noted and recorded, from simple regular transverse grooves or milling over the whole surface or series of punched circles to more complex combinations of transverse and diagonal lines, circles and dots. Patterns in relief such as zig-zag lines and angular meanders were created by cutting or filing a regular sequence of notches. In general, penannular bracelets made of fairly wide bands of metal with some form of decoration appear to be more common in the earlier Roman period.

Bracelets made of bronze chain probably tended to incorporate beads or other additional decoration but, as with necklaces, circumstances in which we can be sure of the use of bronze chain as jewellery are not common.

Non-metallic bracelets

Jet and shale bracelets

Shale and jet were already being used for the manufacture of jewellery in prehistoric Britain, and plain bangles of shale were an established type in the Iron Age. There were sources of shale other than those in the Kimmeridge region of Dorset and they continued to be exploited. Fine-quality jet from Whitby in the north-east became particularly important in the late Roman period. Jet and related materials were of widely varying degrees of suitability for working as polished black ornaments, although they may all have looked somewhat similar when new and glossy. Many jet and shale bangles were completely plain and unadorned hoops depending only on their colour and lustre for their effect. Others have grooved and notched patterns similar to those found on many of the bronze bangles. A common device is the regular notching of each side to produce a reserved pattern on the outer surface of the ring, such as a zig-zag line or a series of raised diamond shapes. A particularly interesting treatment found on some bangles is spiral grooving, carefully finished and shaped to resemble a twisted, roped effect. One treatment that has not yet been noted in Britain appears on several Rhenish examples, namely the insertion of thin strips of gold into the lines and grooves in the jet, producing an elegant black-and-gold pattern.

Not all bangles of these materials are strictly circular in plan. There are octagonal examples, and a number have an oval form. The latter may have been favoured because a rigid hoop of this flattened shape is a little easier to put on and take off as it allows better for the shape of the hand. Many metal bangles could have been flexed slightly if necessary, but this would not be possible with jet. However, glass bangles, equally immovable, are circular, so perhaps there is some other reason for the oval form. Circular bangles in jet and shale were produced on a lathe, but the oval ones must have been carved without mechanical aid.

Flexible bracelets could be made in jet and shale by employing beads carefully designed to produce an articulated band. When found singly, these jet segments can look somewhat strange. A typical form is a flat half-disc (or less than half) with two perforations and a slightly wedge-shaped section whose curved edge is decorated with a grooved and ridged pattern. Placed together in series and, it seems, also graduated in size, such beads form a broad flexible band with a rounded exterior surface decorated with a pattern in relief. There are also simpler articulated jet bracelets made of transversely perforated half-cylindrical or pyramidal beads. Jet beads come in a great variety of forms and were used in many ways, combined with other materials or on their own, and in both bracelets and necklaces. They were a very significant element in the non-precious jewellery of Roman Britain.[36]

Glass bangles

Coloured glass has been used for bracelets in many cultures, and Celtic Europe was one of them. There are many highly decorative glass bangles of sophisticated manufacture from continental Iron Age contexts, but the same is not true of Britain where they remain quite rare finds in the later prehistoric centuries. In general, the fashion for coloured glass bangles seems to have arisen around the time of the Roman conquest and to have been at its height in the earlier centuries of the occupation, but the question of the cultural affinities of the earliest glass bangles in Roman Britain is a contentious one. The arguments concern bangles with a D-shaped or rounded triangular cross-section that are decorated on the highest point of the section with applied cords of glass in contrasting colours, and sometimes also with trails and "eyes" of coloured glass.

Figure 5.33 Dark blue glass bangle with white trails, from London. British Museum. (Photo: author)

121

A painstakingly detailed typology for glass bangles of the early Roman period was devised by H. Kilbride-Jones in 1938, and this work was later modified and refined by R. B. K. Stevenson.[37] Briefly, type 1 bracelets have a D-shaped cross-section and are made of translucent glass encased in coloured glass. Type 2 are lighter bangles with a more triangular cross-section in a variety of colours with one or more horizontal cords of contrasting colours applied on the apex of the section; some also have additional trailed ornament. Type 3 bangles are generally of heavier type, although the plano-convex and subtriangular cross-sections continue, and there are numerous subtypes based on the colour and form of the trailed decoration that is always marvered, that is, rolled flush with the surface.

Both Kilbride-Jones and Stevenson focused mainly on the finds from southern Scotland (indeed type 1 does appear to be peculiar to that area) and regarded the bangles as a native, non-Roman type, while acknowledging that they first appear in the Roman period. There is no evidence for an existing tradition that was simply stimulated or modified by Roman culture, but it is of course possible to envisage a situation in which the increased availability of glass gave rise to a new industry that was wholly native in inspiration, manufacture and clientele. Some of the necessary glassworking skills were undoubtedly present in pre-Roman Britain, as polychrome glass beads were made, albeit not in great quantities, on the island.[38]

Alternatively, we could regard the emergence of this type of personal ornament as being firmly linked to the Roman occupation. The distribution pattern of Kilbride-Jones's types 2 and 3 is not as exclusively Scottish and northern as used to be believed, and some of the earliest specimens of type 2 bangles come from first-century military sites in southern Britain. A very handsome and complete specimen of a type 3 bangle in blue glass with white threads was found in February 1864 "nearly forty feet beneath London's pavement" in Old Steel Yard, Thames Street (Fig. 5.33).[39] The distribution in fact shows a definite connection with early Roman fort sites, and it could be argued that the bracelets were manufactured and distributed from these centres. The glass of which they are made is certainly likely to derive from Roman sources, although that in itself does not preclude native inspiration and manufacture. The hypothesis that the type is Roman rather than British in origin is cogently argued in a paper on the finds from east Yorkshire.[40]

Future finds may well clarify the matter. Glass is a recyclable material, and glass jewellery is likely to be under-represented in the archaeological record except where it was regularly buried with the dead. Like metal, the same raw material can continue in use in various forms over a long period of time. It may be that the absence of Late Iron Age glass bangles in Britain is more apparent than real, the emergence of the type in the Roman period having more to do with easy availability and probably lower value of glass than with a new taste in personal ornament. In any event, the pattern appears to be quite different from that on the Continent, where the Iron Age use of glass bangles appears to die out with romanization, and we can at least say that a fondness for coloured glass bracelets was a distinctively Romano-British taste in the early Roman period.

Glass bangles appear to have fallen out of favour by the late Roman period, although some fragments are found in late Roman and indeed in post-Roman contexts, where we may assume that they were kept as curiosities for their exotic appearance. This is in marked contrast to the jet bangles that were a flourishing type in the late period.

Sizes of jet/shale and glass bangles

Before leaving the subject of glass and jet annular bracelets, there is one important question that needs to be addressed, namely the implications of the sizes of some of the examples. As with all putative bangles, very large examples are known that may have been intended for the upper arm or for wear as anklets. More difficult is the matter of very tiny "bangles".

In the case of simple metal-wire rings, there is in effect an unbroken continuum of diameter from those that could be worn as finger-rings through to infants' and children's bangles to adults' armlets and anklets. Glass and jet finger-rings can easily be recognized as such, and they are different from the thick bangle-like rings of these materials that have internal diameters of 3–4 cm, seemingly improbably small even for a child's wrist. While conceding that some may indeed be bangles for young children, it is worth pointing out that they could have been used in several other ways, for example as hair-ornaments or simply as pendants on necklaces, bracelets or other adornments.

Bone and ivory bangles

Both bone and the far more exotic material ivory were used for bangles in the fourth century, and many examples are recorded from the late cemetery at Lankhills near Winchester, an invaluable source of information on personal ornament at that period.[41] A few ivory examples are known which are carved as complete circles, but most of them, and all of the bone bangles, consist of slender strips that have been bent round into a ring and secured at the join with a metal sleeve, usually of bronze, although silver has also been found. It would probably have been necessary to apply heat to curve the material into this form when making the bangles. It seems curious that they are so plain; both bone and ivory lend themselves to fine carving, and bone objects of other kinds were often highly decorated. The ornamentation of the bronze bangles would have been very easy to reproduce in bone, but this seems not to have been done.

Other bracelets

Strings of mixed beads were sometimes used as arm-ornaments as well as necklaces, and we may also infer the existence of wooden bangles of types similar to those found in glass and jet. It would be surprising if wood, which is well suited to the purpose, were not used in this way, but unfortunately sound archaeological evidence is lacking. Other organic materials such as textiles might also be used as wristbands, but of course this takes us outside the realm of jewellery as such.

Chapter 6

Earrings and hair-ornaments

There is no distinction in English terminology between ear-jewels that are suspended from wire hooks and those that take the form of a ring; even ornaments that are clipped on to the earlobe are still popularly referred to as earrings. Roman earrings belong to two main groups, those based on actual rings perforating the earlobe and those which hang freely from a hook.

Earrings differ in certain respects from the ornaments that have been discussed so far. Like all jewels, they are intended to be beautiful in their own right, but they attract the gaze more directly to the face of the wearer than jewellery worn on the hands and arms or even the neck (necklaces, in fact, are often subtly designed to focus attention on the bosom rather than the face). Finger-rings need to fit the fingers comfortably, so that favourite rings may become unwearable if the owner's hands become thinner or plumper, but treasured earrings made of precious materials can be worn throughout their owner's lifetime. Earrings can also be large and showy without being unduly inconvenient to wear, whereas large and elaborate gem-set rings, long or heavy necklaces, and almost any kind of bracelet can be awkward if the wearer is engaged in any practical activity. They easily interfere with free movement and catch on to external objects, sometimes sustaining damage to themselves or causing pain. Probably the only real hazard involved in wearing dangling earrings is that they fascinate small children. Although men and women have never been dissuaded in the slightest from wearing fashionable clothes and adornments simply because they are inconvenient or even downright painful, there is obviously much to recommend a type of jewel that can be ostentatiously splendid without being in any way impractical.

There is another important aspect of earrings that sets them slightly apart from other jewellery. Rings, bracelets and necklaces need only be slipped onto or draped around the appropriate parts of the body. To wear an earring, the body needs to be specially prepared, and once that preparation has been carried out, earrings must continue to be worn, not necessarily constantly, but at any rate regularly. Nose-rings and studs, which are widespread in African, Asian, South American and Oceanic cultures, are alien to Western tradition (although they are enjoying something of a minor vogue in the late twentieth century), and in Classical times as well as in our own culture earrings are therefore the only popular personal ornaments that require physical mutilation to enable them to be worn. There are, of course, several types of ear-ornament that can be worn without piercing the flesh, and although the sprung clasp of the modern earclip was not used in antiquity, decorations that could simply be hung around the whole ear or compressed on to its lobe or rim can be identified or at least guessed at in certain cultures. But in the Roman world, like our own, the characteristic type of earring was suspended on a wire hook or ring that passed through a hole in the earlobe, specially made for the purpose.

Piercing of the body for the sake of decoration is a recurrent practice in many societies, and although its overt purpose is adornment, there are strong sexual undertones. Some of the more arcane sexual practices of modern Western society involve the piercing of far more sensitive appendages than the earlobe. Metal rings and studs worn in the nipples and genitals of both men and women are considered by some to be erotically stimulating to a degree that justifies the very painful process of piercing and the not inconsiderable risk of infection which it carries.

Compared with these intimate parts of the body, the piercing of the earlobe is safe and virtually painless. Earlobes have few nerve-endings. We have no information from Roman writers about how and at what age girls' ears were pierced, but in all probability it was a simple domestic operation carried out with a needle. Even today, ear-piercing, whether carried out professionally or domestically, occasionally results in infections, and this must have happened regularly in antiquity. But the allergic reactions to the wearing of base-metal earrings – well known in modern times – may have been much rarer then, since the metals most commonly involved, nickel and chromate compounds, were not in use. Copper and its alloys can indeed cause irritation, and the actual friction of metal against the skin can give rise to painful reactions. Gold and silver very rarely cause any problems.

In the Roman world earrings were regarded as feminine adornments. To the occasional male Roman writer who commented on the practice, the only men who would wear such jewellery would be effete and effeminate foreigners from the East. It appears that wearing of earrings by men was acceptable in Persia and parts of Asia Minor, and there can thus be little doubt that however much the austere Roman traditionalist might have disapproved, some men in provincial Roman society would have worn them, but they would have been exceptional. To twentieth-century Europeans, the wearing of earrings by men has tended to have connotations either of a traditional, romanticized and definitely dangerous "other-ness" (pirates, Romanies), or simply a deliberate or imposed anti-Establishment position (hippies, homosexual men). The nuances of "masculinity" and "femininity" in jewellery are difficult to analyse and define even in our own culture; although finger-rings are worn by both sexes, males are expected to exercise restraint, and a man who wears several flamboyant gem-set rings will be regarded as effeminate. Yet a man wearing a more typically feminine adornment, the earring, is inclined to be viewed *by women* as a powerfully masculine rebel. It may well have been the same in the Roman Empire but, as is so often the case, the opinions of women were not recorded.

Earrings in Roman Britain

The evidence for the wearing of ear-jewels in prehistoric Britain is patchy. Certain types of Bronze Age gold ornaments may plausibly be interpreted as earrings, but the identifications are not entirely certain. Open rings can be used as ear-ornaments, dress-ornaments and hair-ornaments, or indeed as nose-rings, leaving aside those that might be wearable as finger-rings too. For prehistoric periods, it can be impossible to define them with any confidence. The Iron Age in Britain has produced little incontrovertible evidence for earrings, but there may still be some problems in recognizing some of the simpler and more ambiguous forms in base metal. This possibility is underlined by the recent history of research on Romano-British earrings.

Until very recently, it was commonplace to state that earrings were rare in Roman Britain, and indeed, if we search only for parallels to the magnificent and often very elaborate gem-set gold earrings depicted in the Egyptian portraits and known from the Mediterranean provinces and the Roman East, we find relatively few. It took the work of one scholar, Lindsay Allason-Jones, to alter this perception, simply by demonstrating that a great many fairly simple penannular rings and loops, mainly in bronze, were in fact earrings that had not been recognized as such in the archaeological literature. Her study, *Ear-rings in Roman Britain,* is a thorough treatment of the subject, and my discussion which follows is based upon it.[1] There may also be more earrings from adjacent Celtic provinces than have yet been recognized.

Allason-Jones's typology is quite a detailed one, and I shall refer to her types, but I shall not discuss all of them or take them in numerical order.

Her types 1, 2, 4, 5, 6, 7 and 8, together with eight subtypes of 2, are all basically penannular rings with tapering ends, and we shall return to them, but we shall look first at some of the distinctive types of Roman gold earring that are known all over the Empire and have also been found in Britain.

Gold ball earrings (type 13)

Large hollow spherical or hemispherical beads of gold sheet surmounted by a small disc to which the wire hook was attached were familiar throughout the Roman Empire. They have been found at Pompeii and other sites and they appear on mummy-portraits. Stylistically, the use of a smooth, unadorned gold surface of this kind seems to be in the Etruscan and Roman Republican tradition rather than that of the Hellenistic world but, be that as it may, the ball earring type is principally an early imperial one. The most typical example known in Britain is a stray find from Colchester that is in private possession.[2] An example of the double-ball variant type is known from Caerleon; it is from an archaeological context datable to the early second to early third centuries, but it may have been made considerably earlier.[3]

Figure 6.1 Gold ball earring from Colchester. Length 4.2 cm. In private ownership. (Photo: British Museum)

Included in Allason-Jones's type 13 are some related but distinct types that are probably later than the typical "Pompeii-type" large ball earrings. A pair from a very small hoard found at Owmby (Lincolnshire) have a simple hook and a hexagonal plate to which is soldered a ribbed hexagonal dome. From the accompanying finds, this pair would seem to have been buried in the fourth century.[4] A single earring from London is in the form of a shallow gold dome with a sunken centre that may have had a setting of some kind; its context was first to second century, but it is some way removed from the classic bead type.[5]

Hercules-club earrings: type 15

A particularly distinctive type of ear pendant is a slender, elongated cone with raised bosses, sometimes outlined in filigree wire and set with gems or enamel. The cone often contains a coloured glass or hardstone setting in the base. Occasionally the sides of the pendant are angled to make a tapered square or hexagonal cross-section, and there are other variants that lack the projecting knobs or filigree bosses and instead have decorative horizontal mouldings.

Figure 6.2 Two club-of-Hercules earrings, from Ashtead, Surrey, and London. These are amongst the rare examples of gold jewels from Roman Britain with enamelled decoration. Length 3.9 cm and 2.9 cm. British Museum. (Photo: author)

There is no doubt that these pendants are highly stylized representations of the club of Hercules, depicted in Roman art as a heavy tapered club with protruding knots. The type has been comprehensively studied by Rudolf Noll, and his work demonstrates that these pendants are found throughout the Empire over a very long period, from Hellenistic times to the fourth century AD.[6] This is not particularly surprising: the design is a suitable and effective one for a suspended ornament, and indeed earrings of much the same shape are still made today by artisans and for customers who may never have heard of Hercules, let alone his club. In antiquity, however, the motif clearly had a talismanic significance that added to its popularity. It has been suggested by Jack Ogden, on the basis of the story of Hercules and Omphale, the club may have been regarded as a love-token.[7]

Not all gold Hercules clubs were used as earrings. They could equally well be worn as necklace pendants, and the two large fourth-century specimens from the Thetford treasure that have already been referred to are likely to have been used in that way. As earrings, they were hung not from an open wire hook but from a closed gold ring with overlapping ends. Allason-Jones lists nine examples from Britain, of which seven are of gold. The one silver example, from Shakenoak (Oxfordshire), is from an early fifth-century context and is rather atypical. More standard are the early (first to second century) gold examples from Walbrook (London), Ashtead (Surrey) and Birdoswald (Cumbria).[8] While the Walbrook earring has brown glass or enamel in some of the wire cells, the other two have the blue or turquoise enamels that are typical of Classical enamelling on gold, and are otherwise known in Britain only on the bracelet from Rhayader.

Gem-set gold rosette earrings (type 11)

Circular or square gold earrings with a decorative openwork gold frame surrounding a gem, sometimes provided with additional pendent orna-ments, constitute another standard Roman type found throughout the Empire. Allason-Jones's type 11 covers the British examples; she includes other, simpler gem earrings that I would not see as quite the same type, although they are obviously closely related. An earring from Silchester, with pelta-shaped petals and a central pierced emerald crystal held in place by gold wire passing through the perforation, is typical.[9] A square exam-ple from Henham, Essex, is very similar and has an emerald bead mounted in exactly the same rather crude fashion.[10] Some have a cell in which the central gem is properly set; an unpublished circular rosette from Brishing in Kent is set with a small conical garnet, and may be rather earlier than the Silchester and Henham pieces.[11] A very crude gold plaque from a gold hoard found at Wincle in Cheshire would seem to belong to the same general type. It is square, and the gold mount is pierced in a haphazard fashion with triangular cut-outs. The gem is lost. The Wincle earring, if indeed it is an earring, evidently had attached pendants, since one wire hook is still soldered to a corner of the plaque.[12]

Figure 6.3 Gold earring from Henham, Essex, with an emerald bead in the centre and pierced surround. In private ownership. 1.7 cm × 1.5 cm. (Photo: British Museum)

The British examples of this type are all quite modest compared with the intricate and elaborate versions that have been found in other prov-inces. Additional drop pendants were often attached to a horizontal bar of curly bracket form. Some startlingly flamboyant variants of this earring type are known, for example an unprovenanced pair in Mainz which incorporate a chain above the main earring disc bearing three smaller rosettes.[13] In wear, the chain could be looped over the ear to display the small rosettes, and although these earrings look over-elaborate in an enlarged photograph, they were probably very pretty when worn. Emeralds, garnets and pearls were especially favoured for the settings and pendent beads.

Other gold and gem earrings

Glass or hardstone beads mounted in a gold frame crimped or rilled like the edge of a pie-crust form a distinctive and quite obvious earring type that is also found in Britain. They can be of various shapes and some are provided with additional pendent drops. Allason-Jones includes them under her type 11. A fine drop-shaped example with a cabochon garnet and two wires for additional pendent beads comes from Bath.[14] Crimped or rilled gold mounts seem to be typical of the middle and later Empire, and are frequently to be found in necklace-pendants, but there is really no reliable dating evidence.

Earrings that consist of clusters of beads threaded on gold wire have not yet been found in Britain. They are known from Pompeii, where there are examples that resemble berries and bunches of grapes, and were still current in the later Empire. The Eauze treasure contains one pair designed as clusters of three large emeralds, and another that is a beaded version of the gold rosettes with a central bead, having a central emerald in a plain rectangular cell and eight pearls surrounding it to form a stylized green-centred white flower. The combination of pearls and emeralds matches some of the Eauze necklaces: not surprisingly, necklaces and earrings were often made, or at least selected, to form a related set or parure.[15]

One of the simplest forms of gold-and-gem earring is simply a hardstone or glass bead threaded on to a gold wire that is extended and bent to form the hook (Allason-Jones type 10). An emerald earring of this type is recorded from Silchester.[16] Single beads, series of beads or complete pendent assemblies could also be attached to a plain ring, or a ring with a hook extension. The latter form, Allason-Jones type 12, is depicted with great frequency in Roman-Egyptian portraits, especially with a series of pearls threaded on the ring. Only six examples, four in gold and two in bronze, are recorded from Roman Britain, and not only is none of these a complete example with surviving beads, but one gold pair is of dubious provenance. Nevertheless, it would not be safe to assume that this popular and fairly simple form was rare in Britain. Gold earrings were probably present in far greater numbers than the archaeological evidence would suggest.

Silver earrings

Lindsay Allason-Jones was able to list 82 gold earrings from Roman Britain in her 1989 publication as against only 25 in silver, virtually all of them being of the simplest open or closed ring types. Although the catalogue does not claim to be a complete corpus, the proportions must be significant. She identified well over 450 bronze earrings. It is possible to think of a variety of reasons why silver was not favoured for ear jewellery, perhaps the most likely being that earrings could be made from a very small quantity of gold, and if a person aspired to something more noble than bronze, it might have been felt worth the extra expense to acquire gold rather than the less precious silver.

Whatever the reasons, the inference would seem to be that silver earrings in Britain may have had more in common with the designs favoured in bronze than gold, and may well have been of local manufacture.

Annular earrings with overlapped ends: type 3

Rings of this form, with the ends overlapped and secured by winding them around the shank, occur as earrings in both precious and base metals, but the majority are of bronze. Naturally it is not always possible to distinguish them from finger-rings of the same construction (Guiraud type 6) or from functional rings that have nothing to do with jewellery, but some have actually been discovered in burial contexts lying on either side of the skull.[17]

Figure 6.4 A group of gold earrings from London: a pair of simple penannular rings, one closed ring and a closed ring with a filigree-patterned crescentic pendant. Width of crescent 1.7 cm. (Photo: British Museum)

At first sight closed rings may seem an unlikely form for ear-ornaments. The rings must be open for insertion in the ear, but once they have been closed by twining one of the ends around the hoop, they cannot easily be removed and reinserted by the wearer on a daily basis and therefore become permanently or semi-permanently fixed in place. Even today, however, it is not unusual for women to keep simple hoop or stud ear-rings in place for long periods. Provided they do not have unduly sharp or bulky elements, they cause little or no discomfort and do not interfere with washing or sleeping. Allason-Jones records over sixty examples of the type in gold, silver, bronze and pewter. Club-of-Hercules pendants are generally attached to this type of ring, and other beads and drops are also found mounted upon them.

Bronze penannular rings: types 1 and 2

The great majority of earrings identified by Lindsay Allason-Jones are open rings of tapered bronze wire. They had been widely overlooked by archaeologists interested in personal ornament, and statements about the rarity of earrings in Roman Britain made by researchers (including the present author) were based on the relative scarcity of gold earrings of the decorative types discussed above. Even the gold examples of the simple pennanular earrings tended to go unnoticed.

The open rings have finely tapered ends that would have facilitated their insertion into the earlobe perforation. Some have angled tips that would have helped to prevent them slipping out but, even so, this type of ring is not very secure. Some still have beads or the remnants of an added pendant, but no doubt others would have been worn without any additional embellishment.

Type 2 is a development in which the wire forming the ring has ridges, projections or beading to make it more decorative and incidentally also less likely to slide out of the earlobe. Eight subtypes (2a–2h) have been defined according to the precise nature of the decoration. These earrings, too, may often have had added elements. There is no clear pattern of either date or distribution, and earrings of these types seem to occur all over Roman Britain. Like the simplest base-metal finger-rings and brace-lets, they would have been simple to manufacture and probably quite cheap to buy.

Bronze pennanular rings: types 4–8

Penannular rings made of a single twisted wire or of two or more strands of wire twisted or even plaited together were also common. They would not have required extra beads or drops to have had a decorative appearance. Although the form lends itself perfectly well to manufacture in gold, the only examples known in gold are imitations of twisted wire made of a thicker wire with surface grooving. There are a few examples of different metals or alloys being combined to produce colour contrasts.

Bronze spiral earrings: type 9

One final earring type deserves mention even though it is not very common. It consists of a bronze wire coiled into a tight flat spiral with one end forming a hook to pass through the lobe. It is not recorded in precious metal although it is another obvious and simple design, and the specimens of the type from Romano-British sites are principally from early contexts, some of them possibly pre-conquest. Typical are examples from excavations in Hertfordshire, at Baldock[18] and at the Roman settlement at King Harry Lane, Verulamium (St Albans).[19]

Ear-studs: type 16

Allason-Jones notes two examples of possible ear-studs, objects like small bronze rivets with straight shanks. It is perfectly possible that such items were worn in perforated earlobes, and there are endless examples of studs with decorative heads that could have been used in this way. However, to function as ear-ornaments, straight studs must include some form of secure stop at both the front and the back of the lobe to keep them in place. The modern butterfly clip is one such device. Another is an arrangement of interlocking rod and tube that is found in some Greek and early Hellenistic ear-ornaments. There is no certain evidence of ear jewellery of this kind in Roman Britain.

Non-metallic earrings

Beads and settings made of glass and hardstone must have embellished many earrings of the types described above, but all too often they have decayed, broken or simply parted company before they are found in the ground. There is also no reason why beads of the other materials that were used in necklaces should not have been used to manufacture earrings – coral, bone and ivory, jet and wood, for instance. Ivory, bone and jet could all have been carved into penannular earrings in their own right, and would not have been any more likely to cause discomfort or infection than the bronze versions which we now know to have been common, but there seems to be no evidence for the use of these materials. There are one or two possible penannular earrings made of glass from Britain. The apparent absence of iron earrings may be due mainly to the poor survival of this metal when it is in the form of thin wire.

Summary: earrings

The existence of a detailed study of earrings in Roman Britain helps us to see the overall picture. The general impression is that most of the earrings in use were of simple and inexpensive designs and materials that may well have been native in origin. While the simple open or overlapped rings, with or without beads and pendants, were made in both base and precious metals, the distinctive and ornate styles in the Graeco-Roman taste, such as gem-set openwork rosettes, were current only in gold. They appear not to have been imitated in bronze, although this would have been perfectly possible. Enamelled bronze is also absent in Romano-British earring design, although enamelled settings could easily have been suspended from hooks or wire rings.

Jewellery worn in the hair

Hair- or head-ornaments fall into two major classes: wreaths, diadems or headbands that are decorative and often also symbolic, and hairpins, which in most cases are primarily functional, serving as they do to secure the arrangement of the hairstyle itself. In Roman Britain, positive evidence for the former class of jewellery is extremely rare, whereas hairpins are commonplace, at least in non-precious materials.

In spite of the appearance of simple leaf-wreaths of gold on many of the Egyptian mummy-portraits, intricate gold wreaths and diadems like those made by Greek and Hellenistic jewellers seem to have been a thing of the past by the time of the Roman Empire. However, jewels intended as necklaces and collars can very easily be worn on the head if fashion dictates such a usage, and in some parts of the Empire and at certain periods headdresses could include jewelled bands or chains. The heavily bejewelled women who were faithfully represented by sculptors in the Syrian city of Palmyra wore turban-like headdresses with two gem-encrusted bands festooned on each side above the temples and a central vertical jewel ending in pendent beads lying on the forehead.

The latter ornament, placed along the centre line of the scalp, was not peculiar to Palmyra in the middle centuries of the Empire, although its mode of use in Palmyra, where it was worn combined with other jewelled chains and bands by adult women, seems to have been characteristic of the area. Known in German as *Scheitelschmuck* or *Scheitelornamente* from their positioning on the crown of the head and along the hair-parting, such pieces have been found in several other areas of the Empire, including one example from Britain, a delicate articulated ladder-like band of gold set with pearls and green glass beads from a child's burial at Southfleet, Kent.[20] At 26 cm long overall, this forehead-pendant is

Figure 6.5 A forehead-ornament as worn by a Palmyrene woman in a stone funerary relief. Second century AD. Palmyra Museum. (Photo: D. M. Bailey)

somewhat longer than most other examples that have survived, but its form, ending in a square glass setting with three drop pendants (two glass "emeralds" and probably a pearl lost from the centre chain), makes it certain that it was worn vertically. In a detailed paper on the Rhineland mother-goddess statues, Lothar Hahl and Victorine von Gonzenbach argued that the ancient representations of forehead-pendants of this type in use implies that in the western Empire they were worn by girls rather than by adult women. They could be combined with a variety of hair-styles, and would appear to have been current over a very long period of time.[21]

The Southfleet pendant is interesting for another reason. In an article published in 1986, Hilary Cool made a case for an early Romano-British goldsmith's workshop, the products of which are represented by the bracelet and the series of jewelled plaques from the Rhayader hoard, the Romano-British Hercules-club earrings featuring glass or enamel decoration, and the Southfleet pendant.[22] There are indeed important elements connecting these objects, not least the fact that they are difficult to parallel closely elsewhere in the Empire. The most convincing argument concerns the strips of sheet gold that cover the rather crude hooks fastening the sections together in both the Southfleet pendant and the Rhayader necklace and which in both cases are embellished with repoussé pelta motifs. A common manufacturing source for these two pieces seems very likely, and it may indeed have been in Britain, but we are still quite a long way from being able to assert this with real conviction. The sample of gold jewellery from Britain is still too small for us to exclude the

Figure 6.6 The hair-ornament from Southfleet, Kent, set with glass and freshwater pearls. Length 26 cm. (Photo: British Museum)

Figure 6.7 Detail of the Southfleet hair-ornament. British Museum. (Photo: author)

possibility that these unusual items of jewellery were imported. The apparent absence of close parallels in other areas is negative evidence that should be treated with caution.

Headbands of textile or leather, or of similar materials with metal or bead decoration, would leave little or no trace, and it is worth commenting on one find from the late Roman cemetery at Lankhills that provides some evidence for the wearing of such items. This is a child's grave in which fragments of gilt-bronze and glass lay around the decayed skull, some bones of which were discoloured by bronze corrosion. There was evidence that the metal and glass elements had been mounted on a leather strip. Some continental parallels are cited by Clarke, but objects such as these are at the very limits of what may reasonably be called jewellery.[23]

Hairpins

Straight pins in metal, bone and jet with more or less decorative heads are very common finds on Romano-British sites and indeed Roman sites on the Continent. In both pre-Roman and early medieval times, long straight pins were used as dress-fasteners, and the suggestion has been made that this use was also current in Roman Britain. While it would have been perfectly possible for some of them to have been used in this way, their principal function was undoubtedly to be worn in long hair to decorate it and secure it in place. Flat brooches, pennanular brooches and fibulae (safety-pin brooches) were in such widespread use that it is difficult to imagine plain straight pins, which are far less effective for the purpose, being employed to any great extent to fasten clothing. Pins have been found beneath or close to the skull in some late Roman burials, indicating that they were worn on the head, for example at Colchester and Lankhills.[24]

Hairstyles worn by adult women in the Roman world ranged from simple buns twisted on the nape of the neck to very complex curled and layered constructions that would have required much time and the assistance of a skilled hairdresser to achieve. The styles worn by empresses and other women in the imperial family would have become familiar throughout the Empire by way of official sculpture and coin portraits, and some of the more distinctive coiffures can therefore be dated quite closely. Women at all social levels, in the provinces as well as the centre of the Empire, undoubtedly imitated some of these styles to the best of their ability and resources.

Probably the most easily recognizable extreme of Roman hairdressing was a mode favoured in the period of the Flavian emperors, the late first century. It consisted of a vertical façade built up out of rows of tight curls above the forehead, with a somewhat anti-climactic basket-like coil of plaited braids at the back of the head. It was not too far removed in concept from some of the more fantastic coiffures of the late eighteenth century. The time that would have been needed to create the curly frontal diadems of hair, and also the problem of keeping the whole erection in good condition for longer than one day, may have been dealt with in many cases by using a partial wig. However, the slightly less imposing versions of the style could certainly have been achieved with the woman's own hair, probably with some kind of supporting structure and perhaps some false curls or padding. It is no surprise that Roman satirical writers commented wryly on the time and effort expended by fashionable women on their hair.

The favoured styles of the imperial ladies of the second, third and fourth centuries were less bizarre, but most of them involved some winding, plaiting and waving of the hair. In addition to the copies of these hairstyles which must have been seen in all corners of the Empire, there would also have been traditional native styles that may have been retained by some provincial women, even if only for certain special occasions. Distinctive local headdresses can be seen in provincial Roman sculpture from many areas, although they are generally in the form of head-coverings rather than the dressing of the hair itself. For example, dedications to the three mother-goddesses in parts of the Rhineland depict them as a young girl with waved hair hanging loose (with a forehead-pendant lying along the parting) and two matrons with high, smooth, halo-like hoods completely covering the hair. There are indications from Britain that simple styles based on plain hanging plaits were worn by some native women, as well as slightly more complex pinned-up braided arrangements.[25]

Nearly all methods of confining or covering long hair require pins or clips of some kind. Plaits that are allowed to hang down can be secured using only thread, but as soon as buns or twists or coils are attempted, pins of various lengths become essential, sometimes in combination with rings or with pads of false hair or wool. However, once long and thick hair has been anchored in some way, it can itself form the basis for additional embellishment, and hairpins can be placed in it that are not utilitarian implements at all but purely head-ornaments. Hairpins can therefore be ambiguous objects, on the borderline between everyday dress equipment and jewellery.

It is not feasible in practice to divide Romano-British hairpins along these lines and to pick out some that are articles of adornment while relegating others to the same status as a modern steel hair-grip intended to perform a useful function as unobtrusively as possible. While the more elaborately decorated and intrinsically valuable pins may safely be classed as jewellery, the plainer ones of humble materials may still have been regarded as decorative however practical they may have been in fastening the hair. Incidentally, the forms of the two modern types of hairpin, the U-shaped pin and the flat, springy hair-grip, were both unknown in antiquity.

In a recent study, Hilary Cool classified the metal hairpins of southern Roman Britain under no fewer than twenty-seven groups.[26] Two of her general points must be noted. She observes, first, that hairpins rapidly became very numerous in the first century, presumably reflecting the spread of Roman styles of dress, and secondly that the average length of hairpins is greater in the early Roman period than in the third and fourth centuries, a fact that accords well with the changes in hairstyles and the ways in which pins were worn. It is in the first and second centuries that we find lavishly piled-up hairstyles and also the tendency to allow pins to project and display their ornamental heads: in the later Empire, hair was worn closer to the head, and pins did not in general need such long shafts.

Detailed typologies are valuable in describing and interpreting excavation finds, and can lead to a fuller understanding of the dating and use of particular classes of artefact, but it will not be necessary to describe all the minute variations of hairpin form here. All that is needed is to distinguish between the highly ornate pins with heads finished as representational carvings and those that have more abstract grooves, mouldings, facets and the like. The materials used included precious and base metals, bone, jet, glass, and undoubtedly wood, although the latter has not usually survived. That some hairpins were made of gold almost goes without saying. Examples both with and without added gems may be seen in some of the

Romano-Egyptian paintings, and actual specimens have been found on the Continent, but no comparable example has yet come to light in Britain, although there is a small number of hairpins that have thin sheet gold applied to the shaped head.

Hairpins with representational heads

One of Cool's classifications covers several varieties of figural heads, namely those in the form of complete human figures, human busts, animal figures and depictions of inanimate objects such as axes (all these are under group 18). Under group 7 we find pins that have a human hand, normally holding some object, as the decorative motif. Pins such as these are found in metal and bone, although not, apparently, in jet, and must have been worn in such a way that the little carved motifs were clearly visible in the hair. The subjects would have been chosen with an eye to favourable symbolism as well as attractive appearance.

One of the most notable silver hairpins from Britain is an example from London that bears a complete miniature statuette of a goddess. It takes the form of a slender shaft topped with a Corinthian column capital supporting a tiny figure of Venus leaning on a pillar and raising her left foot to fasten her sandal.[27] Comparable figurines of Venus in standard poses have been found on silver and gold hairpins from other parts of the Empire: she was a goddess often invoked by women and her image was an appropriate one in jewellery. The workmanship of the London silver Venus pin is not of the best. The little figure is comparatively rough and clumsy in execution, but its diminutive size (the height of the figure itself is 2.5 cm) may be some excuse. Venus is also the deity on a long bronze pin from London; she is depicted in the form of a bust, nude apart from a diadem, with her head turned slightly to the right.[28]

Another goddess appears in a humbler material on yet another pin from London, a 4.5 cm high carving of Fortuna, complete with her attributes of steering-oar and cornucopia, superbly carved in bone.[29] Like Venus, the image of this goddess would have been regarded as protective and fortunate by the wearer. Complete human (or rather, divine) figures as hairpin-heads are exceptional, but bone pins with heads carved in the form of busts, like the bronze Venus pin, are not uncommon, and range from the crude to the very accomplished. Two from London, one in the British Museum and one in the Museum of London, are especially interesting in several respects. They are to all intents and purposes identical, and depict a female bust wearing the high-fronted hairstyle of the first to early second century. A third pin of exactly the same form, but with a slightly smaller carved head, comes from Gloucestershire.[30] The busts on these pins wear a hairstyle of the kind that the pins themselves would

Figure 6.8 A silver hairpin with a figure of Venus leaning on a pillar and fastening her sandal. She stands on a tiny Corinthian capital. The height of the figure is 2.5 cm. (Photo: British Museum)

Figure 6.9 A bone hairpin from London carved with a figure of Fortuna, 4.5 cm high, holding a cornucopia and a steering-oar. The carving is of unusually fine quality. British Museum. (Photo: author)

Figure 6.10 A bone hairpin with a female bust wearing an elaborate late-first-century hairstyle. The height of the bust is 5.5 cm. (Photo: British Museum)

have been employed to adorn. The summit of the coiffure displays a row of points that represent the heads of hairpins. These three pins are clearly from the same workshop, carved and finished in an assured style, and in all likelihood they were made in London, or at least in Britain. They exemplify a total fusion of Celtic and Roman themes, made of a traditional material and probably by a British craftsman, yet intended for use in a Roman fashion and actually depicting that fashion itself.

There are other, cruder bone pins with carved busts and, all too often, the head itself has been lost, the slender neck of the figure being a vulnerable point, but the most fascinating bone hairpin of all from London combines the image of a deity with the motif of a right hand holding a sacred or symbolic object. Found in Moorgate Street in 1912, its head is carved as a right hand supporting a bust of the universal Egyptian mother-goddess, Isis.[31] The goddess's headdress and hair make this identification certain. Below the hand, on the "lower arm", so to speak, is a simple but unmistakable carving of a spiral serpent-bracelet. There are now several individual items of evidence for the worship of Isis in London, including references to her temple, and this small personal object may be added to them. The cult of Isis was established throughout the Empire, and we need not suppose that the woman who wore this pin in her hair, inviting the protection of Isis, was necessarily from abroad, let alone from Egypt itself. It is interesting to speculate where the pin was made, but in our present state of knowledge we cannot be sure.

Figure 6.11 Front and back views of a bone hairpin from Moorgate Street, London, decorated with a hand holding a bust of the goddess Isis. Around the wrist of the hand is a snake-bracelet of type B iv. Height of bust 2.9 cm. (Photos: Museum of London)

Figure 6.12 A silver hairpin from the Walbrook ornamented with a hand holding a pomegranate. Hand 2.2 cm long. (Photo: British Museum)

The Isis pin shows a hand holding a small bust of the goddess as an object of devotion, but hands with eggs or fruit raised aloft between the thumb and index finger, as well as a few holding a larger spherical object, occur regularly as hairpin-heads. One silver example from the bed of the Walbrook, dating to the first or second century, will serve as an example. The hand, quite skilfully depicted, holds a small pomegranate, a fruit that in Roman iconography carries symbolism of eternity, rebirth and fertility. All such hands with fruit or eggs are simply generalized symbols of good omen.[32]

Some pins have been found depicting animal figures, including dogs, bears and birds; an iron pin surmounted by a small bronze bear on a column cap has been classified as a hairpin, but this may be debatable. Hairpins with carvings of inanimate objects are not especially common, but they do appear: one silver pin is known that is topped with a tiny representation of an oil-lamp with green glass insets.[33] Pine-cones are comparatively common motifs, and may simply have been suggested by their similarity to a simple slightly pointed bulbous head, but the Bacchic wand, the *thyrsus*, was surmounted with a large pine-cone, and this religious connection may well have been conscious in the choice of such a pin. In any case, they had a general symbolic value of fertility and good fortune.[34]

Amongst the other representational motifs worth mentioning are handled vases – likewise symbolic of Bacchus, and common on an Empire-wide basis – and complex pierced motifs surmounted with a crescent and

1 The 22 finger-rings from the Thetford treasure. The noteworthy features include the filigree decoration and the use of settings of many colours. Late fourth century AD. (Photo: British Museum)

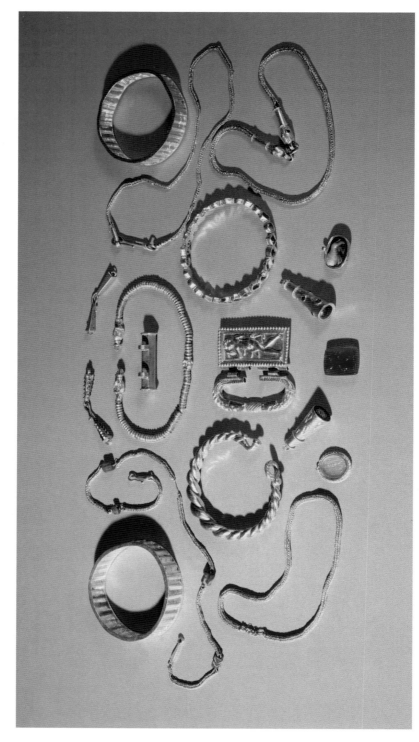

2 Chains, bracelets and pendant from the Thetford treasure. The matching corrugated bracelets at top left and right are paralleled in the Hoxne treasure. The gold buckle in the centre is a particularly rare object. Late fourth century AD. (Photo: British Museum)

3 A selection of eight engraved gems from the second-century Snettisham jeweller's hoard, illustrating typical subjects. They are Bonus Eventus, Ceres, Fortuna, Diana, a dolphin and trident, a stork, a cockerel and a corn-measure (*modius*, with ears of corn and scales). (Photo: British Museum)

4 Enamelled bronze dog brooch. London. (Photo: Museum of London)

5 Enamelled bronze zoomorphic brooch in the form of a horse. British Museum. (Photo: author)

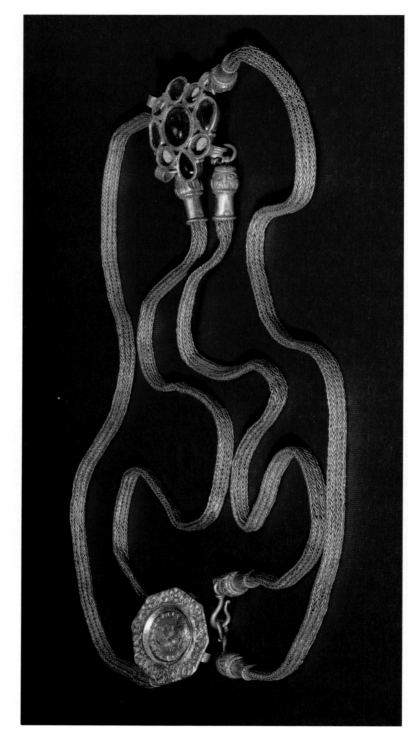

6   The gold body-chain from the Hoxne treasure. One chain-connection is a gold *solidus* of Gratian (AD 367–383) in a decorative mount. The other is a roughly diamond-shaped gold plaque with nine settings for gems. The central gem is a cabochon amethyst. The four elliptical garnets alternate with empty circular settings, probably for pearls. Early fifth century. (Photo: British Museum)

7 A matching pair of gold bracelets in the Hoxne treasure. The hunting scenes are closely similar, but are not an exact match; only the bracelet on the right includes the figure of a *nereid* (sea-nymph). The technique is repoussé work in very thin sheet gold. Early fifth century AD. (Photo: British Museum)

8 Three enamelled dragonesque brooches. The central example is from Norton, Yorkshire, while the other two, a matching pair, are from a Roman grave at Faversham, Kent. Second century AD. (Photo: British Museum)

9 Silver ring with extension incorporating a Bacchic scene, from London. (Photo: Museum of London)

10 The late Roman ring from Havering, Essex, set with a glass gem imitating nicolo, finely engraved with Bellerophon mounted on Pegasus, slaying the Chimaera. Fourth century AD. (Photo: British Museum)

11   The complete group of 19 gold bracelets from the Hoxne treasure. Early fifth century AD. (Photo: British Museum)

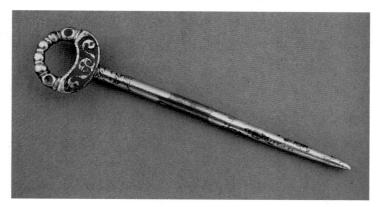

12 The small silver pin with red-enamelled head found in a mid-fourth-century coin-hoard at Oldcroft, Gloucestershire. This tiny object (6 cm long) is extremely important: as an example of enamelling on silver rather than bronze, it is exceptional in Romano-British technology, while its form and decoration provide a link between Iron Age and medieval Celtic design. (Photo: British Museum)

13 Two lozenge-shaped bronze plate-brooches with millefiori enamel. British Museum. (Photo: author)

14 Pierced gold ring from Corbridge, Northumberland, with the Greek inscription ΠΟΛΕΜΙΟΥ ΦΙΛΤΡΟΝ (polemiou philtron) – "the love-charm of Polemios". (Photo: British Museum)

15 Gold ring from an early fourth-century hoard found at Sully Moors, near Cardiff. The cameo setting is a simple representation of the head of Medusa, a powerfully apotropaic image. Third to fourth century AD. (Photo: British Museum)

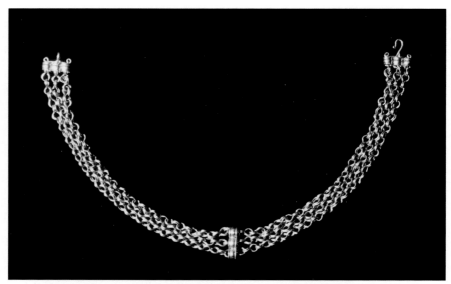

16 A short gold choker of three chains, from near Carlisle, *c.* second century AD. (Photo: British Museum)

17 A very fine Roman cameo depicting the head of Hercules, from Wiveliscombe, Somerset. In private ownership. (Photo: British Museum)

provided with extra dangling wire pendants and punched decoration. Cool identifies the latter (her group 27) as images of military standards, and since they often occur at military sites in the early Roman period and are sometimes tin-plated like many early imperial articles of military equipment, she has suggested that they are not feminine hairpins at all.[35] However, the importance of the crescent as a moon emblem and its ubiquity in female jewellery should also be borne in mind, as should the presence of women in the vicinity of forts and fortresses at all phases of the Roman period. There may be a question mark over this type, but these pins have by no means been excluded as hairpins.

The pins that have heads in the form of an axe-head, however, are a somewhat different matter. Miniature axes and other craft implements certainly had cult significance, and it is quite possible that such pins are not personal ornaments at all, but rather miniature votive items designed to be displayed by inserting their points in some support.

Pins with non-representational heads

The great majority of the many hairpins from Romano-British contexts have heads that are quite simply shaped with decorative baluster mouldings, grooves and cordons, or even without any additional decoration at all, merely a rounded or slightly pointed terminal. Silver and bronze examples may be assumed to be purchased items, manufactured by professional craftsmen, while the simpler bone examples and the presumed wooden ones could easily have been made in a domestic environment. Any reasonably patient and handy person with a sharp knife can make a simple ball-headed or baluster-headed skewer-like pin out of a suitable piece of bone or wood. Jet pins are common, especially in the later Roman period, but they generally have spherical, ovoid or faceted heads (Fig 1.5) rather than elaborately carved motifs, although quite a few are recorded that have heads in the shape of a more or less stylized Bacchic cantharus (a two-handled vase). As we have seen in previous chapters, intricate carvings were executed in certain other forms of jet jewellery. One factor in the rarity of representational carvings on jet pins is that they are most common in the later period, when pins were used less obtrusively as functional items and were not intended to stand above the level of the coiffure as decorative items in their own right. An evocative find which demonstrates the use of jet pins in the hair is a fourth-century woman's burial from York in which the deceased's hair survives, secured in a large bun with cantharus-headed jet pins.[36]

The forms of bone pins have been studied and classified by Nina Crummy on the basis of the many finds from Colchester.[37] One noteworthy feature is that a slight swelling or entasis half-way down the shaft of the pin becomes more usual in the later examples. This swelling, most often seen in bone and jet pins, has been explained as a device to strengthen the shaft, but it is perhaps just as likely to be a way of assisting the shorter late Roman pins to remain firmly anchored in the hair; the longer early pins had less need of it. There is a possibility that pins can be confused with spindles in a few cases. Wood was probably the most common material for spindles, but other substances were used, even silver.

Some hairpins have heads covered or set with different materials; in addition to the gold-headed bone pins already mentioned, there are others with a glass bead forming the head of a metal pin or set in it. Cool classifies these under her group 14. Bone pins with heads made of jet have also been found.

Hairpins made wholly of glass have simple ball heads or sometimes ring terminals. They are inclined to have twisted shafts, which would have given them greater grip and strength. It has already become clear that in spite of its innate fragility, glass was used for items of jewellery such as bangles and finger-rings, and it is therefore not surprising that hairpins were also manufactured in this material. One advantage of glass would have been the fact that it could be in almost any colour. It has been observed that bone pins are sometimes found with green or red staining: while the green colouring can occur naturally during burial through proximity to corroding copper alloys, it is also more than likely that bone

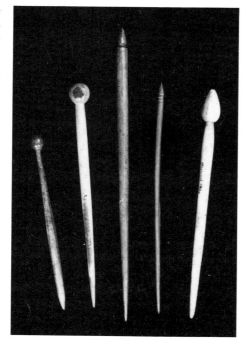

Figure 6.13 Five bone hairpins, all found in London. They display a variety of simple but carefully shaped forms. British Museum. Length of centre pin 13.7 cm. (Photo: author).

and wood ornaments were deliberately coloured in antiquity. One bone pin with a gold-foil covering on the head, from the bed of the Walbrook, and now in the British Museum collection, is a dark-brown colour that may well be artificially induced.[38] Its colour is not due to burial in the river-bed context, since another very similar pin from the same source is much paler.

Finally, there is another type of metal pin, different in form and very possibly also in function, from the great majority of Roman pins. These are the ring-headed "proto-handpins", which are forerunners of a class of dress-pin characteristic of the early medieval period. Cool calls them pins with projecting ring heads (group 17): the ring-shaped head of the pin is offset forward from the shank, and is usually decorated by cast mouldings. This is perhaps the one type of Romano-British pin which is more likely to be a garment-fastener than a head-ornament, although the latter use is by no means excluded. Several examples in bronze have been recorded, but a silver specimen is the most interesting. It comes from Oldcroft, near Lydney in Gloucestershire, and was found in 1972 in a coin-hoard deposited not later than AD 354–9.[39]

The Oldcroft pin is very small, only 6 cm long overall, and its beautifully detailed ring head has a minute scroll pattern reserved in silver against a background of red enamel. The scroll is extremely close in design to some of the enamelled bronze terrets (rein-rings) of the Late Iron Age. This tiny article is extraordinary for several reasons. At the same time it expresses the prehistoric Celtic tradition in enamelling on metalwork and foreshadows the design and craftsmanship of the medieval

Figure 6.14 The enamelled silver pin found with a fourth-century coin-hoard at Oldcroft, Gloucestershire. The enamel is red. Length 6 cm. (Photo: British Museum)

Celtic era. In addition, the fact that it is enamelled on silver makes it extremely unusual in Romano-British jewellery. The Oldcroft pin remains unique, but at any rate we know from its hoard context that it was in use in the first half of the fourth century (without the associated coins, it might well have been dated substantially later). Plainer examples of this type of pin, made of bronze, have been found at the late Roman site of Lydney itself.

The ring-headed pins may have been garment-fasteners. The huge class of brooches, whose prime function was to secure clothing, is the subject of the next chapter.

Chapter 7

Brooches

It would not be too difficult to make a case for excluding brooches altogether from a general discussion of Roman jewellery. It could be argued that, as practical objects designed to fasten clothing, brooches should be placed alongside articles such as late Roman belt-buckles, which are not customarily regarded as jewellery even though they were sometimes very decorative and were occasionally made in precious metals.

Brooches were often rather more than simple clothes-fasteners, however. In spite of being essential functional items in a period when the range of fasteners was comparatively limited, their decorative potential was fully appreciated and exploited, and their prominent position in the costume of the wearer must have ensured that they were often chosen with the care that is applied to the purchase of a jewel rather than a purely utilitarian object. It is also perfectly possible that some types of brooch were primarily decorative, their practical function being minor and secondary. Both fibulae (safety-pin brooches) and penannular brooches (open ring and pin) were in use in Britain centuries before the Roman conquest and continued to be a normal part of dress long after the Roman administration of the island was over. The Roman period therefore represents only a small segment of time in a very long history of use and development.

Bronze brooches are extremely numerous finds from Romano-British sites, and the numbers that exist in museums and private collections, from organized excavations, stray discoveries and the activities of modern metal-detector users, are vast. They lend themselves to minute typological analysis, and the range of variations recognized by specialists is correspondingly extensive. To some degree (although perhaps not as much as some archaeologists might wish), precise typological differentiation is helpful in building up a dated sequence of forms. For those who wish to study brooches in depth, the four volumes published by the late Richard Hattatt are useful sources of reference,[1] and most excavation reports on

Romano-British sites include catalogues and drawings of many brooches. The earlier classification first published by R. G. Collingwood in 1930 is still frequently referred to.[2] I shall not attempt anything approaching a full typological survey here, although I shall refer to most of the major forms.[3]

It is important to remember that although logical sequences of development can be perceived, objects hardly ever evolve in a smooth and unbroken sequence from simple and primitive to complex and sophisticated; human beings are not that rational. So although it is possible to devise a typological sequence that reflects the introduction of certain new features at specific periods, it does not follow that more traditional forms were superseded. Typological analysis is a practical device for studying objects, but we should not imagine that it was part of the thinking of the manufacturers or users of the artefacts.

As a broad overall classification, I propose to draw a basic distinction between fibulae and penannular brooches on the one hand and the so-called plate-brooches on the other. Furthermore, I shall be placing one important Romano-British type, the dragonesque brooch, into the same primary group as the fibulae and penannulars, rather than regarding it as a form of plate-brooch.

Fibulae or bow-brooches are safety-pins, with a hinged or sprung pin engaging in a catchplate and a back or bow that is often, although not invariably, strongly curved so as to provide a larger space between the back and the pin than is available on a modern safety-pin.

Penannular brooches consist of an open ring with a straight or bowed pin moving freely upon it. Plate-brooches are like most modern brooches, namely a more or less flat metal plate with a straight hinged pin at the back leaving quite a narrow space. The functional difference between the fibula/penannular class and the plate-brooches is important: the former are able to take in a fairly substantial fold of fabric, while the latter may be able to encompass only as little as a centimetre-wide strip of quite fine cloth. Many plate-brooches are very small, and although they could indeed be employed to pin two layers of thin fabric or two edges together, there is a strong possibility that they were sometimes worn solely for decoration. Many fibulae display the decoration on the bow to best advantage if they are enclosing a thick pleat of material. The types with fairly narrow heads are apt to tilt sideways if pinned to a thin or narrow strip of material. Modern reproductions of fibulae are rarely satisfactory for this reason, whereas modern copies of Roman plate-brooches can be worn without any difficulty. Penannular brooches of the Roman period are in general quite modest in both size and ornamentation, certainly by comparison with some medieval Celtic examples which are enormous and extremely lavishly adorned.

The combination of Mediterranean and British traditions in the province, the natural evolution of clothing fashions over a period of four centuries, and the different garments likely to be favoured by individuals of different means and occupations all make it difficult to generalize about the costumes worn in Roman Britain. But tunics of simple form, draped garments and cloaks all had to be pinned together, and the variety of textiles used would have required brooches and pins of varying sizes.[4] Wool would have been the most usual fabric, and some surviving fragments give a slight idea of the extensive and sophisticated range of weaves and weights available: Britain was famous throughout the Empire for the *birrus britannicus,* the British cloak. This was evidently a rainproof outer garment, presumably of a heavy and closely woven wool, no doubt developed in response to the climate. Linen was also in widespread use, and both cotton and silk were available in the Roman world, although they were expensive luxuries.

Several brooches might be needed for a single outfit, to secure the basic loose tunic and an outer garment in the form of a cloak, a woman's short cape or a shawl. Women often wore a matching pair of brooches at the shoulders to anchor the outer garment to the tunic. The brooches were evidently joined together by a chain festooned across the chest, helping to hold the gathered fabric neatly and prevent the garment gaping at the neck. Cords or ribbons might also have been used for this purpose, and would not survive alongside the metal brooches. Both men and women needed to pin their garments, but apart from certain brooch types that appear typically on military sites, it is difficult to make any gender distinctions. The use of fibulae in particular diminished very markedly in the later Roman period, and although the reasons for this are not fully understood, they must reflect changes in clothing fashions.

The overwhelming majority of Romano-British brooches are made of bronze, and quite a number of types have never yet been found in any other metal. Scientific analyses carried out in recent years have indicated that the range of copper alloys used was extensive, and that certain compositions were deliberately selected because of their suitability for specific purposes. Iron brooches existed both in the pre-Roman Iron Age and after the conquest, but even allowing for some loss through poor preservation, they were not an important class. Gold and silver are also comparatively rare, but it is interesting that gilding, silver-plating and tin-plating were applied more commonly to brooches than to most other metal personal ornaments.

Penannular brooches

Although fibulae were the dominant form of brooch in the early centuries of Roman Britain, we shall start with the penannular type, which continued in use throughout the period. The fibula was an inspired invention, but the penannular brooch is a natural evolution from a very basic and simple form of fastening.

The simplest way of all to pin cloth is to skewer it with a plain pin. The pin has to have a head to stop it passing straight through the weave, and if the head is a ring to which a string can be attached, then it need not be completely lost when it eventually works itself out of the fabric. Longer pins are more likely to hold securely, but there are practical safety limits on the length of a sharp-pointed needle-like implement that is worn on the person. Another way of improving the stability of a dress-pin is to introduce some type of kink or swelling into the shaft, or to wind and knot a cord around both the head and the point (the probable origin of the safety-pin concept): one type of Iron Age pin has a ring head and a swan's neck curve in the shaft.

Yet another, and better, way of making a plain pin hold firmly is to use it in conjunction with a ring. A portion of cloth is drawn through the ring, and the pin is then passed through it so that it is held tightly and securely against the ring. Dress-pins may have been used in this way more often than we can now infer, since the ring and pin need not have had any obvious visual relationship to one another or have been made of the same material. They were entirely separate objects.

Figure 7.1 A simple penannular brooch, showing how the object was used. British Museum. (Photos: author)

The evolution of the penannular brooch need not have followed precisely the logical progression described here; it is a refinement of the simple ring-and-pin idea that could easily have evolved independently in different times and places. The ring element becomes an open circle with a small gap, and the pin, either straight or arched, is attached to it by means of a loop that allows it to swivel freely. The ring is brought down with its opening over the pin which has been inserted through the cloth, and then the ring is given a slight turn to bring it *under* the pin, closing the circle and creating an assembly like that of the separate pin and annular ring described above. It is an ingenious and effective form of fastener, and versions of it were in use for at least a millennium in antiquity. It is not even a type confined to the ancient world; Berber women may still be seen in Tunisian towns with two large silver penannular brooches on the shoulders pinning their colourful garments.

Small penannular brooches provide little scope for decoration. The terminals flanking the opening in the circle may need to be expanded in some way to prevent the pin slipping free in the unlikely event of the ring turning, and they can be treated in various ornamental ways. The ring itself and the head of the pin provide other minor opportunities for decoration, but it was not until the development of early medieval penannular brooches with flattened and greatly expanded terminals that they became showy pieces of jewellery. Various typologies have been devised based on the form of the terminals, which may be bulbous, flattened, rolled or turned back, cast in stylized animal-head forms or inlaid with enamel.[5]

A few Romano-British penannular brooches were made in silver, and iron examples are also known, but most are very simple bronze pieces. Probably the most decorative Romano-British example is a large penannular brooch found in 1979 at Bath that has terminals decorated with linear designs of birds and fish reserved against a red enamel background, a motif sometimes seen on enamelled disc brooches in Britain and Gaul.[6] This may well be a late Roman piece, and like the Oldcroft pin it foreshadows the medieval evolution of the type in the Celtic West.

Dragonesque brooches

The distinctive and beautiful form of the Romano-British dragonesque brooch has been employed on more than one occasion to illustrate studies of prehistoric Celtic art, and of course it is undeniable that these ornaments do express the continuing Celtic aesthetic in the provincial Roman milieu. Nevertheless, they are Roman products that did not exist in the Celtic Iron Age, and they reflect the interaction of native and Classical elements rather than the Celtic tradition alone. Because they have a fairly flat bronze front, normally with enamelled decoration, they are generally regarded as one of the many zoomorphic forms of plate-brooch, albeit a fantastic one, but they have a strongly curved pin, and functionally they were designed to pin a thick piece of fabric. They should therefore be classified as another variant of the group that includes fibulae and pen-annular brooches.

The form is that of an S-shaped double-headed animal with large upstanding ears and and a curled snout. The beast looks almost the same either way up – the symmetry resembles that seen in a playing-card king or queen. Around the neck of the upper head is the loop of a rather thick, strongly curved pin which, after passing through the fold of cloth, is hooked over the lower "neck". There are S-shaped brooches that have no enamel and no zoomorphic decoration, and others that are decorated only with patterns in relief or openwork motifs, but the standard dragon type is patterned with coloured enamels on the body and usually the head and ears as well. The full range of enamel colours is found, underlining the fact that these brooches are products of Roman-period technology rather than of the pre-Roman Iron Age. The actual patterns, which have been classified and numbered, are also provincial Roman in concept. The majority include squares and lozenges of colour, with or without additional curvilinear design elements. Whether the animal was based on any natural creature or was a total fantasy that grew out of the form is difficult to tell, but if a real animal was in the mind of either the maker or user, the best candidate is probably the hare.

Figure 7.2 Three dragonesque brooches. The matching pair is from Faversham, Kent, while the example in the centre is from Norton, Yorkshire. Length of centre brooch *c.* 7 cm. (Photo: British Museum)

Like some fibulae, dragonesque brooches could evidently be worn in pairs. A pair from a grave at Faversham in Kent was obviously designed as a matching set, their patterns of red and blue enamel the same in every detail. Interestingly, they were not designed as symmetrical pairs with one forming the mirror-image of the other: reversed-S dragonesques do exist, but they are very uncommon. The pin of the dragonesque type, curved like the bow of a fibula, is inclined to be thicker than the pins of other brooch types and this has implications for the nature of the garments with which they were worn: they would have worked best with thick and loosely woven cloth. While the fine, sharp pins of many fibulae and plate-brooches could have been used with reasonable care on fine fabrics like woollen or linen textiles in a close twill weave, the pins of most dragonesque brooches would certainly have damaged such materials. It is interesting to speculate whether dragonesques might have been worn with a particular type of garment.

Dragonesque brooches are strictly Romano-British objects. Only occasional stray examples have been found on the Continent and they were probably taken there as personal possessions. The distribution of known finds may indicate manufacture in the north of the province, but they were not peculiar to that area. They appeared in the first century AD, after the Roman conquest, and probably remained current for some four or five generations. As noted above, several types of S-shaped brooch exist that lack the animal-heads and decoration of the typical dragonesque, and some of them have been quoted as part of the evolution of the type. They include S-shapes of coiled wire and plain leaf-like forms with ends curled in opposing directions, as well as bulky cast S-brooches with swelling trumpet-like forms. Clearly all these S-brooches with more or less flat fronts and curved pins merely looped around one end are related to each other, but the dating evidence is not precise enough for us to present a clear and unequivocal sequence of development; many of the different types may be contemporary variants, and in particular those using coiled wire could very easily be a variant made domestically rather than by a professional bronzesmith.

Detailed analysis of both the enamelled decoration and the overall shape of the brooches has been undertaken and used as a basis to argue for their manufacture in specific discrete areas of the territory of the Brigantes, a large tribal area covering what is now northern England.[7] It is undoubtedly true that dragonesque brooches can be stylistically grouped, and that we may well be seeing the products of specific artisans or workshops, but it seems wildly over-optimistic to claim that these can be precisely located and dated. What is certain is that there is no obvious Iron Age predecessor, nor is there a Classical (or Roman provincial) type that was introduced to form the immediate inspiration for the development of these decorative fasteners. Dragonesque brooches are an indigenous Romano-British creation, and as such are significant indicators of the cultural interaction of Roman and native.

Fibulae

The most typical clothes-fastening device of the Iron Age and Roman period was a bronze bow-brooch or fibula. The simplest safety-pin consists of a single wire with a sharp point at one end, a hooked catch at the other to capture the point, and a sharp angle where the wire bends back on itself. The addition of one or two coils to form a simple spring at that angle improves and controls the tension on the pin. Such a device is a one-piece fibula. The modern utilitarian safety-pin illustrates one of the simplest forms of fibula, using a single wire for both pin and bow, coiled once only at the spring, but featuring the addition of a separate foot and catchplate. Alternatively, a similar pin can be made from two pieces of metal, a separate pin and bow. Although this method allows for more creative ornamentation of the visible section, it does necessitate a method of attaching the pin effectively and tensioning it so that the point of the pin is firmly pressed into the catch. Two-piece fibulae can be made with springs like the one-piece variety, but it was also possible to have a simple hinge where the pin was attached. Fibulae had come into use in some areas of Europe as early as 1200 BC, and many different refinements of manufacture and decoration had evolved by the Roman period.

Figure 7.3 Drawing showing the construction of a one-piece fibula. (Drawing: author)

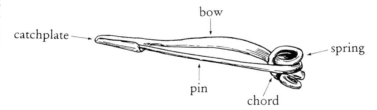

The hinge or spring end of the brooch has been referred to here, following the normal convention, as the head, and the catchplate end as the foot; Roman fibulae are normally illustrated vertically in archaeological reports, with the spring or hinge at the top and catchplate and pin-point at the bottom, but it should be noted that this was not the way they were worn. Representations in sculpture show that fibulae securing garments in the region of the shoulders were habitually worn at an oblique angle with the "head" downwards. This is not necessarily a crucial matter, and it is more than likely that there were occasions when they were pinned in at other angles, especially if they were not intended to be an important visual feature of the costume, or were to be covered by an outer garment. When we come to consider some of the more elaborately decorated brooches, however, it is useful to remember that the design was conceived with this "head-downwards" orientation in mind.

The advantages of a safety-pin over a plain dress-pin are obvious – when in good condition, it is more efficient and less likely to be lost or to injure the wearer. However, the springs or hinges of all brooches are subject to considerable strain in wear, and it must have been common for them eventually to loosen or snap; furthermore, the pin mechanism at the head of the brooch may sometimes have caught up threads of cloth and caused damage to the garment, or at least made the brooch difficult to unfasten. The modifications made to fibula design over the centuries and the several types of spring or hinge mechanism that were in use concurrently during the Roman period imply that manufacturers were constantly searching for improvements. It is important to understand that there is no single, clear-cut typological sequence of improvement. All the designs worked, as did the penannular brooches that remained in use throughout the period, and the opposing impulses of honouring tradition and seeking innovation would have played their part in the popularity of specific brooch types at any given time.

One development of the ancient fibula was to elaborate the spring into several spiral coils on both sides of the head of the brooch. The section of wire that passes across the spring from one outer end to the other is termed the chord, and it could either be stretched over the top of the spring (external) or be turned under the bow (internal). The bilateral spring created a more resilient fastener with an attractively balanced appearance in use. This development suggests some interest in the visual effect of the object as well as its functional efficiency. Bilateral spring mechanisms could also be employed in a two-part brooch, although they required a reliable method of attachment.

The use of a hinge rather than a spring in a two-part fibula made it possible to create a narrower and neater head. Although a hinged pin looks far simpler than a spring, its manufacture requires rather more precision. Experiments with hinged pins had already been made in pre-Roman times, but it was in the Roman period that they became common on many varieties of fibula and almost standard on plate-brooches. The pin of a hinged brooch has to be made with a suitably flattened area pierced in exactly the right place with a hole of the right size, and there must also be a small lug or stop to press against the body of the brooch and provide the right amount of pressure when the pin is closed. While this presented no technical difficulty, hinged brooches may have been a little slower to make. More importantly, when the tension lug wore down, a hinged pin would become slack and inefficient and would need to be replaced.

The decorative potential of the fibula was always secondary to its practical value, but it was none the less perceived and exploited at a very early stage, and by the time Britain became a Roman province, there was already an extensive range of brooch types in use both on the Continent and in Britain. Bronze fibulae were therefore very far from being a new and exotic class of object introduced by the Romans. The varieties discussed below are simply a selection of the types used in Roman Britain, and I make no apology, in a survey of jewellery that is particularly concerned with the visual qualities of personal ornament, for concentrating more on the decorative effect of the brooches than on the typologically significant details of the pin mechanisms and overall construction.

One-piece and thistle brooches

Some of the many new types of brooch that became current in the early years of the province were still simple one-piece forms with a bilateral spring and internal chord (passing under the bow). They are often known to archaeologists as "Nauheim derivatives". One-piece fibulae evolved from continental Iron Age predecessors similar to those used in pre-Roman Britain, but they were considerably less decorative than many pre-Roman forms: with their light, thin bows and minimal decoration, they are simply practical fasteners with little ornamental value, and they scarcely qualify as jewellery. Many were made of iron, a metal that was seldom used for brooches after the first century AD.

If the "Nauheim derivatives" were not intended for show, the same cannot be said of another continental type that was in limited use in Britain in the middle of the first century, the thistle or rosette brooch. There can be no doubt that these brooches were intended to be a prominent and ornamental feature of the costume. A large circular or diamond-shaped plate forms the central feature of the bow; the short, strongly arched upper bow emerges from it, and the broad, expanded foot continues beneath, covering the catchplate, while the spring is concealed by a broad tubular cover. All frontal parts of the brooch are richly ornamented with ribbed mouldings and incised detailing. Variants of the form include simplified examples in which the decorative disc was simply applied to the front of a smoothly curved bow; these variants occasionally have a small boss of enamel in the centre of the rosette-like disc. Certain later types further exploited the decorative potential of the wide foot, and the Aesica brooches discussed below represent a particularly interesting development of the thistle form. Some continental thistle brooches bear the name of the manufacturer discreetly stamped on them, but this feature is even more characteristic of another type, known as the Aucissa type, from the name of their best-known maker.

Aucissa and Hod Hill brooches

Stamps giving the name of the individual maker or a workshop are familiar on certain classes of mass-produced Roman pottery, but they also occur regularly, if less frequently, on certain bronze and iron items such as pans and knife-blades. Aucissa was not the only brooch-maker to have marked some of his products, but name-stamps of this kind occur only on certain types of brooches, and it seems likely that there was some military connection in the manufacture and supply. Whether this was so or not, Aucissa brooches appear to have been made in Gaul, and they are found principally on early military sites in Britain. The pin is hinged, not sprung, and the bow, which is a flat strip of metal decorated with ribs and other details, has a high, semicircular arch. There is a short foot ending in a knob, and at the hinge end the metal is rolled forward to enclose an axis bar, generally made of iron rather than bronze. If a maker's name is present, it is stamped across the head. Aucissa is a Celtic name, as are the others that are sometimes found, for example Atgivios and Tarra.[8]

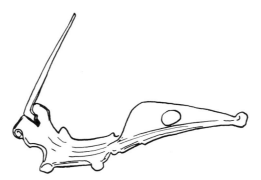

Figure 7.4 A brooch (Hod Hill type) with hinged pin. (Drawing: author)

This type of brooch died out well before the end of the first century, along with another early military type that was closely related, the Hod Hill brooch, named after an Iron Age hillfort in Dorset where the conquering Roman army subsequently built a fort of their own. Hod Hill brooches have much less deeply curved bows than Aucissas, and they feature a variety of ribbing and lateral knobs and extensions to the bow. They were very often tin-plated, and would therefore have matched other items of bronze military equipment of the period, many of which were also tinned. If the fibulae were regarded as part of a soldier's accoutrements, their claim to be considered jewellery must be at best quite tenuous. However, there are certain examples of the type, one of them from Britain, which tend to undermine this view.

One of the recurrent characteristics of jewellery throughout the ages is its tendency to be worn for sentimental reasons and to embody messages of remembrance and affection; the subject has already been discussed in Chapter 3. Love-inscriptions have been recorded on brooches of a variant Hod Hill type, a form in which the upper part of the bow is a smooth rectangular field unbroken by grooves and ridges. A fibula of this type from Richborough, Kent, has four lines of lettering in a lightly pecked technique reading SI AMAS EGO PLUS – "if you love (me), I love (you) more".[9] The same inscription is recorded on a French find, and there is a brooch of precisely the same form from Geneva which has a different motto, declaring that the wearer (or giver?) "burns with love for you".[10]

The imagination immediately conjures up a romantic scenario involving a handsome Roman soldier and his woman, no doubt a beautiful young Briton with a passionate Celtic temperament, who has presented him with this small, practical item, unobtrusively but clearly inscribed with a message that will remind him daily of her devotion. Alternatively, it may have been a gift from the soldier to his lady, or indeed it may have been a token of love between two men: in any case, the sentiment expressed in the inscription makes it something much more than an everyday item of equipment, and it must be classified quite positively as jewellery.

Colchester brooches

Returning hastily from the realm of the historical novelist to that of the archaeologist and to the typology of fibulae, a separate strand of development may be seen in the so-called Colchester type and its many derivatives, both of which have more solid and smoothly curved bows than the varieties described above. Colchester brooches are one-piece brooches with an external chord above the bilateral spring mechanism. The latter is held in place by a hook or spur bent forward at the top of the bow. This was a potentially decorative feature that may have provided the inspiration for the characteristic "headstud" of the type of that name, described below. By the late first century and the early second, a number of different designs had become popular. They were based upon the Colchester shape but had become very much more decorative, with cast, and in many cases enamelled, embellishment combined with the knobbed foot found on the Aucissa type.

Aesica brooches

Aesica brooches were related to the thistle form. They are named after a particularly splendid example from a remarkable hoard of jewellery found in 1894 at Great Chesters, Northumberland, the Latin name of which was *Aesica*. This hoard was unfortunately discovered under conditions that make the circumstances and date of its deposition impossible to reconstruct; it includes rings, a silver necklet and a huge brooch of the trumpet type. "The" Aesica brooch is also of considerable size (10.6 cm long), and is made of gilded bronze. As on the true thistle brooches, the bow is P-shaped in profile and there is a very broad expanded foot as well as a circular feature in the centre of the bow that recalls the disc or rosette of the thistle type. But instead of the regular ribbed decoration of its Continental predecessor, the Aesica brooch is embellished with swirling curvilinear patterns in relief on head, bow and foot. The designs are unmistakably Celtic, recalling such objects as the terminals of British Iron Age torcs.[11]

Figure 7.5 Bronze fibula of Aesica type, from Lincolnshire. Length 5.1 cm. British Museum. (Photo: author)

Humbler examples of the Aesica form are known, but they are fairly rare, and some of them also display relief decoration that can be classified as native rather than Roman, although it is usually much simplified and fragmented compared with the lush and confident scrolls of the Aesica brooch itself. Some are tin-plated, and they are generally quite small brooches. Typically the curved upper part of the bow has lateral knobs or points, and the pin mechanism may be either sprung or hinged. Fibulae classified as the "bow and fantail" type are related, but they are further removed from the construction of the thistle brooch, and lack the Celtic scroll ornamentation.

Headstud brooches
Together with the trumpet-brooches described below, these are typical of the robust and rather florid brooches that were extremely popular in the second century, and must have been worn by both sexes and at many social levels. Headstud brooches are normally adorned with coloured

enamel along the bow and on the central round stud at the head end; they may have either sprung or hinged pins and wire loops or cast rings at the head (that is, at the lower end as worn) which served as a purpose-made attachment for the chain or cord joining a pair. The presence of this feature implies that it was normal to wear two of these brooches together, but its absence on some other types should not be taken to prove that they were not worn in that manner; it would have been a simple matter to attach a chain or cord to the head or bow of most fibulae. At the foot or catchplate end is a profiled moulding. On some examples, enamelling is applied even to the wings at the spring or hinge end and to the circular base of the foot moulding.

Figure 7.6 A brooch of headstud type from Faversham, Kent. Red enamel remains in the pattern on the bow. Length 6.3 cm. British Museum. (Photo: author)

The patterns of enamelling on this type consist of squares, rectangles or lozenges of colour along the bow and the obvious rings or segments on the stud. On brooches of the trumpet type, however, simple geometric patterns are often augmented by more ambitious and distinctive curvilinear patterns.

Trumpet-brooches

Although trumpet-brooches had identifiable continental predecessors, in their true form they were a characteristically Romano-British design. They survive in very considerable numbers, and were clearly in extremely widespread use during their heyday. The origins and chronology of the type have been the subject of conflicting theories, but they were certainly current in the late first and second centuries.[12]

The name derives from the swelling expansion of the head, thought to be reminiscent of a trumpet mouth. This expansion covers either a sprung or hinged pin attachment. Roughly mid-way along the bow is a knobbed moulding, and in most cases the foot terminates in another moulding similar to that found on headstud brooches. The waist moulding on the

Figure 7.7 Pair of silver trumpet-brooches from Chorley, Lancashire, with the fine silver foxtail chain which was worn with them. There is some damage and loss to both the brooches and the chain, but they are of exceptional quality. Length of lower brooch 6.6 cm. (Photo: British Museum)

bow is often in the form of a double stylized acanthus capital, that is, it resembles two Corinthian column caps placed head to head. A great variety of decoration was employed; the basic form of the bow was cast, and some examples have cast surface embellishment in low relief. Engraved and enamelled ornament was also common, while pierced designs were sometimes worked in the catchplate. Over and above all this, trumpet-brooches were made in silver and even silver-gilt as well as bronze. There is therefore every reason to believe that some gold trumpet-brooches existed, but no example has yet come to light.

Two pairs of trumpet-brooches from Lancashire and Northumberland respectively and a single example from Carmarthen illustrate the type at its finest in precious metal. One of the pairs is from the mid-second-century Backworth treasure, which has already been mentioned repeatedly; the trumpet form is sometimes called a Backworth-type brooch. They are large (about 10.3 cm long including the heavy cast head-loop) and are of completely gilded silver to give the appearance of gold. They are handsome and imposing, but by no means the most beautiful specimens of their type. No joining chain was found in the group, and it is interesting to speculate whether, if it existed, it would have been of silver or gold. The cast and engraved decoration includes clearly detailed petalled or acanthus mouldings in the centre of the bow, a series of regular curved transverse lines flanking the central angle or arris along the front of the bow, and a swirling curvilinear pattern on the head with "eyes" and pointed lobes at each side: the catchplates bear a tripartite engraved device with similar eyes and lobes. These details are unmistakably Celtic in origin; the catchplate design is a Celtic triskele, a triple-armed whirligig that has been adapted to the asymmetrical and elongated shape of its background. Related patterns are found, not engraved but cast in crisp relief, on the beautiful pair of silver trumpet-brooches from Chorley, Lancashire. These were found with a length of beautifully made silver foxtail chain long enough to have been worn in a double festoon between them. The Chorley brooches are slender and elegant, with sharp fluted mouldings on the lower part of the bow and raised zig-zag and milled mouldings at the central acanthus knob and the foot. The one surviving head-loop also has a plate with rows of milled or beaded relief. They give an impression of highly developed and sophisticated taste. Both the Backworth and Chorley fibulae were found associated with coins that date their burial to around AD 140.

The parcel-gilt Carmarthen brooch is a heavier and more opulent specimen, full and rounded where the Chorley brooches are slim and sharp.[13]

Figure 7.8 The pair of brooches from the Backworth treasure; the trumpet type is sometimes named after these. They are silver, wholly gilded, and are very large. Length 10.3 cm. (Photo: British Museum)

Figure 7.9 The Carmarthen trumpet-brooch. The parcel-gilding on the silver emphasizes the decorative pattern in high relief. Length (excluding loop and rosette) 6.3 cm. (Photo: Carmarthen Museum)

It has intricate scroll decoration of almost baroque exuberance, cast in relief and standing out in silver against a gilded background. Both the acanthus moulding at the waist of the bow and the knob at the foot are finely petalled, and the straight part of the bow bears a lobed running S-meander scroll on each side of the central line. Elements of this are repeated in the pierced catchplate and on the highly elaborate moulded pattern on the head. The large cast head-loop has a splendid cupped silver-gilt flower or rosette set on it, concealing the point where the loop separates to encompass the head. The carefully judged balance of yellow background and reserved white relief is typical of Celtic art, but the date of the object, in spite of the claims of pre-Roman manufacture made in the definitive publication, must fall within the Roman era. Apart from the fact that there is every reason to believe that the trumpet-brooch form did not emerge until after the Roman conquest, the technique used for the gilding (mercury-gilding) was probably a Roman introduction. Clearly this sumptuous brooch and its lost companion would have been a valued piece of jewellery, and its owner, whatever his/her own ethnic origins, was undoubtedly able to appreciate the Celtic love of curves and scrolls.

Amongst the numerous surviving bronze trumpet-brooches are many that feature vivid enamel inlay in red, blue and other colours. Enamelled patterns on the lower part of the bow are generally based on geometric zig-zag or lozenge patterns, but the flaring head of the brooch sometimes displays a curvilinear lobed ornament similar to that cast or engraved on the precious-metal examples described above. There are obvious similarities with the colourful decoration of many of the headstud brooches, but it is possible to detect a greater element of traditional Celtic taste in the trumpet-brooch enamelling.

By contrast, some examples are quite plain, and there are some in which the neat petalled moulding at the waist has been reduced to an amorphous swelling. In the Collingwood classification there are subdivisions of his type R to cover these variations of form. One of the strangest trumpet-brooches is the monstrous specimen from the Aesica hoard, just over 19 cm long and ill-proportioned, with a wide rectangular head covering the spring of the pin, and a huge pad-like foot. In spite of its absurd size it is undoubtedly a functional item. Collingwood remarked drily that "the purchaser was no doubt induced to buy it by being told that it was the largest brooch in the world".[14] It is difficult to imagine a pair of brooches like this in use; they would seem to be more likely to drag a garment down to the owner's feet than to secure it neatly on the shoulders, but ostentatiously large pins and brooches are found in many cultures and obviously gave pleasure to people with flamboyant tastes.

The trumpet-brooch form also served as the basis for some other aberrant types. Some small brooches classifiable as trumpets from the characteristically flared head have a disc or crescent, enamelled or otherwise decorated, in the centre of the bow instead of the double acanthus moulding; this form may be combined with a foot in the form of an open crescent rather than the normal column-base shape. It is also amongst these variant trumpet-headed fibulae that we find a few examples with silver filigree wire inlaid in the bronze to form linear patterns and combined with areas of enamel. An intriguing trumpet-brooch variant is one in which the centre of the bow is developed even further than in the crescent-plate variety so that it takes on the shape of a winged insect, its head indicated by the knob-like foot of the brooch. The wings are enamelled, and the insect appears to be a fly rather than a bee or wasp. Plate-brooches were frequently made in zoomorphic shapes, and these trumpet-headed fly brooches are an interesting link with them. The fly has no obvious symbolic significance, and it may well have developed from the crescent merely as a visual conceit.

Trumpet-brooches exhibited great vitality and inventiveness of design and employed a noticeably wider variety of materials and decorative techniques than are to be found in most fibulae. We know little about how the

Figure 7.10 The fly-shaped variant of the trumpet-brooch. The enamel is mostly lost from the wings of this example, found in Lincoln. Length 3.5 cm. British Museum. (Photo: author)

manufacture of such articles was organized, but moulds providing clear evidence of the manufacture of both trumpet-brooches and penannular brooches have been found in excavations at Prestatyn in North Wales.[15] This is not to say that the site was necessarily a major source of these ornaments. Such essential and everyday articles as brooches would have been made all over the country, and it is also possible that some craftsmen may have been peripatetic. It takes some knowledge and experience to identify fragments of bronze-casting moulds, and it is more than likely that many such objects have been found in the past, even in deliberate excavation, and discarded unrecognized.

Late Roman fibulae

It is extremely difficult to say how long brooches such as the trumpet and headstud types continued to be manufactured and worn. In general, they are thought not to have outlasted the second century. If this is so, the overall picture is of a bewilderingly large variety of fairly short-lived types of bow brooch in use in the first century, diminishing to a smaller selection in the second, and reducing sharply in the third and fourth centuries not merely to very few types but to far fewer fibulae of any kind. The same development took place in the adjacent Gaulish provinces.

The reasons for this are not clear, but are likely to be complicated. The most obvious factor is a change in clothing customs and fashion, but there is probably more to it than that. A similar pattern can be seen in other aspects of material culture, for example the range of pottery in use. During the first two or three generations after the conquest of Britain in AD 43 there was constant change and development. There was a tremendous influx of people and goods from the Continent, and the wholesale changes in every aspect of life were so great and so rapid by the standards of antiquity that it is difficult for us to envisage them. Modern scholarship tends to emphasize the underlying continuity of life in Britannia, and to stress that the rural peasant of the second century AD lived in much the same way as his or her Iron Age ancestors and medieval descendants; this is perfectly true but, paradoxically, it does not alter the fact that the changes wrought by the Roman conquest were greater than anything that were to happen up to, and probably including, the Industrial Revolution. By the middle of the second century, these changes had crystallized and settled. Britain, however vibrant its substratum of Celtic tradition may have been, had become Roman, and Roman ways came naturally to people of wholly Celtic pedigree. By the late Roman period changes were afoot again in all parts of the huge Empire, and the native elements in the hybridized culture of Roman Britain were once more in the ascendant, operating within a framework of *romanitas* that had become the norm.

This is obviously not the place to enter into a detailed discussion of this difficult and contentious area of social history: everything would be very much clearer if we had more to go on than the limited evidence of archaeology. For example, there are important cultural and social messages in the use of different languages (in this case, Latin or British Celtic), and in aspects of daily life and behaviour as basic as the different traditions of food and cookery. These are impossible for us to observe and analyse from archaeological evidence alone. Clothing is a social and cultural indicator, but can be perceived only partially through the evidence of contemporary images and the surviving objects that constitute only one aspect of the whole.

Whatever the factors may have been, by the fourth century there was really only one important type of fibula, the crossbow brooch. Penannular brooches continued to be used in Britain, as did certain forms of plate-brooch. Small fibulae known as knee brooches (from the form of the bow, which resembles a bent knee and lower leg) were fairly widespread on the continent in the third century, and were imported in some quantity and probably also made in Britain. Some of them were decorated, and a few bear inscriptions prominently enamelled on the bow itself, in particular the good-luck motto *utere felix,* literally "use (this) happily".

Crossbow brooches

The evolution of the late Roman crossbow brooch has been systematically analysed on the basis of south German finds by E. Keller, and it is not necessary to enter into the finer details.[16] Crossbow brooches were an international late Roman type, and they were worn by men, including, or perhaps especially, men in positions of authority. There is evidence that the finest and most valuable specimens were worn by individuals in the very highest echelons of society: although it has been quoted in practically every discussion of crossbow brooches ever written, attention must be drawn to the famous ivory diptych preserved in Monza, north Italy, which depicts Stilicho, the military ruler of the Western Empire under the Emperor Honorius, with his wife Serena and son Eucherios. Stilicho and Eucherios are both depicted with crossbow brooches of a specific and recognizable design clasping their cloaks high on the right shoulder.[17] These ivory plaques would have been carved around AD 400. There are many other fourth- and fifth-century representations of crossbow brooches in use, for example the portrait of Secundus and Proiecta on the Proiecta Casket, the large highly decorated silver box from the Esquiline treasure.[18]

The characteristics of the mature crossbow brooch include its weighty and imposing appearance, a bow that is markedly P-shaped in profile, and the transverse bar at the head giving rise to the "crossbow" effect; at the head of the bow and the ends of the crossbar are three large knobs, often with a slightly pointed shape like an onion. As the pin was not sprung but hinged, these side extensions were not required for any functional reason. Earlier P-shaped brooches and the initial phases of the crossbow form itself were fairly light and slender, but the fully evolved crossbow fibula can appear exceptionally large and heavy. Its actual weight was sometimes reduced by making the principal elements hollow rather than massive.

Crossbow brooches were made in precious metals as well as bronze, and the comparatively large areas they provide for decoration were used for a variety of ornamentation including inscriptions. Many crossbows display ingenious features such as imaginative and carefully executed safety-catch mechanisms designed to lock the pin securely into the catchplate. This ingenuity extended to include a neat method of replacing damaged pins: the hinge and axis bar was completely enclosed in the tubular crossbar, but on some examples, one of the side knobs was the head of a screw that itself formed the axis bar, and could be removed to insert a new pin. The known examples of screw stud all have left-hand threads.[19]

One of the finest gold crossbow brooches from Britain reveals this latter feature. It is an elegantly decorated object, with a series of filled zigzags in black niello inlay along the arris of the bow and foot, and applied cusps or volutes along the sides, exactly like those visible on Stilicho's brooch. The pointed onion terminals are faceted. This handsome piece of jewellery was discovered in Scotland (the Moray Firth) in 1847.

Figure 7.11 Gold crossbow brooch from the Moray Firth, with niello-inlaid ornament. Length 7.5 cm. (Photo: British Museum)

Figure 7.12 The Moray Firth crossbow brooch with one arm removed to show the screw mechanism. (Photo: British Museum)

Also from Scotland is an incomplete example of an inscribed gold cross-bow brooch in *opus interrasile:* it was found in the 1780s at Erickstanebrae (Dumfries and Galloway), and is now in the Los Angeles County Museum.[20] The inscription reads IOVIAVG/VOTXX, and refers in all probability to the twentieth anniversary of the accession of the Emperor Diocletian, which took place in AD 303. On the inside of the bow is a scratched graffito reading FORTV, probably an abbreviation of the owner's name. Valuable gold and silver objects were presented by the Emperor to courtiers and senior officials on special anniversaries, and soldiers also received a bonus in bullion; an inscribed brooch such as this would undoubtedly come into the first category. Inscriptions on high-quality gold rings and fibulae expressing loyalty to the Emperor are recorded quite frequently in the late Roman world.[21]

Another gold crossbow brooch from Britain was found in 1844 at Odiham, Hampshire; it is rather less elegant than the Moray Firth brooch, but of equally fine quality. An example of a typologically somewhat earlier gold crossbow, probably of late third-century date, was found in a rather curious hoard of jewellery from Wincle, Cheshire.[22] Silver cross-bows have also survived from Britain. A fine example from Bath has a distinctive pattern in niello inlay on the bow. Along the narrow front edge of the bow and the centre of the foot is a series of arrowhead motifs in niello, but while one side of the bow bears rows of zig-zag ornament, the other has a totally different design, a wave meander.[23]

There are many bronze fibulae of this late type, some of them gilded. When new, only the closest examination would have revealed that these were not made of gold: if gold crossbow brooches had some significance aside from the obvious one of wealth – that is, if the wearing of a gold crossbow implied high status and authority – the gilded examples may have been intentionally deceptive. It is more likely, however, that they were merely, in time-honoured fashion, intended to give an impression of somewhat greater affluence than that actually possessed by the wearer. Hollow construction may also have been for the purpose of achieving the maximum amount of brooch for the minimum quantity of metal, but the size of some of these brooches was such that their weight would have been impractical if solid.

A bronze crossbow brooch from Elton, Derbyshire, illustrates one of several safety-catch gadgets that are found on these late brooches. It consists of a swivelling arm that could be closed to seal the opening of the catchplate once the pin was in place.

The decoration of many crossbow brooches is typical of late Roman metalwork, with the deeply cut circle-and-dot motifs and chip-carved notches. Although gold-plating, inlaying of bronze with silver, and niello inlay all occur, enamelling is not found at all. It is not clear how many of the crossbow brooches found in Britain were made in the province, and it is conceivable, although not very likely, that they were all imported.

These characteristically late fibulae are found in late Roman treasures from other provinces, for example in the Ténès find,[24] but they are absent from the two major treasures of this period from Britain, those from Thetford and Hoxne. There are, however, some examples from useful late contexts, for instance from some of the burials in the late Roman cemetery at Lankhills.[25] It is not possible to date the fully developed crossbow form closely; it probably changed little throughout the course of the fourth century and into the fifth.

The most remarkable and probably the latest crossbow brooch known from Britain is a unique piece in silver that is unfortunately without any recorded history or provenance; it was acquired by the British Museum in 1954 and was said to be "from Sussex".[26] There is no particular reason to doubt this information, although it is frustratingly vague, and analysis has revealed a metal composition that is wholly compatible with a late Roman date. The object is a crossbow variant with a sprung pin instead of the usual hinge and arms finishing in profiled reel-like knobs rather than the normal spheres or "onion" knobs. The bow is shaped into the form of a stylized animal head, a boar or just possibly a horse, with an upstanding mane and glass-set eyes, and at the head of the brooch covering the spring is a disc that has a large dotted monogram cross upon it, the developed form of the Christian monogram that emerged later than the basic Chi-Rho device. The foot of the brooch tapers to an abrupt and quite narrow

Figure 7.13 Two views of the silver crossbow-brooch variant from Sussex, with a disc bearing a monogram cross and a stylized boar's head with glass eyes. Length 6.7 cm. (Photos: British Museum)

end, and has deep oblique grooves to give a twisted appearance. It is very easy to imagine the Sussex brooch as a native product of the early fifth century, contemporary with such ornaments as the three Brancaster-type rings from Amesbury.

Plate-brooches

Like their modern counterparts, Romano-British plate-brooches would appear to have been worn primarily for their visual effect. Most of them were quite small and were made of bronze or brass with enamelled decoration. The pins were more often hinged than sprung. There were scores of different forms, including an extensive series of zoomorphic shapes, and the types seem to have been common to several northern provinces, so that we find precise parallels to British examples not only in the adjacent provinces of Gaul but further afield, for instance in Pannonia (present-day Hungary).

The range of form and decoration that is found in Romano-British plate-brooches can be paralleled in other decorative metalwork of the period. The technique of making enamelled bronze objects was exacting, and we can assume it to have been a highly specialized skill; the bronze-workers and enamellers would not have confined their output to brooches, but would undoubtedly have manufactured a range of enamelled articles. These would have included the sealboxes, buckles, studs and "mounts" of uncertain use which abound in Romano-British contexts. Enamelled discs with a central projection at the back rather than a brooch-pin may have been intended for attaching to other metal items or to leather, and were not necessarily for human adornment, but they are found in designs that correspond closely with those of certain disc-brooches.

Even some plate-brooch types which were not designed to have enamel inlay can be paralleled closely in objects that the archaeologist tends to describe as "mounts" because all that can be inferred about their original function was that they were supposed to be attached to some other object.

Discs and other geometric shapes
Many of the simplest plate-brooches are quite small enamelled discs, not infrequently less than an inch (2.5 cm) in diameter. The pin on a brooch of this size will be able to pick up only about 1 cm of fabric, since allowance has to be made for the space occupied by the hinge lugs and the small catchplate attached to the back of the plate. The clearance between the

pin and the plate may be half a centimetre or less, and the fabric therefore has to be fairly thin. Many of the animal-shaped plate-brooches were of similar dimensions. A penannular brooch of this diminutive size is able to take in a much wider and thicker piece of woven textile, as can the occasional miniature fibula. The largest disc-brooches are around 5.5 cm in diameter, and they would naturally have a pin as long as that on a medium-size fibula, but they are rare compared with the small specimens. Combined with the fact that the enamelled inlay found on so many of them is often colourful to the point of gaudiness, their limited efficacy as fasteners leads one to infer that small disc-brooches were intended less for use than ornament.

Enamel can decay and change colour during burial, and this deterioration, combined with the brown or green patina of the copper alloy, means that the present condition of most of these brooches conveys little impression of their original brightness. The range of enamel colours, which were more opaque than those of most modern enamels, included several shades of blue and blue-green, red, orange and yellow, green, black and white. Blue and red were the most popular. In addition to the plain colours, inlays of millefiori enamel were used, consisting of minute squares of colour containing an integral coloured pattern. These were often crosses or chequer patterns, but there were also flower rosettes and spiral scrolls and minute tree-like designs. Individual millefiori elements were usually around 2–3 mm square. The enamel was set into cells cast in the metal, although more than one colour was sometimes used in a single area without any metal wall for separation.

Contrasting with the enamel colours was the golden bronze or, in some instances, the silvery white of tin-plating. The simplest disc-brooch patterns are concentric zones of coloured enamel demarcated by cast ridges or walls of bronze, but designs based on stars or rosettes were especially favoured. Some have circular spots of colour on a contrasting background, and there are a few with more imaginative triskele patterns or circular wave designs. There are a few plain disc-brooches that display an all-over chequered surface in millefiori enamel.

The basic disc shape was varied in a number of ways. One of the most common was the addition of projections around the circumference, usually in the form of small round lugs that were themselves enamelled. Often one of them was a cast ring that would have served to attach a chain or cord to the brooch. Pointed projections, giving an overall star shape, are occasionally found, and the centre of the disc can be open to make a ring brooch, or raised and domed. Some flat discs had added decorative studs in the centre that stand out from the surface, while others seem to be so prominent that they must, again, be designed as attachment points. A few brooches have zoomorphic elements in the round on such projecting

studs – birds and dolphins are known. Central "hubs" and cut-out patterns were used to make wheel shapes, which are known in a wide variety, with and without enamelling.

Lozenge- or diamond-shaped plate-brooches had many of the same features as the circular specimens, with similar enamelling and often with edge projections. Both forms were sometimes provided with two more prominent projections to which the hinge and catchplate were attached; the central enamelled plate could be raised above the level of the projections, and the final result was then an elongated brooch that was not significantly different from a fibula. This range of forms includes many with square or rectangular enamelled plates, and the projecting lugs are often zoomorphic in a generalized sense – they are not identifiable as a particular animal, but have a vaguely reptilian appearance. Crescentic enamelled plate-brooches are known, although they were not common. The true crescents have the pin attached across the points, so that the hinge is behind one point and the catchplate behind the other. There are also crescentic plates that have an extra central point to enable the pin to be attached there, and these should more properly be described as pelta-shaped, after the Amazonian shields which are a recurring device in Roman art.

Wheel-shaped plate-brooches have been mentioned, and there were other openwork enamelled forms made up of combinations of rings, squares, lozenges and so forth. Openwork brooches without enamelled inlay were also current in a variety of forms including some asymmetrically curved arrangements of Celtic trumpet-scrolls. The swastika is found both as a freestanding form and as an openwork pattern in a square; it was a geometric figure widely used in Roman decorative art, and obviously still carried some of its prehistoric sun-symbolism.

A few small enamelled rectangles are known with abstract or zoo-morphic patterns reserved in bronze against coloured enamel. Some of these are close in form to the shield-shaped brooches mentioned below, but those with animal designs are plain rectangles: fishes and hares are the creatures that have so far been noted on British examples.

Zoomorphic brooches

A great many small plate-brooches were made in animal shapes, and inter-preting the significance of these is something of a challenge. On the one hand, it is important to remember that most animals had symbolic over-tones in Roman art and religion, so it is possible to argue that at least some of these ornaments could have signified something over and above the straightforward representation of a particular creature. But is this too solemnly academic an approach to objects that may have been intended simply as cheerful spots of colour on a garment? The vivid colours of enamel would have been esteemed in a way that is hard for us to envisage, since we are constantly surrounded by bright colours. Perhaps the brooches had no deep significance at all, but gave pleasure in themselves as similar animal ornaments have done up to the present day. Their naïvety is certainly more appealing than the vulgar ostentation of some of the expensive precious-metal and gemstone animal ornaments that were made in the 1920s and 1930s. The best way of trying to assess the signifi-cance of zoomorphic brooches may be to attempt some analysis of the subjects they represent, along with the brooches made in the forms of cer-tain inanimate objects. When the range of subjects is compared with those common in Roman and Romano-Celtic iconography generally, a somewhat unexpected picture emerges: animals that were important and frequently depicted in art are rare amongst these brooches. As always, it is vital to remember that the examples that have been lost, survived the ages, have been found again and, above all, have been made known in the archaeological literature must be a minute proportion of those that were in use in antiquity.

The first point which seems curious is that enamelled bronze brooches in the shape of humans (or deities) are almost unknown. In theory, since a person could carry the image of a god or goddess on an engraved gem-stone, or in the form of a name on a piece of jewellery, it would not be in the least surprising to find small plate-brooches that depicted, say, Mars or Minerva, or perhaps a trio of mother goddesses. Apparently they do not exist. But having said that, a god figure does form part of one of the most common varieties of small zoomorphic brooch from Britain, namely the horse-and-rider brooch.

At least thirty-five horse-and-rider brooches have been recorded from Britain, and the real number must be much higher.[27] They are all quite similar to each other; around 2.5–3 cm long, they present a very simplified image of a prancing long-tailed horse with upstanding mane. The head and torso of the rider are seen above the horse's body, and in some, but not all, his leg and foot project below it. The group faces to the right, like most zoomorphic brooches. The enamel inlay is disposed in simple shapes, usually three main cells following the form of the object. On a few of the more elaborate examples, it is possible to make out what may be a sword in the hand of the rider.

Figure 7.15 A typical horse-and-rider brooch. This example is from Woodyates, Dorset. British Museum. Length 2.7 cm. (Photo: author)

Horse-and-rider brooches appear to be specifically Romano-British, and they are moreover concentrated on certain sites that are known to have had temple precincts, for example Hockwold-cum-Wilton in Norfolk and Hayling Island in Hampshire. It is very tempting indeed to link this image of a mounted warrior with the Romano-Celtic rider god, who was probably regarded as an aspect of Mars conflated with a native deity, and is sometimes represented in sculpture and small bronze statuettes in Roman Britain.[28] If the connection exists, we might envisage these brooches as being like pilgrim badges, souvenirs that could be purchased at the appropriate temples and worn as a proof of a visit to the shrine.

Horses alone also feature in a fair number of zoomorphic brooches, many of them quite similar in appearance to the mount of the rider god. A few are rather charmingly embellished with coloured spots of enamel. There are also horse-brooches without enamel inlay. Horses are not as common a subject as dogs, however. Hounds and hares, together or separately expressing the idea of the hunt, are amongst the most fundamental themes of Roman art, and can be found in numerous versions in provincial art as well. Many of the running-hound brooches – at least twenty are recorded from Britain, with others from abroad – are enamelled in a single colour, blue or red, with spots of a contrasting hue. It is not always

Figure 7.16 A horse brooch with enamel spots. Length 3.3 cm. British Museum. (Photo: author)

easy to distinguish hares from hounds; the latter are shown with longer tails and may wear collars (although this feature has not been noted on brooches), but both are depicted with very long ears. Many of the hares are sitting or squatting, and there is one variety in the form of a compact sitting hare with two smaller hares enamelled within its body, presumably to suggest a female with young. Another variant is a hare brooch with stripes applied not in enamel but in black niello; there is an example from London and a virtually identical one from Luxembourg.

Figure 7.17 Zoomorphic enamelled brooch in the form of a hare. Length 2.7 cm. British Museum. (Photo: author)

While hares and hounds express in a general way the theme of hunting, it may not be too fanciful to see some special meaning in the comparatively common depiction of hares, which evidently had some significance in Celtic religion. Deer, especially red-deer stags, were another standard subject in provincial Roman art, but they occur very rarely in the brooches we are considering. Also fairly uncommon are the lions and leopards that were likewise standard themes; leopards or panthers were creatures of Bacchus. Dolphins were also Bacchic animals, and they are ubiquitous in Roman art; again, they are infrequent in the enamelled brooches, and there is no standard type such as the horse-and-rider or hound types. A tiny silver dolphin-brooch from London (without enamel) is not unique, but it is the only one of its kind from Britain. Fishes are more common than dolphins, a reversal of the position in Roman iconography generally.

Figure 7.18 A small silver brooch in the form of a dolphin, from London. Length 3.2 cm. (Photo: British Museum)

There are no known bull or ram brooches, and very few in the form of boars. When we turn to birds, the same slightly unexpected distribution of species is seen. Eagles and peacocks do occur, the eagles sometimes depicted in the act of devouring a hare, and there are two or three strutting cockerels in profile and a considerable number of unidentifiable flying birds seen from above, perhaps pigeons or doves. Eagles, peacocks and cockerels all have specific connections with major deities (Jupiter, Juno and Mercury respectively), while doves are connected with Venus. By far the most common bird amongst the brooch menagerie, however, is a three-dimensional representation of a stylized swimming duck (I shall refrain from classifying it as a sitting duck), its back decoratively enamelled and the pin attached beneath its hollowed body. Ducks were undoubtedly important in Celtic mythology, although it is difficult to define their significance precisely, and images of ducks, often holding a round object in their beaks, occur in a wide range of pre-Roman and Romano-Celtic contexts. Ducks, or sometimes perhaps swans, were also used ornamentally in certain classes of Roman silver tableware, for example in a distinctive class of fourth-century spoon that features a short, coiled handle terminating in the head of a water-bird.

Almost as common as the ducks are sitting chickens designed and decorated in exactly the same way. They have curved tails, and have been described as cockerels, but their heads and the sitting pose are far more suggestive of a broody hen than a cock. The tails always have a small perforation that was presumably intended for the attachment of a chain or cord.

Figure 7.19 Two "sitting chicken" brooches, the one in the foreground from Brough (Cumbria), the other from Lincoln. Length 3.9 cm and 4.6 cm. British Museum. (Photo: author)

A few monsters are known – hippocamps, capricorns and *ketoi* (the Classical sea-serpent), and the occasional frog-brooch has been noted, but there are no snakes, notwithstanding their popularity in other forms of jewellery. One exceptional brooch, from Baldock, Hertfordshire, is of a hare being hunted by another animal;[29] the theme of a hound running down a hare is found in all kinds of small decorative items, but brooches of this design are not common, and no example has yet been noted from Britain. However, the Baldock brooch is more remarkable still, because the predator is not the usual hound but a cat. It has stripes, probably originally defined with niello rather than enamel. This object is not only a unique brooch but is also the only known representation of a cat from Roman Britain. The European wildcat (*Felis silvestris silvestris*) was native to Britain, but it is quite likely that the domestic cat, which probably evolved principally from the North African species *Felis silvestris libyca*, was first introduced in the Roman period. Of course it is not possible to say whether the Baldock brooch represents a wild animal or a domestic one.

Figure 7.20 A bronze brooch from Baldock, Hertfordshire, with tin-plating and probably niello inlay, depicting a cat catching a hare. Length 3.3 cm. (After Stead & Rigby 1986)

Overall, the distribution of subjects that are common or rare, or the absence of some subjects, seems quite out of step with what we might expect if the choice depended on religious significance on the one hand, or mere visual appeal on the other. The same unexpected balance characterizes the smaller group of brooches that represents inanimate objects.

Brooches in the shape of objects

It would be easy to make a long list of inanimate objects that had apotropaic and religious significance in the Roman world and would have been images well suited to the design of brooches – Bacchic vases, clubs of Hercules, the caduceus (a winged, snake-entwined staff) of Mercury, steering-oars, cornucopiae and thunderbolts come to mind.

It comes as something of a surprise, therefore, to discover that the most common object-shaped enamelled brooches in Roman Britain would appear to have been those in the form of a pointed and hobnailed shoe- or sandal-sole. They are generally enamelled in one colour, often blue, with spots of another colour inset direct in the background enamel, presumably to suggest nail heads. Brooches of this variety were equally popular in other Celtic provinces, but it is difficult to know why. Like all of the brightly coloured trinkets in this class, they would have looked attractive pinned on to a fabric of a soft and subtle shade, but why a shoe-sole? There was surely a reason for their popularity that escapes us. There could be a military link, or the nailed sole could be connected with the idea of travel, and thus with protection from the dangers of travel, but there might be some much more obscure concept to which we have no key at all.

Figure 7.21 Enamelled sandal-sole brooch from London. Length 4.4 cm. (Photo: Museum of London)

Other object-shaped brooches include a few that are in the form of an axe. Miniature axes were a recurrent votive subject in certain cults, so we can say with confidence that these brooches are likely to have been associated in some way with a shrine. The pilgrim-badge analogy suggested for the horse-and-rider brooches could apply equally in this case. A characteristic shield-shape including the central boss is also found in a number of plate-brooches, mostly enamelled but a few without added colour. Some are so stylized that their interpretation as a shield depends on knowledge of the other, more certain examples, but in any case, a military connection of some sort seems undeniable. While the typically Bacchic cantharus or two-handled pedestalled vase is not a standard plate-brooch type, there are a few brooches both from Britain and elsewhere depicting a one-handled jug. This subject, again, is of unknown significance.

In general, then, the subjects favoured by the manufacturers and purchasers of enamelled plate-brooches made in the shapes of animals or inanimate objects raise a number of questions about meaning and use. The range of representations suggests something other than a simple predilection for pretty ornaments, but it is clearly not related in a straightforward way to the symbols of the standard Graeco-Roman cults. We are probably justified in seeing a fairly strong Celtic preference at work, not only in Britain but throughout the Celtic provinces. If so, the iconography of these small decorative objects deserves rather closer attention than it has yet received.

In Chapter 1, I referred to the way in which fashion trends in modern trinket jewellery can be inspired by cartoon characters or particular advertising campaigns that would be wholly impossible for anyone to interpret except from within that culture itself. Even allowing for the fact that twentieth-century mass media can disseminate popular knowledge of such ephemeral trends in a way that could not even remotely be approached in antiquity, there may be a parallel. A widely known story, parable or saying, a famous decorative or natural feature of an important place, a symbol associated with some popular game or activity, all these could give rise to a symbol that would work well as a badge, and would have clear meaning to others in the same society. We can amuse ourselves working out possible meanings for some of these little brooches, but there is no way of knowing whether we are anywhere near the truth. The most that an archaeologist or jewellery historian can venture to say is that the little enamelled bronze animals and objects that were pinned to the clothing of many Roman Britons are every bit as interesting in their own way as the superb gold ornaments flaunted by the wealthiest women in that society.

Other plate-brooches: chateleine brooches

Before trying to sum up some of the points that have emerged from this survey of brooches, there are three remaining varieties of plate-brooch that deserve special mention. The first of these is the so-called chateleine type, an enamelled brooch which incorporates a set of small toilet implements. Toilet utensils such as tweezers, nail-cleaners and tiny spoon-shaped tools that are probably ear-cleaners were in common use in the Roman provinces, and they are not infrequently found as sets placed together on a ring. The chateleine brooches, richly decorated in enamel, are more elaborate versions of such sets. The brooch part of the assembly is usually a disc with a centre boss and three or five border discs, with a segment cut off straight at the base and provided with lugs to hold a bar. A row of small toilet implements, enamelled to match the brooch, is suspended from the bar. In addition to the implements described above there are toothpicks and other items, perhaps for the preparation and application of lip- or eye-makeup or some other cosmetic purpose. The spoon-shaped ear-scoops might also have been used for removing unguents from small containers. Chateleine brooches are not especially common amongst Romano-British finds; fifteen were known to Richard Hattatt.[30] One of the best-preserved examples retains all six implements and is finished in mid-blue and yellow enamel.

These objects were utterly unsuitable for practical purposes, and it is hard to believe that they were intended for use at all. A simple wooden or bone toothpick is far more convenient and effective than an elegantly enamelled bronze one that is firmly attached to a brooch and five other

small implements. The simpler bronze chateleine sets are carried on a plain ring like a key-ring, and would therefore have been quite easy to use. The chateleine brooches are gadgetry of the most blatant kind, but they are undoubtedly pretty and intriguing: utilitarian items arranged as a compact and comprehensive set still exercise a strong appeal.

It is an entirely hypothetical suggestion, but it seems possible that for some women in the Celtic provinces, a brooch of this kind somehow symbolized acceptance of *romanitas* in the form of the Roman standards of personal hygiene which were a significant element in the culture. Another possibility is suggested by a modern parallel: in the 1950s, most young girls sooner or later received as a gift a handsome manicure set packaged in a leather wallet. Probably very few of them ever used the mysterious selection of tools that the kits contained, but the gift was intended to imply that the girl was now a young woman who would be interested in such matters as well-cared-for nails and hands.

Repoussé disc-brooches

Some small disc-brooches were decorated with an applied front plate bearing a raised design worked in repoussé technique. One very homogeneous group has a tightly coiled Celtic triskele motif within an outer beaded border (e.g. Fig. 7.24). In the spaces between the curled lobes of the three elements of the triskele are three additional leaves or lobes, sometimes stylized to simple crescents. A particularly fine example of the type with an applied plate made of gilded silver instead of the more usual bronze comes from South Shields.[31] There is no reliable archaeological evidence for the dating of this group.

While the triskele brooches belong very obviously to the Celtic artistic tradition, another important class of disc-brooch with applied front plate reveals a combination of Roman inspiration and Celtic execution. These have pictorial scenes of a mounted figure and three soldiers, or a single figure leading a horse, designs that were recognized many years ago as being based on coin-reverse types of the Emperor Hadrian (AD 117–38).[32] Specifically, they were inspired by series of coins issued in AD 134–7 honouring the provinces and the provincial armies. Around twenty are recorded from Britain, although many are in very damaged condition. Those that are better preserved show very clearly that the thin repoussé plates were not made by shaping them over an actual coin: there are considerable variations, including changing the Emperor's quietly standing mount into a prancing charger and providing both Emperor and soldiers with shields.

Disc-brooches made in this embossed technique may have been commoner than now appears; solder generally decays after burial, and once detached, the thin sheet-metal of the front plaque is very fragile and unlikely to survive intact. There are, in fact, quite a few back-plates and pins extant that have lost the decorated face.

Gilded brooches with glass settings

One important plate-brooch form remains to be discussed: it looks disconcertingly like some nineteenth- or early twentieth-century brooches. Oval or circular bronze brooches with gilding and impressed ornament on the face, tin-plating on the back, sprung pins and a central oval or round cell containing a conical glass setting, or a truncated cone with or without an intaglio device, were evidently a Romano-British fashion in the third century, and at least a hundred examples have been noted. They were cast with concentric ridges alternating with zones of punched decoration – lines, crosses, circles, S-shapes – to create a textured effect. The glass gem in the centre was often of a very dark shade of blue, brown or green that appears black. Flat, bevelled settings are also found, some of them plain, others with a simple moulded stick-figure in intaglio similar to those that appear in some of the glass ring-settings, but there is at least one known example that has a properly engraved paste setting. It is a find from Abbotts Ann, Hampshire. The gem is a layered light and dark blue glass imitating nicolo, a banded onyx cut in the same plane as the coloured bands, and the device cut on it is a female head, probably of the goddess Diana, in a style of engraving that tends to confirm a third-

Figure 7.23 Two gilt-and-glass brooches from Uley, Gloucestershire. Although both of these are circular, oval examples are more common. Diameter 3.3 cm and 3 cm. (Photo: British Museum)

century date.[33] Obviously closely related to these brooches are oval plates with an enamelled border surrounding a large glass setting with a crude bust in intaglio.

The gilding seems to be an invariable feature, although it has often been worn and damaged, and may be visible only in the more protected areas. The brooches must surely be direct imitations of a prototype in precious metal with a hardstone setting, and although no oval gold brooch with a plain or engraved gem has yet been recorded from a Romano-British site, we can infer the existence of the type from a handsome specimen in Cologne, said to have been found there. It features a large carnelian engraved with Apollo leaning on a pillar, and is set in a gold frame of twisted and beaded wire.[34] Although the style of the gem is attributed to the first century, the object as a whole may well be later. Unfortunately its context is not known. Oval gem-set gold necklace-pendants of very similar appearance are known from elsewhere in the Roman world, and it was in the third century that highly ornamented rings with gems of truncated conical form were especially popular; both could be regarded as visually related to the gilded oval brooches. If precious-metal versions were made in Britain, their absence from the archaeological record is hardly surprising in view of the lack of major third-century treasure hoards from the province.

Celtic elements in brooches

Although the foregoing discussion should have demonstrated that brooches were not always solely utilitarian items and therefore fully deserve their place in a survey of jewellery, it is clear that they do nevertheless differ in some interesting respects from the other personal ornaments worn in Roman Britain. In particular, several references have been made to decoration in a traditional Celtic style on certain types of brooch; the characteristic swelling curvilinear scrolls do not appear on other Romano-British jewellery, even those objects that were undoubtedly manufactured in the province. The frequent use of enamelling on bronze is another feature that is common on brooches of several kinds but unusual on other forms of contemporary jewellery.

The development of Celtic art from prehistory down to the early medieval period is far too complex and specialized a subject to go into here, and it has in any case been extensively analysed elsewhere: there are several well-illustrated books to which the interested reader can turn, for example *Celtic art* by I. M. Stead, and the comprehensive study by Vincent and Ruth Megaw, also entitled *Celtic art*.[35]

If we consider the repoussé disc-brooches with triskele designs, it is not difficult to find extremely close parallels for the motif and its treatment both from the pre-Roman Iron Age and the early medieval period. Pre-Roman examples include the circular face of a gold torc-terminal from Clevedon, Avon, the far more elaborate triskele of the Brentford "horn-cap" and the Tal-y-Llyn shield-mount, all dating to the first century BC, while a variety of stunningly beautiful developments of the theme can be found in Irish metalwork and book illumination of the sixth to eighth centuries AD and on the ornamental escutcheons of the Celtic bronze hanging-bowls found in Anglo-Saxon contexts.[36] The modest little triskele brooches of the Roman period in Britain take their place in a tradition that remained unbroken over many centuries. It is not unreasonable to ask ourselves why this type of design is absent on objects such as jet necklace-pendants, made of a local material and surely by native craftsmen.

Dragonesque brooches cannot be related so precisely and directly to pre- and post-Roman objects; they are entirely of their period, and yet in their creation of a zoomorphic form out of an abstract design (or vice

Figure 7.24 A small disc-brooch from Brough (Cumbria), with a repoussé plate bearing a triskele design. Diameter 2.4 cm. British Museum. (Photo: author)

Figure 7.25 The triskele pattern on the end of a gold torc-terminal from Clevedon, Avon. First century BC. Diameter 3.5 cm. (Photo: British Museum)

versa), they, too, are part of the underlying spirit of Celtic art. The same curves and palmettes appear in the enamelled or cast decoration of some trumpet-brooches, and in the ornamentation of fibulae of the Aesica type.

Why do these native tastes, so attractive to modern perceptions, emerge overtly only on items such as trumpet fibulae, disc-brooches and the beautiful enamelled dragonesques, and largely fail to appear in the vast range of rings and bracelets and necklaces in precious and base metal that must certainly have been made by Romano-British craftsmen? One reason may be the tendency for objects that had been introduced for the first time by the Romans to be identified as such and adopted without much alteration, while those that were already part of Celtic culture retained native features in spite of evolving and changing under the influence of Roman ideals. It is very noticeable that architectural innovations such as mosaic floors and painted walls invariably bore Classical decorative themes, as though the idea of using these new techniques to embody native images was simply not thought feasible; it may also have been true that the people who wished to impress others with their cosmopolitan polish would have felt that native elements in their domestic decoration would spoil the effect. This motivation could well have operated in the case of high-quality gold and silver rings and necklaces and bracelets.

Another connected factor might have involved the workshops and craftsmen who made the brooches. The traditions and methods of bronze-smiths were separate from those of workers in gold and silver, and of course there would have been far more bronze foundries than goldsmiths' workshops. The Roman conquest was unlikely to have had much effect on bronzesmiths, except perhaps to bring them even more custom. They would have continued to make similar artefacts for the same customers and for new customers at almost every social level. Furthermore, many of the same types of object were familiar to and needed by both indigenous and immigrant clients. The changes in material culture would indeed have been merely a natural evolution.

Goldsmiths, on the other hand, were obviously a much rarer breed, and they would have been working only for the wealthiest and most powerful elements in tribal Celtic society, possibly even being directly employed by local chieftains. The changes caused by the Roman takeover would have been total and abrupt, and if the craftsmen wanted to stay in business, they would have needed to adapt very rapidly to manufacturing and repairing the types of article required by new customers. The outward appearance of international chic would also quite quickly have become desirable for the wealthier elements in British society if they wished to integrate successfully into the new order. Thus massive gold torcs were totally replaced by delicate gold necklaces, but bronze safety-pins could still be made, purchased and worn by almost anybody without carrying any complex social and ethnic messages.

Hypotheses such as these may well be simplistic when we have so little idea about the organization of manufacture. But whatever the reasons, we are able to perceive the interaction of native and Roman far more clearly in brooches than we can in other types of jewellery, even when the latter were made in non-precious materials. Fibulae and other brooches therefore have a special place in expressing the nature of Romano-British culture and society.

Chapter 8

The manufacture of Roman jewellery

In the foregoing chapters I have attempted to build up a picture of the types of personal ornament worn in Roman Britain and the interest that they hold for the archaeologist and the art historian. In this final section it remains to say a little about the nature of the craftsmanship required to create the jewellery. Ancient technology is a vast field of research, and its study in depth requires scientific training and often practical craft experience as well. My purpose is merely to give some idea of the main techniques that were used to make and decorate items of personal adornment during the Roman period in Britain.

For a more complete and detailed discussion of the subject of ancient jewellery manufacture, the reader should refer to the essential work *Jewellery of the ancient world* by Jack Ogden, and the same author's short introduction *Ancient jewellery*. There is also a useful section on materials and techniques, with an emphasis on precious metals, in the late Reynold Higgins's *Greek and Roman jewellery,* and an excellent introduction to the wider subject of Roman craftsmanship in the essays that make up *Roman crafts,* edited by Donald Strong and David Brown. Approaching the subject from another angle, that of the practising artist and jewellery maker, Oppi Untracht's *Jewelry concepts and technology* is an encyclopaedic and highly relevant source of information.[1]

Modern methods of study, in particular examination under very high-power magnification, are often able to reveal details about ancient manufacturing processes that could not have been detected in the past, but it is important not to become too complacent about our discoveries. One common pitfall applies not only to research on ancient technology but to all theorizing about the past, namely the danger of thinking that there is only one solution to each problem. There may be several. If it is possible to demonstrate that a particular effect was achieved in a certain way, it does not automatically follow that every object of that kind at that period was made in the same manner. It is especially important to be aware of this in case different methods of manufacture should eventually turn out to be significant in defining finer degrees of differentiation, for example indicating contemporary manufacture in diverse areas.

The advice and input of modern craftsmen is an invaluable source of information but, again, it must be treated critically. Modern artisans have their own traditions, and while they may be able to suggest and demonstrate an excellent method of making a given ancient artefact, we cannot always go on to assume that the object was indeed made in exactly that way. Time was a less important factor in antiquity than it is now. Some procedures favoured by modern workers will have been chosen because they are quicker than another equally effective method, and the Roman craftsman would not necessarily have preferred the faster way. Finally, it must be borne in mind that ancient craftsmen learnt their skills at a far earlier age than is customary in modern Western society. Procedures that seem almost impossibly precise and time-consuming to a modern artist who started to practise his or her craft at the age of sixteen or eighteen may have been quite feasible for a person who was already an experienced master by the age of twelve. A tombstone found in Rome in 1631 commemorates a young slave jeweller named Pagus, who died at the age of twelve years, nine months, thirteen days and eight hours. In spite of his youth, Pagus was described in his moving epitaph as being skilled in the working of gold and the setting of jewels.[2]

The existence of the necessary metals and many other materials for jewellery manufacture in Roman Britain has already been commented upon in Chapter 2. However, metals and glass are recyclable resources, and scrap was always a significant source of material for metalworking, so that even if the raw materials had not been obtainable in Britain, manufacturing could still have been carried out on an extensive scale. Nevertheless, actual evidence for workshops is as yet very patchy. Some industries leave evidence that is difficult for even the most primitive archaeological methods to miss, for example the firing of pottery; others can be missed extremely easily even by sophisticated excavation methods. A goldsmith need not necessarily leave any archaeologically detectable traces. There is one inscription from Roman Britain, found at Malton in North Yorkshire, that refers to a goldsmith, but without it there would have been no way of inferring the manufacture of gold items in that area.[3] All we can say in the present state of knowledge is that during the centuries of Roman rule in Britain there would certainly have been a great many workshops making items of jewellery in various materials.

Metals

The principal metalworking techniques were already ancient by the Roman period. The basic shaping processes varied according to the metal: gold of high purity is very soft and malleable, so that quite complex shapes can be produced by cold working, whereas casting was a standard method in bronzeworking, and even the working of sheet bronze necessitated regular annealing (heating) of the metal to restore its flexibility. Iron, which has a melting point of 1525°C, could not be cast at all in the Roman period, so that even delicate iron ornaments such as brooches and rings were forged. The melting points of gold (1063°C) and silver (960°C) presented no technical problems for the Roman craftsman; the melting-points of various copper alloys vary according to the precise composition of the metal (for example the melting-point of pure copper is 1083°C, but a bronze containing 10–12 per cent tin melts at around 1000°C) and modern analytical techniques have shown very clearly that specific mixes were consciously chosen for their suitability for different manufacturing processes.[4]

Although traditional hand fabrication methods are still used by many artist jewellers, modern commercial gold jewellery is mostly cast or made from cast and soldered components; not only is casting a time-saving mass-production method, an important consideration in modern Western economies, but "gold" containing as little as 37.5 per cent of the precious metal (9 carat) cannot be manipulated by pressure alone, as can

Figure 8.1 A small stone inscription from Malton, North Yorkshire, which refers to a goldsmith. Length 33 cm. (Photo: Yorkshire Museum)

gold that is over 90 per cent pure, which was the norm in gold jewellery of the Roman period. Much Classical gold jewellery was made from a combination of sheet gold, cut or formed into three-dimensional shapes, and gold wire used in various ways, functionally as chain, or decoratively as filigree. Cast elements were not common.

Casting was used more routinely in the creation of silver and bronze ornaments, but wire and sheet-metal techniques such as repoussé ornament were also important in the working of these metals. Casting was the principal method for making solid shapes in bronze, although for items such as brooches, cast blanks would still have required a great deal of secondary working with chasing tools. Open (one-piece) moulds, piece moulds with two or more sections and lost-wax (*cire perdue*) casting were all in use in the Roman period, and the method used in any given case would have depended on the judgement of the craftsman. The lost-wax method was widely used for objects of complex shape such as bronze statuettes. It involves making an archetype or model from wax, investing (covering) it in clay and then firing it to bake the clay and melt out the wax. The resulting hollow mould is finally filled with molten metal. When the metal has cooled and hardened, the mould is broken. Obviously each mould can be used only once.

The concept of piece-moulds was well established in the Roman period and was often used in making such objects as terracotta statuettes and lamps. It was also employed for some bronze castings, such as finger-rings and brooches; an unused two-piece mould for a bronze trumpet-brooch was found at Prestatyn, in addition to other metalworking debris.[5]

Embossed decoration on sheet metal was produced by using punches of various kinds. At its simplest, freehand raised designs on the front of the sheet can be made by laying the metal on a yielding, resilient surface, such as pitch, wax or clay, and hammering with suitably shaped tools from the back. For working gold of high purity, metal tools are unnecessary: bone or hardwood implements would have sufficed. Some finishing of the design from the front is usually necessary as well, and a sharp distinction between *repoussé* work, carried out from the back, and *chasing*, executed from the front, is not really meaningful. In the same way, the formal distinction between chasing and engraving, in which metal is cut away rather than deformed and rearranged, is rather less clear in practice than in theory.

From the basic process of raising relief designs freehand from the back, other more complex possibilities suggest themselves. If the punch, instead of having a simple rounded head, is itself made with a relief design on the head, that design can be transferred in its entirety to the sheet metal and will be reproduced on the front of the work. Sheet gold could also be laid over a high-relief form made of wood or metal, and could be shaped over it from the front. In Roman jewellery, thin three-dimensional forms made of sheet gold, for example some finger-rings, were often backed or filled with sulphur to support them, as otherwise they would very easily have been damaged and dented in wear. Sulphur melts easily and when cool solidifies without contracting.

Alternatively, the sheet metal could be driven from the back into a hollow mould. Globular gold beads were made by working the metal into a hemispherical mould, and then soldering two of the resulting half-spheres together. Intaglio moulds of this kind could be of very complex shapes. A method akin to the striking of coins may also have been used on occasion. The silver bracelets and rings from the Snettisham jeweller's hoard appear to have been made in that way: the cast silver bar, much thicker than sheet metal, may have been hammered into an open die with the design in intaglio to produce the details of the snake-head terminals. A die from Alchester that could have been used for this purpose is in the Ashmolean Museum.[6]

Surface decoration

The many methods of creating three-dimensional forms in sheet metal could be used as described to make the basic elements of a piece of jewellery, or they could be employed as a means of adding surface ornamentation; the Romano-British disc-brooches that have a plain front to which a repoussé-decorated plate of thin sheet is soldered exemplify the latter usage. Many other forms of surface decoration were used. Tracers and punches were used to impress lines and other shapes so as to form patterns on metal, and wire filigree and granulation were also applied to create intricate patterns. The rectangular gold plaque from Colchester with a portrait of the Empress Faustina the Elder includes repoussé work in low relief and piercing of a simple kind, together with filigree wire. Openwork or piercing in gold was a specialized and very skilled decorative method used in the later Roman period, and forms of decoration that involved colour contrasts included the plating of one metal with another and inlay in niello and enamel.

Wire filigree in provincial Roman gold and silver jewellery consists of different types of wire soldered to a solid background or, in some cases – as in the hoops of some late Roman rings – supported on a framework so minimal that they become a lacy openwork structure. The wire may be plain, twisted or beaded, and is often combined with minute gold spheres. Technically the attachment of such grains of gold or silver to a base may be termed granulation, but it is not nearly as fine as the granulation that is found on Etruscan goldwork; the individual globular grains on provincial Roman gold and silver objects are fairly large, ranging from about 0.5 mm to as much as 2 mm in diameter. They were consequently comparatively easy to handle and place individually.

Many examples of wire filigree are illustrated in the preceding chapters, from the spiral volutes on the shoulders of many late Roman rings to the elaborate plaited wire seen on the enamelled gold bracelet from the Rhayader group. The Snettisham jeweller's hoard provides examples of the same techniques in silver. One of the recurrent motifs in Romano-British jewellery is the use of a round blob of gold or silver set within a circle of beaded wire; this appears regularly on snake-rings like those from Backworth and Snettisham and also as the central feature on wheel clasps.

The technical skills required for this type of decoration were the manufacture of fine wire and precise control of the delicate process of soldering: incompetent soldering would reduce the crisp and detailed relief ornament to a blurred and amorphous mass.

Solder is an alloy with a lower melting-point than the metals to be joined. The addition of very small amounts of silver or copper to gold will lower the melting-point of the metal and produce a suitable solder; heat would have been applied using a flame-source such as a small furnace or an oil-lamp directed by means of a blowpipe. But special methods must have been developed to deal with the attachment of the minute grains of gold used in the finest pre-Roman granulation, and these may well have continued in use for the small-scale, although not microscopic, work of the Roman period. One soldering method that works for fine granulation was developed and patented by H. Littledale in 1934.[7] Known as "colloidal hard soldering" or "diffusion bonding", this is an elegant technique that simultaneously solves the problems of holding the elements in place and attaching them permanently to the base: an adhesive of organic glue combined with copper hydroxide is used to hold the grains in place, and when heated, the copper salt turns to copper oxide and the glue to carbon; the carbon then absorbs the oxygen from the copper oxide, leaving a layer of copper that at 890°C combines with the surrounding gold and forms a joint. This, and related, methods must have been in use in antiquity together with more conventional soldering methods.[8]

Wire

The normal method of making wire today is by *drawing*: a metal rod is pulled through holes of ever-decreasing size in a drawplate until it reaches the desired diameter. The manufacture of wire in antiquity has been extensively studied, and it now seems virtually certain that drawn wire was not made within the period we are concerned with here but was first developed in the West around the eighth century AD. The best summary

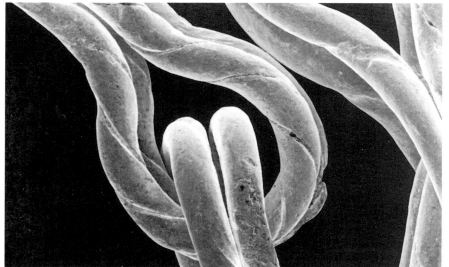

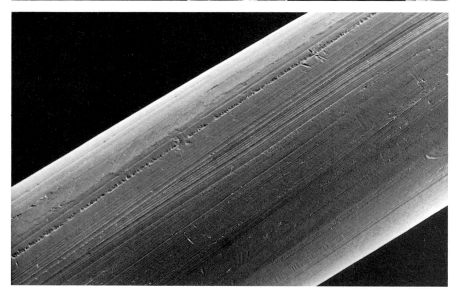

Figure 8.2 Wire made (a) by twisting techniques and (b) by drawing, both seen through an SEM (scanning electron microscope); the former displays helical seams, the latter has straight parallel lines. The twisted wire is a link from a late Roman gold necklace found at New Grange, Co. Meath, Ireland, while the drawn wire is modern. (Photos: Department of Scientific Research, British Museum.)

of the methods of manufacture and the history of the study will be found in Jack Ogden's paper "Classical gold wire: some aspects of its manufacture and use".[9]

Wire can be made simply by hammering, but obviously this is a somewhat crude method when the aim is to produce very fine wire of regular cross-section. Fine gold or silver wire was made in antiquity by twisting and rolling techniques, either by twisting a thin strip or ribbon of metal until it became a coiled tube like a paper drinking-straw and then rolling it between two flat surfaces (wood is hard enough to roll gold wire) until it was compressed into a solid cylinder, or alternatively by starting with a thicker strip that was simply twisted and rolled; the former method has been termed *strip twisting* and the latter *block twisting*, although it is unlikely that the ancient craftsman made any such distinction – the manual processes were virtually the same in practice. These methods of wire manufacture leave distinct helical seams on the completed wire that can easily be seen on many gold examples. Drawing, on the other hand, leaves straight grooves along the length of the wire. The distinction and the visible traces that are left by the different methods used to be one way of detecting modern fakes of ancient gold jewellery. Some skilled forgers have long since caught up with the state of knowledge, and now use twisted wire.

Wire with a beaded or milled appearance, imitating a row of tiny grains of metal, can be produced by several different methods. The simplest is to roll a single-edged blade across the wire at intervals. This tends to result in a somewhat irregular series of transverse grooves. A tool with a concave U-sectioned edge will produce more regular spherical beads in the wire. Both regular rounded beading and more haphazardly grooved wire are found in Romano-British gold and silver jewellery, and various types of beaded wire continued to be popular in much medieval jewellery. Two wires twisted together, and then used in juxtaposition with a pair twisted in the opposite direction, create a miniature plaited or herringbone effect that is also seen in Roman filigree work. Fragments of twisted wires were included amongst the scrap silver in the Snettisham jeweller's hoard.

Pierced work

From applied decoration we move to decoration that was cut into and through the metal. Fine piercing was a technique that was to all intents and purposes confined to gold jewellery, and it is typical of the later Roman period and of Byzantine work. Although often referred to as *opus interrasile*, there is no good evidence for this term having been used in antiquity for the lacy pierced patterns to which it is now applied, and it is probably wiser to avoid the Latin term.

The technique of manufacture is very clearly described on the basis of examination of ancient examples and modern experiment in a paper by Jack Ogden and Simon Schmidt, "Late Antique jewellery: pierced work and hollow beaded wire".[10] Some simple cut-out patterns were evidently made by using only a tiny chisel blade, but the finest work was first pierced using a circular punch; the round holes with the slight burring of their edges on the interior surface can clearly be seen on the pierced gold bracelets in the Hoxne treasure. The exact shaping of the tiny holes from the front of the work seems to have been executed using a tool with a finely tapered triangular point. This created bevelled notches that modelled the curves and angles required; in the case of the most delicate Hoxne bracelets, the technique produced a network of slender stems and tendrils and leafy forms. Each phase of producing an overall pattern in this extremely intricate technique must have required the greatest skill and care. The positioning of the first round holes had to be exact, and the subsequent notching of the holes to produce the design had to be precisely judged, especially when we consider that the detail of the patterns was often asymmetrical and curvilinear, not regular and geometric.

Pierced work of this nature is one of the outstanding achievements of Roman and Byzantine goldworking, and the discovery of the Hoxne treasure proves that ornaments made in this technique were known in Roman Britain, although doubtless their possession was confined to the wealthiest members of society.

Chains

Chains have already been described to some extent in Chapter 5. Whether in precious or base metal, the most typical Roman chain was not the obvious type that consists of one round or oval link passed directly through the next and soldered closed. Many Roman chains are based on the principle of preformed links that require no further soldering once they are assembled and connected to each other.

One very common form is a figure-eight loop-in-loop construction with a 90° twist in each link. The single loop-in-loop or foxtail, which could be of large, slender loops giving a very open effect, was made by compressing the first ring to an elliptical form and folding it in half; the second link was likewise compressed and folded and then passed through the ends of the first. The chain which results from this process is square in section. Double loop-in-loop construction is made by passing each elongated link simultaneously through the end-loops of the two previous

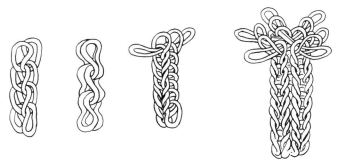

Figure 8.3 Diagrams illustrating single, double and triple loop-in-loop (foxtail) chain construction. (Drawings after Ogden 1982)

links. This creates a denser chain. By starting with two or three elongated links attached and laid across each other, more complex "cords" can be created. A threefold loop-in-loop is difficult to describe; it is started on three elongated links soldered together to form a regular six-looped star or rosette shape. Additional links are then passed through either single opposite pairs of end-loops or two at a time (single or double loop-in-loop), consistently following a clockwise or anti-clockwise direction. The resulting chain, which looks like a knitted cord, has six faces.[11]

Flat straps such as those that make up the body-chain from the Hoxne treasure are foxtail chains linked side to side. Much finer versions were used in Hellenistic and Etruscan jewellery, the links being made of extremely thin wire.

The same chain types were made in silver and in bronze, although the bronze versions tend to be fairly coarse. Bronze chains could also be made using cut metal strip opened up into a flat, ribbon-like link and then folded into the next as a single loop-in-loop. This method eliminated all soldering. S-shaped links with a central 90° twist were also common in base metal, and they were also generally bent into position without being soldered in place.

Plating and niello

Silver and bronze artefacts were sometimes gilded. In some cases this may have been in order to give the impression that the entire article was made of gold and was therefore of higher value than was actually the case, but gilding was also used purely decoratively as a means of producing a colour contrast. The silver-gilt trumpet-brooches from the Backworth treasure are completely gilded, while the brooch from Carmarthen has a carefully designed pattern of plain silver and gilt that follows and emphasizes the relief scrolls.

Several methods of gilding were known in the Roman period: the subject is succinctly summarized in Andrew Oddy's "The gilding of Roman silver plate", with numerous additional references.[12] Gold foil, which is thin gold sheet, may be attached to a silver surface by physically folding it over edges or into grooves; this method was still used on some Roman silver table-vessels with decorative relief motifs partially gilded to emphasize the details. Gold leaf, which is exceedingly thin, was usually applied using an adhesive, while diffusion bonding, involving the gentle heating of gold leaf and the substrate metal, was also employed. However, true fire-gilding (mercury gilding) was introduced in the early Roman period, and this was the method normally selected for silver-gilt and bronze-gilt jewellery such as the brooches mentioned above. In mercury-gilding an amalgam of gold and mercury is spread over the cleaned surface of the basic metal, and then gently heated so that the mercury evaporates, leaving a thin layer of gold bonded to the surface of the work.

Similar methods – the physical ones of applying and attaching silver sheet, or combining silver with mercury and heating – can be used for silver-plating,[13] but silvering seems to have been rather less common than gilding in the Roman period. Tin-plating, however, was quite frequently used on bronze objects, particularly military equipment of the earlier period. There is a fairly obvious practical reason for this: bronze would have needed regular polishing to keep it bright, whereas a tinned surface would have required far less care; silver or silver-plated bronze were presumably more costly than tin-plated metal.[14]

Bronzes with a relatively high tin content may appear silvery in colour without having been deliberately tinned. This can occur either through concentration of tin on the surface during the cooling of the alloy at the time of manufacture or as a result of burial, corrosion affecting the copper more severely. Actual tin-plating was a comparatively simple process, however, entailing only the placing of pieces of tin on the copper-alloy surface with a suitable flux and then heating to 232°C, quite a low temperature. Tinning was used on the interior surfaces of some bronze pans and on the military fittings referred to above. These include certain brooches, particularly the first-century Hod Hill type. The round and oval plate-brooches with gilded faces and a central glass setting were normally tinned on the back, also probably to make cleaning unnecessary on an item that was intended to look like gold. Tinning is found likewise on some other plate-brooches, including those that have enamelled surfaces.

Before considering the use of enamel in jewellery, another device to produce colour contrasts should be noted, namely the use of black metal sulphides set into incised patterns or inscriptions on a metal surface. This is niello inlay. The most beautiful and dramatic use of niello is found on some silver table utensils of the Roman period in which the lines are as intense and precise on the white metal as a pattern drawn in black ink on white paper.

The technical aspects of the material have been summarized by Susan La Niece.[15] Niello is found on Roman gold, silver and bronze jewellery as well as on silver plate (table utensils). Sulphides combining silver and copper have been analysed on some late Antique objects, but earlier Roman examples tend to be based on silver or copper only, and moreover, copper sulphides are generally used on bronzes and silver sulphides on silver and gold objects: there is no technical advantage in this, and it probably merely reflects the scrap metal most easily available to the craftsman. In fact, there were considerable practical problems with the niello compositions used in the Roman period. Heating either silver or copper sulphide to melting point, which would have made the niello easier to apply, not only causes it to revert to its metallic form and lose the characteristic black colour, but in the case of copper would have taken it above the melting point of the backing bronze. The material must therefore have been applied as a compacted powder, and it would not have formed a perfect bond with the metal, so there was some danger of it eventually working loose. Niello inlay has indeed been lost from some objects that it originally embellished, but it has also survived on many others, including brooches of various kinds: two of the fine late crossbow brooches mentioned in Chapter 7, the gold example from the Moray Firth and the silver one from Bath.

The colour contrast of black niello and the background metal, whether gold, bronze, or most effective of all, silver, produces a decorative effect that appeals to modern taste; even when the applied pattern is an intricate one, there is an impression of sophistication and restraint. The polychrome effect of enamelled metal objects, on the other hand, seems to us to be cheerfully gaudy, but our attitude to bright colours is jaded by familiarity, and the perceptions of people in antiquity may have been different from our own.

Enamelling

Whatever the aesthetic perception of enamelled jewellery may have been, the techniques required for making it were fairly demanding. The subject is discussed in several sources, including Bateson's *Enamel-working in Iron Age, Roman and sub-Roman Britain*, Ogden's *Jewellery of the ancient world*, and in chapter 3 of Strong & Brown's *Roman crafts*.[16] The compositions of Roman enamels have recently been analysed and studied by Julian Henderson.[17]

Enamel is a vitreous substance, a form of glass, and it is fused or bonded to a metal base by the action of heat. Reference works describe several different types of enamelling on metal,[18] but the definitions are based on modern practice and cannot always be applied precisely to the methods used in antiquity. The principal distinction is drawn between *champlevé* enamel and *cloisonné*. In the former, the glassy material is used to fill cells that have been cast or cut out of a solid metal base. After melting and cooling, the enamel is polished flush with the metal. In cloisonné enamelling, cells are built up for the coloured inlay by soldering thin walls of metal to a flat surface, so that the enamelled areas are raised above the original level of the metal. Although it is commonly stated that the cloisonné technique is not found in Roman provincial work, filigree enamelling is undoubtedly a form of cloisonné and is found, albeit rarely, in Roman Britain: it was a very ancient technique, employed not only in Hellenistic jewellery but also much earlier in the Classical lands. The bracelet from Rhayader with filigree wire has a scroll pattern of beaded wire enclosing small areas of blue and green enamel, and some of the Hercules-club earrings also have enamel set in the drop-shaped areas marked out with wire. In general, these rare examples of enamel on gold are blue and green, although the gold earring from the Walbrook is set with a brownish enamel – if that is indeed its original colour. It is perhaps worth pointing out that many enamels decay easily and/or fall away from the metal if the bond is incomplete, so that there might be unrecognized examples of enamelling on gold jewellery from Roman Britain. As has already been noted in Chapter 6, enamelling on silver is extremely rare in provincial Roman work; the proto-handpin from Oldcroft is the only example that comes to mind. With its comparatively low melting point, silver would certainly have been less easy to enamel than bronze or gold, but if the appearance of enamelled silver had been widely admired and sought after, it would not have been too much of a problem to make it.

The use of gold in itself indicated the filigree enamel method, since the metal was usually thin: in the case of a robust bronze brooch, it was more practical to cast the form with hollows already roughly prepared for enamel. We cannot say for certain where the enamelled gold items were made, but although the Rhayader bracelet has many echoes of Hellenistic tradition in its design, we should certainly not exclude the possibility of manufacture in Britain.

Enamelling on bronze was a continuation and development of an established Iron Age Celtic tradition. The earlier pre-Roman enamelled objects in Britain were most typically horse-trappings and weaponry rather than jewellery, and opaque red was at first the only colour used. By the Roman period, the objects that were decorated with enamel included many types of bronze brooch and some small vessels, and a wide range of colours was available – several shades of red, blue and green, plus yellow, orange, black and white. Although Roman vessel glass came in a number of hues, the material used for enamelling metal had additional compounds added to intensify the colours, lower the melting-point and render the enamel more opaque. Many medieval and modern enamels are intended to be translucent so that the underlying metal, which may be decoratively textured, is visible through the glassy colour, but Roman enamels were in general designed to be intense and solid blocks of colour.

The enamel may have been applied in the form of a frit, that is, the partially fused raw materials of glass (for example silica, soda, lead oxide and a colourant), or alternatively as a paste made with ground glass. This was pressed into the hollows prepared on the bronze item. With an appropriate chemical composition, heating to around 650°–750°C would have been sufficient to soften the enamel to a point where it would flood the area intended for it and attach itself to the underlying metal. Even if a true bond with the metal was not achieved, the keying of the floor of the cell and the slight undercutting of its sides would help to ensure that the cooled enamel stayed in place. A furnace may have been used, but a charcoal fire and possibly the use of a blowpipe would probably have been adequate to produce the temperatures for the relatively short times needed. Bateson drew a distinction between simple enamelling, in which each hollowed cell contains a single colour, complex enamelling, where more than one enamel occupies a single cell without dividing walls of metal, and millefiori, which is a special case, but in effect a variant of the "complex" category.[19]

The simple enamels require little comment. On some brooches, a single colour only is found, but it is far more usual to find two or three. Blue and red were the most common colours. The complex enamels fall into several categories, and the juxtaposition of different enamel colours without any dividing wall or septum of metal suggests that the material may have been applied in a fairly solid form. If loose powders had been used, it would not have been possible to keep clear divisions between the colours as they softened and flowed. One of the complex styles may be seen on the shoe-sole brooches and on some of the hare- and hound-brooches: the whole surface is a large area of one colour which has distinct contrasting circular spots set in it without any metal walls. The spots on these small brooches are usually around 2 mm in diameter. The background could have been laid as a paste and the spots set in position as small solid sections from a rod of the appropriate colour, the whole being fired together. This method was used successfully in experiments carried out by Bateson.[20] Alternatively, the background enamel alone could have been heated until it was plastic enough to press the circular sections into it, followed by a final heating, cooling and polishing.[21] Different craftsmen may quite possibly have employed different methods.

Many circular plate-brooches were made with concentric rings of enamel. Examples are found with one solid colour to each ring, but alternating small squares of contrasting colour within the circular areas are even more common, and it seems more likely that they would have been made by setting small squares of solid glass rather than contiguous square areas of paste or powder. The placing of tiny solid squares was certainly the only possible method in the case of Bateson's third category, millefiori enamelling.

Millefiori enamel inlay was used on many plate-brooches and studs, and also on some very decorative small bronze vessels, probably inkwells; the effect, combined with plain enamels, is both technically impressive and visually attractive. The techniques for making millefiori or mosaic rods and sections were current in the manufacture of vessel-glass in the Roman

Empire. In effect, the decoration of objects with millefiori enamel involved metalworking, glassmaking and gem-cutting skills; the thin slices of patterned glass were made by cutting sections from a millefiori glass rod or cane and then treating them as small pieces of enamel to be attached to a metal substrate. The glassmaking side of the process will be described below; the enamelling aspect was essentially similar to that of using any solid glass fragment and attaching it as firmly as possible to a metal base, or bedding it in an enamel background. Experiments carried out by Bateson demonstrate that there was no real difficulty in using tiny sections of millefiori direct on metal as a simple enamel; the heat required to fuse them to the bronze was not great enough to cause serious distortion of the intricate coloured pattern.[22] There are also evidently some instances of millefiori sections being set in a base of red enamel rather than being bonded directly to the substrate, but this technique was less common than the simpler one of direct application.

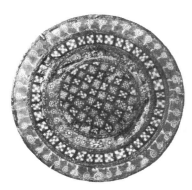

Figure 8.4 A millefiori enamelled bronze stud found in a bronzesmith's hoard at Chepstow, Gwent. Diameter 5.1 cm. (Photo: British Museum)

Bateson distinguished several basic patterns in the millefiori elements used in jewellery. The most common are various chequerboard designs of varying complexity, often within a solid border of a contrasting colour, but rosettes or flowerets were also frequently used and spirals and a fern or "Christmas tree" design also occur. The individual sections of millefiori used on brooches and similar objects were around 2–3 mm square and between 0.5 and 1 mm thick. In some designs, many of these tiny plaques would be used to produce a solid area of millefiori or a complete ring of variegated colour.

Exactly the same millefiori patterns are found on plate-brooches and studs from Britain and many other provinces, and they are repeated on the very rare bronze vessels that are decorated in the same technique, such as the exquisite hexagonal *pyxis*, probably an inkpot, from a second-century grave at Elsenham, Essex.[23] This suggests that the millefiori rods and sections were a highly specialized product manufactured in a limited number of workshops and bought in by the enamellers. The method of making the millefiori inlays was part of the craft of glassmaking, which also had other contributions to make to jewellery.

Glass

A detailed treatment of glassmaking technology in the Roman period lies outside the scope of this book; the principal use of the material was in the manufacture of vessels, and the invention of glass-blowing in the first century BC had revolutionized the process, leading to a level of mass-production that made glass far more widely available than formerly. But other traditional ways of working glass were not abandoned, and some of them are directly relevant to the uses of glass in jewellery. The reader wishing to study the subject of Roman glassmaking in greater detail will find an ideal introduction by Jennifer Price in Strong & Brown's *Roman crafts*. Glass as a component of jewellery is briefly summarized in Jack Ogden's *Jewellery of the ancient world*.[24]

Glass can be worked in a molten, plastic or solid state according to its temperature. Metals can be cast when molten, and cut, shaped and decorated in other ways when cold; semi-precious stones can be ground and drilled and engraved. The plasticity of hot glass enables it to be manipulated in numerous additional ways, by drawing, pinching, impressing, marvering (rolling on a smooth hard surface) as well as blowing. The manufacture of millefiori canes depends on the ability of glass to be stretched or drawn out into long threads when hot. A patterned section like those that were applied to enamelled plate-brooches was cut when cold, using a metal wheel, from a cane made up of the desired combination of coloured rods heated and drawn out to the required size. Sections of millefiori or mosaic glass were also used in the manufacture of highly decorated polychrome glass bowls. The process is very clearly illustrated by W. Gudenrath in the British Museum publication *5000 years of glass*.[25]

Multicoloured canes of glass can also be twisted when hot to make spiral threads, and the glass finger-rings described in Chapter 3 were made from such canes – clear glass with spiral threads of opaque yellow, bent into a ring and given a bezel of dark blue or green opaque glass. Pressed into a mould, such bezels could form a cameo image.

Glass bangles could have been made in precisely the same fashion, from a plain or polychrome glass rod, but in fact the distinctive Romano-British bangles described in Chapter 5 were made in a completely different way, described succinctly by Jennifer Price: "The bangles were made in one seamless piece, being produced by gathering a lump of molten glass on a pointed metal rod, pushing a second rod into the centre alongside the first rod, and then spinning and manipulating the two rods in order to widen the aperture symmetrically."[26] The trails and cords of contrasting colours were applied and marvered flush with the surface. This method of manufacture could also be used for certain glass beads, although others were formed by moulding, by wrapping threads of glass around a wire or possibly even by drilling the central hole in the same way as with hardstone beads; there were, and still are, many different methods of making glass beads.

Glass "gems" were produced in a variety of ways, either by exploiting the distinctive characteristics of glass or by treating the cold glass in exactly the same fashion as the hardstone that it resembles visually. The simple glass settings with crude intaglio stick-figures found in some Romano-British bronze rings were made by moulding the glass rather than cutting or engraving it, but there were several methods that could have been used. Scrap glass of any kind supplied the raw material and must have been widely and cheaply available in the province; many of these settings are of the natural pale green colour that was used for so many glass vessels. Although various translucent light green quartzes were used as settings (for example plasma, prase and chrysoprase), they were not particularly common compared with jasper, carnelian and other darker or more opaque stones, especially after the first century; the standard green glass was probably not intended to simulate these stones but was rather accepted in its own right. The moulded glass gems could have been cast in small moulds with the design in relief, but a simpler method would have been to make them as drops of molten glass deposited on a smooth surface (just as glass gaming-pieces were made) and impressing the design on them with a suitable punch when the material was at a plastic stage. Some shaping and grinding would probably have been needed to fit them into the bronze setting, where they would have been bedded in adhesive. It would also have been possible to set a plain glass "drop" in the ring and then heat it in situ until the punch left an incuse impression on it.

The lapidary techniques of cutting and drilling with abrasives and metal wheels and points were used for high-quality glass gems, and these were sometimes made with the deliberate intention of imitating specific gemstones, in particular the various distinctive forms of banded agate. Glass imitations of nicolo, cut so that the contrasting layers lie horizontally, would have been extremely difficult to distinguish from stone when new. To create the distinctive effect of a motif cut through the light layer into the dark one, the glass had to be engraved, not moulded. Careful examination, and in some cases actual analysis, is needed to identify some of these engraved settings as glass rather than stone.

Engraved gemstones

The various types of quartz that were most commonly used as engraved settings in Roman jewellery were hard enough to survive well in wear, but could still quite easily be cut and engraved using metal tools with an abrasive such as emery (aluminium oxide). Simple bow-drills had been in use since remote antiquity, but the Roman gem-cutter would have used a horizontally mounted lathe-like drill and a series of tiny metal wheels or points. Careful examination under magnification reveals microscopic details that establish what type of tool was used: a point rotated against the surface of the stone held against it leaves concentric microtraces, while a wheel leaves a hollow with parallel linear microtraces. The process is very clearly explained by Marianne Maaskant-Kleibrink in her analysis of the engraved gems from the Snettisham Roman jeweller's hoard.[27] Not only can the method of manufacture be ascertained, but an expert observer can even distinguish between the styles of different crafts-men within the products of a single workshop, as in the case of the Snettisham gems. Very fine gem-engraving of the first century BC made use of rounded points to create smoothly rounded forms in intaglio, but provincial work of the second century AD, like the small Snettisham carnelians, consisted only of linear, sketchy, wheel-cut forms, collections of straight lines of varying width and depth forming cartoon-like images, most of them no more than 4 or 5 mm high. The extreme degree of stylization means that a good deal of knowledge is often needed even to identify the tiny motifs precisely.

However stylized the images, the placing of the minute straight grooves required extraordinary manual precision, and many people find it hard to believe that the work was done without the use of magnifying aids. The property of magnification in hardstones or glass of suitable shapes was obviously familiar to the Romans, but there is no evidence at all that lenses were used in processes such as gem-engraving or, come to that, very intricate goldworking. While good eyesight was certainly required for many aspects of jewellery-making, a delicate and steady touch was even more essential: minute work cannot be achieved even using a powerful binocular microscope if the craftsman's hands are not steady. Youthful craftsmen would have had both the visual and manual skills needed, but if the reader remains unconvinced, it must be pointed out that gem-engraving had in any case to be done by touch alone. At the moment when the gem was held against the tiny spinning wheel, its surface would be wholly obscured by the slurry of emery and oil that enabled the metal to cut into the stone.[28]

Other materials

Most of the other non-metallic materials used in Romano-British jewellery were worked mainly by carving. Jet, bone and wood could have been shaped and polished with very simple tools and methods. Painting and dyeing were probably also used for some ornaments made of these substances, but we have no direct evidence because the pigments do not survive burial in normal conditions.

Afterword

The systematic observation and description of antiquities builds up a body of knowledge that helps to further our understanding of how and where the objects were made and how and by whom they were used. We still have a long way to go in this direction, and new approaches and methods are still evolving. It is in effect impossible for any single individual to combine the skills and experience of the scientist, the art historian, the archaeologist and the practical craftsman which are all directly pertinent to the study of ancient jewellery and other artefacts; the frontiers of knowledge can best be extended by the combined efforts and the productive co-operation of many researchers with different areas of expertise.

In Chapter 1 I attempted to set out some of the difficulties of understanding and interpretation that beset us even when dealing with something as apparently accessible and attractive as Roman jewellery. In the survey of types that forms the body of this book, I hope I have been able to convey an impression of the special qualities peculiar to jewellery found in the Roman province of Britain in the first to fourth centuries AD. In so far as it displays Classical characteristics, Romano-British jewellery testifies to the place of Roman Britain as a vital element in a great ancient empire, while at the same time the native, Celtic traits illustrate the cultural continuity within the history of a small European island. On another level, Romano-British jewellery is simultaneously part of the worldwide history of personal ornament and also of the complex material culture of Britannia. The study of personal ornament is not a frivolous or trivial pastime, but is an area of scholarly research that is essential to the overall understanding of any ancient society.

If there is a lesson to be learnt from this, it is that jewellery and all ancient artefacts need to be perceived in context rather than in isolation. Although archaeology depends on collecting, it is a great deal more than the amassing of a series of objects. The museum collections that grew up before scientific methods of excavation were devised, and the stray finds made by lucky accident or deliberate search today still have much to tell us. Future scientific developments may yet wring more information from them, but they can never be as informative as material that is found and recorded with due attention to its context and associations. The methodical approach of modern archaeology, even when applied to apparently commonplace finds, can often cast light on the unprovenanced *objets d'art* of older collections. In this respect, work in Roman provinces such as Britain has a particularly important part to play. Detailed recording is a demanding and time-consuming task, requiring skill and experience, but it is only by going beyond the simple response of enthusiasm for new and appealing finds to the discipline of serious research that we will gain the reward of enhanced understanding.

In trying to learn about the remote past we do the best we can with unavoidably incomplete data. Within the last few decades great advances have been made in the scientific study and analysis of antiquities, and there are doubtless new discoveries yet to be made; methods of excavation and recording will also be refined as time goes on. It will be a sad thing indeed if the beneficial results of these increasingly precise tools of research are hopelessly undermined by the uncontrolled and chaotic removal from the ground of the raw data, the ancient artefacts themselves. Yet this is what will happen if the current passion for extracting metal antiquities willy-nilly from the soil, and trading and dealing in them as individual curios, continues unchecked. Every ancient artefact that is bought and sold as an isolated trinket, with no record of or regard for its provenance, let alone its archaeological context, is one piece lost from the huge jigsaw of knowledge that has all too many pieces missing already.

If the overall picture of jewellery in Roman Britain which I have tried to convey in the foregoing chapters has brought any pleasure and enlightenment to the reader, then he or she should be aware that amateur students of the past as well as professionals can further that growth of knowledge by exercising a mature and responsible attitude towards the material culture of earlier times. Most people who feel a special kind of pleasure in unearthing and owning a tiny fragment of antiquity, such as a coin or a small bronze brooch, also have the intelligence and sensitivity to realize on reflection that unless it is tempered by restraint, this gratification of their own interest can all too easily reduce the information available to those in the future who will feel the same urge to be in contact with the past. We need to do our best to ensure that future generations are allowed not only to enjoy the timeless and inspiring beauty of ancient jewellery but also to learn as much as it can tell us about the way of life of our ancestors who made and wore it.

I can do no better in conclusion than to quote the final sentence of Edward Hawkins in his paper on the Backworth treasure published as long ago as 1851:

> Isolated objects are of little value; a collector may accumulate a number of amusing and elegant specimens, but it is only by combination, concentration, and comparison, that an entertaining collection can be converted into an instructive museum, and Archaeology erected into a science.[1]

Four treasures from Roman Britain

Two hoards of the second century AD and two of the late fourth to early fifth century have been mentioned repeatedly in the discussions of rings, bracelets and other ornaments in previous chapters. They are the finds from Backworth and Snettisham, both dating to the middle Empire period, and Thetford and Hoxne, belonging to the very end of Roman rule in Britain. The Hoxne treasure came to light while this book was being planned, and had not yet been fully studied and assessed at the time of writing. All four assemblages contain items other than jewellery, either coins or silver plate (tableware) or both, and a succinct description of each hoard will help to place the jewellery that it contains into a fuller context and explain its importance.

The Backworth (Tyne and Wear) treasure

Neither the date nor the place of discovery of the so-called Backworth treasure is known: the objects apparently came into the possession of a silversmith in Newcastle-upon-Tyne in 1811. They were understood to be from somewhere in Northumberland or Durham, and were presumably recent finds at that time. A "small silver dish" and all but one of the approximately 280 silver coins said to have been found with the jewellery and plate had been sold and dispersed long before the British Museum was able to acquire the greater part of the group in 1850.[1] The single surviving coin is a *denarius* of Antoninus Pius issued in AD 139. Although we cannot be certain that this was the latest coin in the hoard, a date for the burial of the cache around the middle of the second century AD is consistent with the typology of the jewellery and the silver vessels.

The Backworth treasure as preserved consists of a deep silver skillet with a decorated handle, a much-mended plain silver mirror that was very possibly used to cover the pan and its contents, three silver spoons, two large silver-gilt brooches, six finger-rings (five gold and one silver), a gold bracelet and two gold necklaces.

The skillet or saucepan has a very elaborately ornamented handle with floral motifs and scrolls in relief picked out in gilding. It also bears a bold inscription with letters inlaid in gold reading MATR.FAB DVBIT.[2] This legend indicates that the vessel was a votive gift to the mother-goddesses from one Fabius Dubitatus. The pan was very harshly cleaned at some time before 1850, probably to remove corrosion on the outer surface, and if there was any additional inscription, for example a note of the weight, it would have been lost. The three silver spoons are typically first- to second-century types, one a round-bowled spoon, the other two with pear-shaped bowls and slightly offset handles; one has been extensively restored.

The two silver-gilt trumpet-brooches are described in Chapter 7, and the necklaces are fine examples of chains with wheel clasps (one with a central glass stud) and small crescent pendants. The bracelet is a flexible chain with a wheel clasp and hollow gold beads. One of the gold rings is a splendid example of a type B iv serpent-ring, complete with gold balls surrounded with beaded wire; the silver ring is of similar type, but damaged, and may never have had the central spheres. Two rings are of Henig type IV with nicolo settings engraved with ears of corn on one and a trussed fowl on the other, and there is a handsome Henig type II with a nicolo depicting an actor portraying a genius of death, with a symbolically downturned torch. The sixth ring has no gem, but the hollowed bezel (perhaps originally intended for a setting?) bears an engraved inscription reading MATR/VM.CO/COAE; like the dedication on the skillet, this records a gift to the mothers.[3]

Figure A.1 The Backworth treasure. The disc on the left is a silver mirror. Only one of the original hoard of coins was kept with the group. Both silver spoons and jewellery are typical of first- and second-century forms. (Photo: British Museum)

All the signs are that the Backworth treasure represents material presented by Roman worshippers at a shrine of the mother-goddesses somewhere near the area around the eastern end of Hadrian's Wall in the second century AD. It is therefore quite different in nature from the Snettisham hoard, but because it is of similar date, the designs of the rings and necklaces are very much the same. The brooches must be of Romano-British manufacture, and there is every reason to believe that the gold snake-ring, so close in style to the silver examples from Snettisham and elsewhere, is also a British product. It is impossible to be certain about the necklaces; certainly silver examples were made in Britain, but the type was universal in the Empire.

It would be good to know more about the background of this important assemblage, but it is a comparatively early find, and we are probably fortunate that it has survived as a group at all.

The Snettisham (Norfolk) Roman jeweller's hoard

Found in August 1985, this treasure consists of a small grey pottery vase only 17.5 cm high that contained a surprisingly large number of silver and base-metal coins, unmounted engraved gems, small items of silver jewellery and silver and gold scrap, over 350 objects in all. The rim of the pot was noticed during building work by Mr George Onslow, who, after removing it and investigating its contents, reported the discovery and handed the find over to the local museum in Kings Lynn. The archaeologists of the local archaeology unit were able to establish that there were no other buried hoards in the vicinity and no immediate traces of Roman occupation. There is every reason to believe that the hoard, now in the British Museum, is complete. It is fundamentally different from any of the other jewellery treasures in Roman Britain because it is evidence of a jeweller's workshop.[4]

The inventory comprises 89 finger-rings, of which 46 are snake-rings of types B ii and B iv, 5 snake-bracelets (B ii), 11 pendants and other necklace elements including wheels and crescents, plus fragments of chain and clasps, 5 silver bars, and scrap silver sheet, bar and wire. The coins number 110 in all, 83 of them being silver *denarii* and the other 27 being base-metal issues, mainly *sestertii*. To the 110 engraved carnelians that were found loose in the group should be added 17 that are set in silver rings of Henig type II. No other type of gemstone was present, but a burnishing tool also found in the hoard is made of a translucent quartz. The hoard also included a small enamelled bronze seal-box in very corroded condition.

Figure A.2 The
Snettisham Roman
jeweller's hoard. The
rings, chains, pendants
and bracelets are grouped
according to type. In the
foreground is the
collection of engraved
carnelian settings, and at
the left, towards the back,
the ingots and groups of
scrap silver. The small
pot in the centre, 17.5 cm
high, contained all the
objects. (Photo: British
Museum)

The silver ingots are bars of square cross-section, and they were obviously prepared by the jeweller for use in manufacturing his products. There is good reason to believe that the silver coins may themselves have been part of his stock of raw material; while the latest coin was an *as* of Faustina I, posthumously issued in AD 155, the bulk of the silver coins (74 out of the total of 83) were late first-century *denarii* minted under the Emperor Domitian (reigned AD 81–96). This is not a normal pattern in such hoards, and the fact that *denarii* of the late first century were known to be of high purity, usually around 93 per cent fine, while the mid-second-century silver coins are about 85–7 per cent silver, makes it seem very likely that the good-quality coins were being hoarded for melting down. The cache also contains six small pieces of gold scrap, one of them a broken finger-ring of very simple, plain form; the gold scrap all has a substantial proportion of silver in it, resembling Late Iron Age gold more than that of the Roman period. It is a matter of some interest and speculation as to whether some connection can be demonstrated between this Roman-period evidence of the working of precious metal and the major hoards of much earlier Iron Age gold and silver from Snettisham.

All the gems are quite small, averaging about 1 cm in length, and the devices on them are cut in a simple, linear style evidently within one workshop but by three separate hands.[5] The most frequent images are of Bonus Eventus and Ceres, but Fortuna, Minerva, Mars, Mercury and other deities also occur, along with birds and other animals. Few of the gems show signs of wear.

The importance of this treasure lies not in the quality or value of the jewellery, which is very modest, but in the fact that it constituted a closely dated second-century workshop group. It is not possible to say whether the gem-engraver worked with the silversmith or whether the latter bought in his ring-settings, but there can be no doubt that the whole undertaking was Romano-British and quite local to the area where it was found. Stylistically, the jewellery is firmly in the Classical tradition, with snake jewellery, wheels and crescents, and engraved stones.

The Thetford (Norfolk) treasure

The Thetford treasure came to light under very unfortunate circumstances in November 1979. The finder, Mr Arthur Brooks, was using a metal-detector without the landowners' permission on a building site at Gallows Hill, outside Thetford; he came upon the treasure in failing light late on a November afternoon, and all the subsequent events suggest that he was more than a little bewildered and intimidated by his remarkable discovery and took some very bad advice. The discovery was not reported to the authorities but was concealed, and attempts were made to dispose of items by private sale; it is highly probable that some items were overlooked during the hasty digging-up of the treasure, and it is possible that others may have gone astray subsequently, so the full inventory of the treasure must always remain unknown. Rumours of the find had spread by the spring of 1980, but it was not until May of that year that it was declared to the authorities, and in the intervening months the findspot had been built over and was not available for archaeological investigation. The finder, who was a sick man at the time of the discovery – a fact that may go some way towards explaining his poor judgement – was terminally ill in hospital by the time the hoard came for study to the British Museum at the end of May 1980, and died at the beginning of July without being able to give detailed information about the circumstances of the find. This story is sad in both human and academic terms, and it means that there are many details that we can never know about one of the most astonishing treasures of the late Roman period.

The British Museum was able to acquire the hoard, and the full catalogue was published 1983.[6] On stylistic grounds, on the basis of the forms of the spoons and on some of the jewellery, the suggested date for the burial of this material is in the final decade of the fourth century AD; parallels from the Hoxne treasure now provide support for this judgement.

The collection consists of 1 gold belt-buckle, 22 gold finger-rings, 4 gold bracelets, 2 Hercules-club pendants or earrings, 2 gem-set pendants, 1 large unmounted engraved gem, 5 gold necklaces and 2 separate pairs of gold necklace-clasps, 1 gold tubular amulet-pendant, 4 separate beads (3 of green glass, 1 of emerald), 3 silver strainers, 33 silver spoons of two types and 1 cylindrical lidded box made of turned shale; 81 objects in all. No coins were reported, although it is possible that some were found. It seems likely that the objects were placed in some kind of container, quite

Figure A.3 The Thetford treasure as displayed in the British Museum. The silver spoons, of types similar to those in the Hoxne hoard, are in the right- and left-hand panels, with the gold jewellery in the centre. (Photo: British Museum)

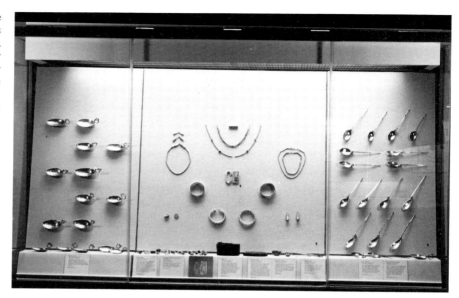

possibly a wooden box, traces of which would simply not have been observed by an amateur digging the material out hastily, especially in poor light.

All the silver spoons belong to characteristically late Roman forms. Sixteen of them are about the size of modern tablespoons with short coiled handles terminating in the head of a water-bird, a duck or swan. The other 17 have smaller oval or pear-shaped bowls, rather larger than a modern teaspoon, and have long slender handles ending in a point. The point where the handle joins the bowl is offset, with a decorative open-work feature. Like many late Roman spoons, most of these have niello-inlaid inscriptions either in the bowl or on the handle, but instead of the Christian signs and mottoes that are common at the period, these inscriptions are pagan, referring to the relatively obscure and minor god Faunus, his name combined with Celtic by-names which testify to local worship in Britain.

The jewellery is opulent and colourful, using amethysts, garnets, emeralds, various quartzes and glass settings in the rings and one of the bracelets. Some of the rings (discussed in Ch. 3) have extraordinarily elaborate zoomorphic modelling of the shoulders or intricate incised designs on the hoop. The engraved gems were re-used from earlier jewellery, and the unmounted carnelian with Venus and Cupid (described in Ch. 4) had been cut down for resetting, while an onyx cameo of a lion had already been set more than once.

The necklaces include one with emerald and glass beads, and one matching pair of bracelets is of a distinctive type otherwise paralleled only in the third-century Lyons hoard and now in the late-fourth-century group from Hoxne. Much of the Thetford jewellery exhibits little or no sign of use. It is impossible to reach a full interpretation of this treasure; it is difficult enough in the case of hoards that are completely preserved and properly recorded, but the Thetford story is so incomplete that many different hypotheses could be made to fit it. What we can say for certain is that the silver plate records a Celtic cult of a minor pagan deity in Britain at a time when the Empire was firmly Christian, and that the jewellery demonstrates the presence, and possibly even the manufacture, of extremely showy and valuable personal ornament in late-fourth-century Britain, a point that has now been emphasized by the contents of the Hoxne treasure. Whether the gold and silver belonged to private individuals or had some link with an actual cult centre is very difficult to decide.

The Hoxne (Suffolk) treasure

The most recent major Romano-British find of jewellery, plate and coins, the Hoxne hoard was located on 16 November 1992 by Mr Eric Lawes, who behaved with admirable good sense and restraint and notified the authorities promptly. As a result, the bulk of the cache was professionally excavated in a single day, 17 November, by members of the Suffolk Archaeological Unit under the direction of Judith Plouviez. Many of the context groups were raised in blocks that were fully excavated in the laboratory once the material had come to the British Museum for study. The entire hoard was sorted, cleaned and stabilized within a month of its discovery, and the immediate involvement of professionals has resulted in the preservation of objects such as tiny fragments of decorative bone and wood box-inlay.[7]

At the time of writing, work on the treasure is still at a relatively early stage, so this summary can only be a provisional one. The group consists of some 200 gold and silver objects and over 15,000 coins, 569 of which are gold *solidi*. The gold jewellery comprises 6 chain necklaces, the body-chain described in Chapter 5, 3 finger-rings and 19 bracelets. Of the latter, the most important is the openwork bracelet bearing the name of "Lady Juliana", but several of the other bracelets are of outstandingly fine workmanship; four bracelets, a matching set, are similar in style to the matching pair in the Thetford treasure, made of gold sheet corrugated and crimped to resemble basket-work.

The silver objects are mainly spoons and ladles, but there are also five small plain bowls, two small vases with decoration in relief and four hollow statuettes that are also containers to be used at table; one of these is in the form of a bust of a late Roman empress. One very large silver vessel is represented only by a single handle, a splendid silver statuette of a tigress with black stripes inlaid in niello. Originally the tigress would have been paired with another zoomorphic handle (a male tiger?) on a decorated amphora-shaped silver vase with a long slender neck. The 20 round-bowled ladles divide into two sets of 10, one of them gilded, while the 75 spoons belong to the two types represented in the contemporary Thetford assemblage as well as several other late Roman silver treasures. Christian symbols, Chi-Rho monograms and monogram crosses, and personal names are found on many of the spoons, while others have very decorative gilded representations of dolphins and mythical sea-panthers. There are also several toilet implements, for example partly gilded tooth-picks incorporating zoomorphic elements (dolphins, elegant ibises and a charming tiny spotted leopard) in their design.

The coins form by far the largest hoard of its date yet found, and they enable us to date the deposition of the Hoxne treasure to the final phase of Roman Britain; in fact, after AD 407. The largest major Roman treasure of this very late period from Great Britain is the hoard from Traprain Law in south-east Scotland, excavated in 1919.[8] Although contemporary, the Traprain treasure is from outside the frontiers of the Roman Empire and in many respects is not comparable with Hoxne. It is a so-called *Hacksilber* hoard, the silver plate having been chopped up into bullion, and contains no jewellery relevant to our present study.

All the objects comprising the Hoxne hoard were buried within a wooden box or chest, and there were other smaller containers within this. Traces of cloth and of other organic packing material (grass or hay) were found, but all the wood itself has perished.

The Hoxne treasure undoubtedly belonged to an extremely affluent family, quite possibly one that owned estates in several provinces. Although no Roman occupation is recorded in the area where the treasure came to light, there is a somewhat nebulous record of an eighteenth-century find of a large treasure of late Roman coins from Eye, which is close to Hoxne. Future work will undoubtedly produce more information on this very significant find; for the moment, it enables us to confirm the date assigned on stylistic grounds to the Thetford treasure. A treasure such as this also illustrates very vividly the dangers of building too many theories on the absence of certain types from Britain, or indeed the number or distribution of a type within the province: the Hoxne hoard has more than doubled the number of late Roman silver spoons known from Britain, while it has raised the number of top-quality pierced-gold bracelets from none to four.

Summary

It may seem invidious to pick out these four groups from the many associated finds of jewellery that have been discovered in Britain, but they are all assemblages that have specific information to give, and the different circumstances of their discovery are also instructive. More such finds will undoubtedly be unearthed in the future: we can only hope that those who come upon them will do everything in their power to ensure that all the relevant information is preserved and safeguarded.

Notes

Introduction

1. R. A. Higgins, *Greek and Roman jewellery* (London, 1980), p. 192.
2. This subject is studied with wit and erudition by Alison Lurie in her book on the language of clothes (A. Lurie, *The language of clothes* (New York, 1981)).

Chapter 1

1. The name of these anklets has been used as the title of a fascinating book dealing with the experience of women in modern Egypt (N. Atiya, *Khul-Khaal: five Egyptian women tell their stories* (Cairo, 1984)). Nayra Atiya writes in her preface, "The khul-khaal of the book's title are heavy silver or gold anklets, not unlike shackles, worn by married women. These are often removed when they are widows. They are an image appropriate to the content of this book because of their symbolic as well as material meanings" (p. xxviii).
2. The history and definitions of the words are clarified in S. Piggott, "Bronze, Britons and Romans: an early antiquarian problem", in *Between and beyond the walls: essays on the prehistory and history of North Britain in honour of George Jobey*, R. Miket & C. Burgess (eds) (Edinburgh, 1984), pp. 117–18.
3. Tacitus, *Agricola* 12.5.
4. For an explanation of the nature of jet and other black materials and their use in Roman Britain, see L. Allason-Jones & D. M. Jones, "Jet and other materials in Roman artefact studies", *Archaeologia Aeliana* (5th ser.) **22**, 1994, pp. 265–72.

Chapter 2

1. For example, V. Megaw, *Art of the European Iron Age* (Bath, 1970), R. Megaw & V. Megaw, *Celtic art* (London, 1989) and S. Moscati (ed.), *The Celts* (Venice, 1991).
2. Megaw & Megaw, *Celtic art*, p. 20.
3. P. Connolly, *Hannibal and the enemies of Rome* (London, 1978), pp. 64–5.

4. Illustrated in numerous books and publications, e.g. Megaw & Megaw, *Celtic art*, fig. 179.

5. Cassius Dio, *Roman History* 62.2.

6. See the discussion in V. Maxfield, *The military decorations of the Roman army* (London, 1981), pp. 86–8.

7. Waldalgesheim: Megaw, *Art of the European Iron Age*, nos. 124–7.

8. V. Rigby, personal communication.

9. G. Jones & T. Jones (trans.), *The Mabinogion* (London, 1949), p. 110.

10. I. Stead, "The Snettisham Treasure: excavations in 1990", *Antiquity* **65**, 1991, pp. 447–64.

11. Higgins, *Greek and Roman jewellery* still provides an excellent broad survey of the history of Classical jewellery. D. Williams & J. Ogden, *Greek gold: jewellery of the classical world* (London, 1994) is lavishly illustrated and authoritatively written, and is now the best standard work on ancient Greek jewellery.

12. A good selection of floral jewellery of various dates is brought together in section 10 (pp. 148–53) of T. Murdoch, (ed.) *Treasures and trinkets: jewellery in London from pre-Roman times to the 1930s* (London, 1991), the catalogue of an exhibition at the Museum of London.

13. F. H. Marshall, *Catalogue of the jewellery, Greek, Etruscan and Roman, in the Departments of Antiquities, British Museum*, reprint 1969 (London, 1911), nos. 1845–6.

14. This unprovenanced bracelet is in the Schmuckmuseum at Pforzheim, Germany, and has been reproduced in many general works on jewellery: see e.g. F. Falk (ed.), *Schmuckmuseum Pforzheim: von der Antike bis zur Gegenwart* (Pforzheim, 1980), no. 40.

Chapter 3

1. F. H. Marshall, *Catalogue of the finger rings, Greek, Etruscan and Roman, in the Departments of Antiquities, British Museum*, reprint 1968 (London, 1907).

2. F. Henkel, *Römische Fingerringe der Rheinlande und der benachbarten Gebiete* (Berlin, 1913).

3. H. Guiraud, "Bagues et anneaux à l'époque romaine en Gaule", *Gallia* **46**, 1989, pp. 173–211.

4. M. Henig, *A corpus of Roman engraved gemstones from British sites*, 2nd edn (Oxford, 1978).

5. G. Taylor & D. Scarisbrick, *Finger rings from ancient Egypt to the present day* (London, 1978).

6. Henkel, *Römische Fingerringe der Rheinlande und der benachbarten Gebiete*; H. Guiraud, "Un aspect de la bijouterie romaine: les bagues serpentiformes", *Pallas* **22**, 1975, pp. 82–7.

7. From Great Russell Street; see Marshall, *Catalogue of the finger rings, Greek, Etruscan and Roman, in the Departments of Antiquities, British Museum*, no. 1137.

8. D. Zienkiewicz, *The legionary fortress baths at Caerleon* (Cardiff, 1986), vol. II, fig. 47, no. 21.

9. The subject is fully discussed with reference to the Roman Empire as a whole in M. Henig, "Continuity and change in the design of Roman jewellery", in *The*

Roman West in the third century, A. King & M. Henig (eds) (Oxford, 1981), pp. 127–44.

10. Chesterford and Feltwell rings: British Museum, P & RB, registration nos. AF 437 and 1937.3-15.2.

11. New Grange rings; see J. P. C. Kent & K. S. Painter (eds), *Wealth of the Roman world* (London, 1977), nos. 231–5.

12. C. Johns & T. W. Potter, *The Thetford treasure: Roman jewellery and silver* (London, 1983).

13. *ibid.*

14. A. Comarmond, *Description de l'écrin d'une dame romaine trouvé à Lyon en 1841* (Lyons, 1844).

15. Henig, *A corpus of Roman engraved gemstones from British sites*, no. 790.

16. See, e.g., Kent & Painter, *Wealth of the Roman world*, nos. 141–3, and Marshall, *Catalogue of the finger rings, Greek, Etruscan and Roman, in the Departments of Antiquities, British Museum*, nos. 1205–7.

17. M. Henig & J. Ogden, "A late Roman gold ring and other objects from Richborough", *Antiquaries Journal* **68**, 1988, pp. 315–17.

18. The Burgate ring is an unpublished recent find, with late silver coins (*siliquae*) and fragments of late Roman silver spoons; the other examples are referred to in Henig & Ogden, "A late Roman gold ring and other objects from Richborough". See also the illustration of the Wantage ring in M. Henig, *The art of Roman Britain* (London, 1995), fig. 103.

19. The Silchester Senicianus ring: G. Boon, *Silchester, the Roman town of Calleva* (Newton Abbot, 1974), fig. 18, no. 4; and P. Finney, "Senicianus' ring", *Bonner Jahrbücher* **194**, 1994, pp. 175–96).

20. The Elsenham grave-group is in the British Museum, registered under the sequence P.1992.12-1.1 and P.1992.12-2.1-43 in the Department of Prehistoric and Romano-British Antiquities. It is not yet published.

21. C. Johns, "Some unpublished jewellery from Roman Britain", *Jewellery Studies* **5**, 1991, pp. 55–64, no. 5.

22. M. Henig & H. Chapman, "A Roman silver ring from London", *Antiquaries Journal* **65**, 1985, pp. 455–7.

23. D. Charlesworth, "Roman jewellery found in Northumberland and Durham", *Archaeologia Aeliana* (4th ser.) **39**, 1961, pp. 1–36, no. 95.

24. Marshall, *Catalogue of the finger rings, Greek, Etruscan and Roman, in the Departments of Antiquities, British Museum*, no. 1184.

25. E. Riha, *Der römische Schmuck aus Augst und Kaiseraugst* (Augst, Switzerland, 1990), no. 166.

26. Marshall, *Catalogue of the finger rings, Greek, Etruscan and Roman, in the Departments of Antiquities, British Museum*, no. 815.

27. Ilchester: *ibid.*, no. 267. Chichester: A. Down, *Chichester Excavations III* (Chichester, 1978), p. 9, fig. 10.48, no. 2.

28. Henkel, *Römische Fingerringe der Rheinlande und der benachbarten Gebiete*, nos. 818–73.

29. H. B. Walters, *Catalogue of the silver plate, Greek, Etruscan and Roman, in the British Museum* (London, 1923), no. 230.

30. RIB 2422.9.

31. L. Allason-Jones & B. McKay, *Coventina's Well: a shrine on Hadrian's Wall* (Gloucester, 1985), no. 32; RIB 2422.28.

32. C. Jones, "Romano-British jewellery", in Murdoch, *Treasures and trinkets: jewellery in London from pre-Roman times to the 1930s*, pp. 30–31.

33. Murdoch, *Treasures and trinkets: jewellery in London from pre-Roman times to the 1930s*, no. 55.

34. C. Johns, "A Roman gold ring from Bedford", *Antiquaries Journal* 61, 1981, pp. 343–5, pl. LVIII, a, b, c.

35. *ibid.*, pl. LVIII, d, e; Charlesworth, "Roman jewellery found in Northumberland and Durham".

36. Henig, *A corpus of Roman engraved gemstones from British sites*, no. 772.

37. Henkel, *Römische Fingerringe der Rheinlande und der benachbarten Gebiete*, nos. 818–73.

38. C. Jones, "Romano-British jewellery", pp. 29–30.

39. C. Johns, *Sex or symbol? Erotic images of Greece and Rome* (London, 1982), ch. 3.

40. Henig, *A corpus of Roman engraved gemstones from British sites*, no. 773.

41. *ibid.*, no. 742; RIB 2423.19.

42. Kent & Painter, *Wealth of the Roman world*, no. 140.

43. Marshall, *Catalogue of the finger rings, Greek, Etruscan and Roman, in the Departments of Antiquities, British Museum*, no. 82; RIB 2422.8, also Henig, *A corpus of Roman engraved gemstones from British sites*, no. 785.

44. *ibid.*, no. 759.

45. Whitwell: R. Bland & C. Johns, "A Roman hoard from Whitwell", *The Rutland Record* 14, 1994, pp. 151–8, fig. 13.

46. Henig, *A corpus of Roman engraved gemstones from British sites*, no. 790.

47. Marshall, *Catalogue of the finger rings, Greek, Etruscan and Roman, in the Departments of Antiquities, British Museum*, no. 208.

48. O. M. Dalton, *Catalogue of the early Christian antiquities and objects from the Christian East in the Department of British and Mediaeval Antiquities and Ethnography of the British Museum* (London, 1901), no. 207.

49. S. Bland & S. Boyd, *Handbook of the Byzantine Collection, Dumbarton Oaks* (Washington, 1967).

50. The reader who wishes to pursue the subject of Romano-British Christianity should refer to the standard work, C. Thomas, *Christianity in Roman Britain to AD 500* (London, 1981), and also to D. Watts, *Christians and pagans in Roman Britain* (London, 1991), which includes important recent discoveries but is somewhat more subjective in tone. C. F. Mawer, *Evidence for Christianity in Roman Britain: the small finds* (Oxford, 1995) is an invaluable catalogue which scrutinizes all allegedly Christian objects from Britain.

51. C. Johns, "A Christian late-Roman gold ring from Suffolk", *Antiquaries Journal* 64, 1984, pp. 393–4.

52. Thomas, *Christianity in Roman Britain to AD 500*, p. 131.

53. C. Johns, "A Roman Christian ring from Brentwood, Essex", *Antiquaries Journal* 65, 1985, pp. 461–3.

54. Thomas, *Christianity in Roman Britain to AD 500*, p. 131; Finney, "Senecianus' ring".

55. K. Shelton, *The Esquiline treasure* (London, 1981), no. 1.

56. M. Henig, "An early Christian signet ring from the Roman villa at Moor Park", *Hertfordshire Archaeology* 9, 1983, p. 184.

57. I am indebted to Lindsay Allason-Jones for enlightenment on this point. Her current work will eventually clarify some of the problems in identifying the

sources of jewellery made of jet and related materials. See Allason-Jones & Jones, "Jet and other materials in Roman artefact studies", pp. 265–72.

58. Henig, *A corpus of Roman engraved gemstones from British sites*, no. App. 206; also M. Henig, "A glass ring from Shakenoak", *Oxoniensia* **42**, 1977, pp. 260–61.

59. Murdoch, *Treasures and trinkets: jewellery in London from pre-Roman times to the 1930s*, nos. 465–6.

60. L. Allason-Jones & R. Miket, *The catalogue of small finds from South Shields Roman fort* (Newcastle, 1984), nos. 7.86–7.102.

61. Murdoch, *Treasures and trinkets: jewellery in London from pre-Roman times to the 1930s*, no. 501.

62. Henig, *A corpus of Roman engraved gemstones from British sites*, no. App. 207.

63. Henig, in M. McCarthy, T. G. Padley, M. Henig, "Excavations and finds from The Lanes, Carlisle", *Britannia* **13**, 1982, p. 88.

Chapter 4

1. M. Henig, "Antique gems in Roman Britain", *Jewellery Studies* **5**, 1991, pp. 49–54; Zienkiewicz, *The legionary fortress baths at Caerleon;* M. Maaskant-Kleibrink, *Catalogue of the engraved gems in the royal coin cabinet, The Hague: the Greek, Etruscan and Roman collections* (The Hague, 1978), M. Maaskant-Kleibrink, *The engraved gems, Roman and non-Roman (Description of the collections in the Rijksmuseum G. M. Kam at Nijmegen)* (Nijmegen, 1986) and M. Maaskant-Kleibrink, "Three gem-engravers at work in a jeweller's workshop in Norfolk", *Bulletin Antieke Beschaving* **67**, 1992, pp. 151–67.

2. E.g., in a beautiful ring from Colchester, Johns, "Some unpublished jewellery from Roman Britain", no. 11.

3. The confusing terminology for semi-precious forms of quartz is helpfully explained in M. Sax & A. Middleton, "A system of nomenclature for quartz and its application to the material of cylinder seals", *Archaeometry* **34**, 1992, pp. 11–20.

4. This point is discussed in Zienkiewicz, *The legionary fortress baths at Caerleon*, with reference to the Caerleon assemblage, pp. 120–21.

5. Johns, "Some unpublished jewellery from Roman Britain", no. 13.

6. Henig, *A corpus of Roman engraved gemstones from British sites*, no. 362.

7. *ibid.*, nos. 558 and 552.

8. Zienkiewicz, *The legionary fortress baths at Caerleon*.

9. Henig, *A corpus of Roman engraved gemstones from British sites*, no. 352.

10. The Warlingham ring is illustrated in T. W. Potter & C. Johns, *Roman Britain* (London, 1992), p. 149, fig. 59; for the Vindolanda example, see Henig, *A corpus of Roman engraved gemstones from British sites*, no. App. 148.

11. Marshall, *Catalogue of the finger rings, Greek, Etruscan and Roman, in the Departments of Antiquities, British Museum*, no. 1476; Henig, *A corpus of Roman engraved gemstones from British sites*, no. App. 150.

12. *ibid.*, no. 359; G. Boon, "An Isiac intaglio from Wroxeter rediscovered", *Antiquaries Journal* **62**, 1982, p. 356.

13. Johns & Potter, *The Thetford treasure: Roman jewellery and silver*, no. 13.

14. Henig, *A corpus of Roman engraved gemstones from British sites*, no. 362.

15. Murdoch, *Treasures and trinkets: jewellery in London from pre-Roman times to the 1930s*, no. 58.

16. For a series of these, see Henig, *A corpus of Roman engraved gemstones from British sites*, nos. 373–94.

17. M. Henig, *The Content family collection of ancient cameos* (Oxford and Houlton, Maine, 1990).

18. Henig, *A corpus of Roman engraved gemstones from British sites*, no. 729.

19. *ibid.*, no. App. 30.

20. *ibid.*, no. 743.

21. *ibid.*, no. 735; Allason-Jones & Miket, *The catalogue of small finds from South Shields Roman fort*, no. 10.1.

22. Johns & Potter, *The Thetford treasure: Roman jewellery and silver*, no. 39.

23. Henig, *A corpus of Roman engraved gemstones from British sites*, no. 732.

24. Unpublished and in private hands at the time of writing.

25. M. Henig, "Caracalla as Hercules? A new cameo from South Shields", *Antiquaries Journal* **66**, 1986, p. 378, pl. lxiv a.

26. Tacitus, *Agricola* 12.5.

Chapter 5

1. Marshall, *Catalogue of the jewellery, Greek, Etruscan and Roman, in the Departments of Antiquities, British Museum*, no. 2716.

2. A. Evans, "On two fibulae of Celtic fabric from Aesica", *Archaeologia* **55**, 1896, p. 179.

3. J. Curle, *A Roman frontier post and its people: the fort of Newstead in the parish of Melrose* (Glasgow, 1911), pl. 87, no. 34.

4. Low Ham mosaic: see Henig, *The art of Roman Britain*, pl. IX.

5. J. P. Bushe-Fox, *Fourth report on the excavations of the Roman fort at Richborough, Kent* (Oxford, 1949), no. 91.

6. Murdoch, *Treasures and trinkets: jewellery in London from pre-Roman times to the 1930s*, no. 169.

7. Comarmond, *Description de l'écrin d'une dame romaine trouvé à Lyon en 1841*.

8. D. Schaad et al. (eds), *Le Trésor d'Eauze* (Toulouse, 1992), nos. 2–4.

9. G. Clarke, *Pre-Roman and Roman Winchester: Part II, the Roman cemetery at Lankhills* (Oxford, 1979), grave no. 183.

10. Murdoch, *Treasures and trinkets: jewellery in London from pre-Roman times to the 1930s*, no. 462.

11. *ibid.*, no. 464.

12. H. Chapman, "Three Roman objects from the City of London", *Transactions of the London and Middlesex Archaeological Society* **25**, 1974, pp. 273–7.

13. Murdoch, *Treasures and trinkets: jewellery in London from pre-Roman times to the 1930s*, pp. 166–7.

14. N. Crummy, *The Roman small finds from excavations in Colchester 1971–9*, Colchester Archaeological Report 2 (Colchester, 1983), nos. 807–9; J. Ogden, *Jewellery of the ancient world* (London, 1982), fig. 6.6, p. 120.

15. P. Bastien & C. Metzger, *Le Trésor de Beaurains* (Wetteren, Belgium, 1977); Schaad et al., *Le Trésor d'Eauze*.

16. Johns & Potter, *The Thetford treasure: Roman jewellery and silver.*

17. The type is discussed in R. Noll, "Zwei römerzeitliche Grabfunde aus Rumänien in der Wiener Antikensammlung", *Jahrbuch des Römisch-Germanischen Zentralmuseums Mainz* **31**, 1984, pp. 443–54.

18. This statuette has frequently been illustrated, see e.g. Potter & Johns, *Roman Britain*; pl. XI.

19. A. Lawson, "Shale and jet objects from Silchester", *Archaeologia* **105**, 1976, pp. 241–75.

20. Vindolanda: R. Birley, *Vindolanda, a Roman frontier post on Hadrian's Wall* (London, 1977), pl. 46–7; Colchester: J. W. Brailsford, *Guide to the antiquities of Roman Britain* (London, 1964), fig. 26, p. 56.

21. H. Newman, *An illustrated dictionary of jewelry* (London, 1981), p. 46.

22. Brailsford, *Guide to the antiquities of Roman Britain*, fig. 6, p. 13.

23. Marshall, *Catalogue of the jewellery, Greek, Etruscan and Roman, in the Departments of Antiquities, British Museum*, no. 2789.

24. P. Rashleigh, "Account of antiquities discovered at Southfleet in Kent", *Archaeologia* **14**, 1803, pp. 37–9, pl. viii, nos. 3 and 4.

25. Marshall, *Catalogue of the jewellery, Greek, Etruscan and Roman, in the Departments of Antiquities, British Museum*, nos. 2782–3; RIB 2424.1, 2.

26. Marshall, *Catalogue of the jewellery, Greek, Etruscan and Roman, in the Departments of Antiquities, British Museum*, nos. 2797, 2798–9.

27. B. Pfeiler [= B. Deppert-Lippitz], *Römische Goldschmuck des ersten und zweiten Jahrhunderts nach Christi, nach datierten Funden* (Mainz, 1970), pl. 17.

28. Marshall, *Catalogue of the jewellery, Greek, Etruscan and Roman, in the Departments of Antiquities, British Museum*, no. 2875.

29. J. Heurgon, *Le Trésor de Ténès* (Paris, 1958), pl. V, 2.

30. Comarmond, *Description de l'écrin d'une dame romaine trouvé à Lyon en 1841*, pp. 2, 3 and 4.

31. Crummy, *The Roman small finds from excavations in Colchester 1971–9*, no. 1610.

32. Marshall, *Catalogue of the jewellery, Greek, Etruscan and Roman, in the Departments of Antiquities, British Museum*, nos. 2793, 2794.

33. Kent & Painter, *Wealth of the Roman world*, nos. 233, 234.

34. Heurgon, *Le Trésor de Ténès*, pl. V, 3.

35. See, e.g., Allason-Jones & Miket, *The catalogue of small finds from South Shields Roman fort 1984* and Clarke, *Pre-Roman and Roman Winchester: Part II, the Roman cemetery at Lankhills.*

36. For good discussions of jet jewellery, see Allason-Jones & Miket, *The catalogue of small finds from South Shields Roman fort*, pp. 302–25 and Crummy, *The Roman small finds from excavations in Colchester 1971–9*, pp. 25–8, 36–7.

37. H. E. Kilbride-Jones, "Glass armlets in Britain", *Proceedings of the Society of Antiquaries of Scotland* **72**, 1938, pp. 366–95; R. B. K. Stevenson, "Native bangles and Roman glass", *Proceedings of the Society of Antiquaries of Scotland* **88**, 1956, pp. 208–21; R. B. K. Stevenson, "Romano-British glass bangles", *Glasgow Archaeological Journal* **4**, 1976, pp. 45–54.

38. M. Guido, *The glass beads of the prehistoric and Roman periods in Britain and Ireland* (London, 1978), class 9 beads.

39. British Museum, P & RB, 1899.5-8.72.

40. J. Price, "Romano-British bangles from East Yorkshire" in *Recent research in Roman Yorkshire*, J. Price & P. Wilson (eds) (Oxford, 1988), pp. 339–66.

41. Clarke, *Pre-Roman and Roman Winchester: Part II, the Roman cemetery at Lankhills*; the bone and ivory bangles are discussed on pp. 312–13.

Chapter 6

1. L. Allason-Jones, *Ear-rings in Roman Britain* (Oxford, 1989a).
2. Johns, "Some unpublished jewellery from Roman Britain", no. 1.
3. Allason-Jones, *Ear-rings in Roman Britain*, no. 16.
4. C. Johns, "A group of late-Roman jewellery from Owmby-by-Spital, Lincs.", *Archaeology in Lincolnshire and South Humberside*, 1979, pp. 87–8; Allason-Jones, *Ear-rings in Roman Britain*, nos. 50–51.
5. *ibid.*, no. 45.
6. Noll, "Zwei römerzeitliche Grabfunde aus Rumänien in der Wiener Antikensammlung".
7. J. Ogden, *Newsletter of Society of Jewellery Historians*, no. 9 (1980).
8. Allason-Jones, *Ear-rings in Roman Britain*, pp. 11–12, nos. 46, 5 and 2.
9. *ibid.*, no. 59.
10. Johns, "Some unpublished jewellery from Roman Britain", no. 4.
11. Unpublished and in private possession.
12. C. Johns, H. Thompson, P. Wagstaff, "The Wincle, Cheshire, hoard of Roman gold jewellery", *Antiquaries Journal* 60, 1980, pp. 48–58, no. 8.
13. B. Deppert-Lippitz, *Goldschmuck der Römerzeit im Römisch-Germanischen Zentralmuseum* (Bonn, 1985), no. 73.
14. Allason-Jones, *Ear-rings in Roman Britain*, no. 3.
15. Schaad et al., *Le Trésor d'Eauze*.
16. Allason-Jones, *Ear-rings in Roman Britain*, no. 58.
17. For example, *ibid.*, nos. 27–8, from Colchester.
18. I. Stead & V. Rigby, *Baldock: the excavation of a Roman and pre-Roman settlement* (London, 1986), nos. 202–5.
19. I. Stead & V. Rigby, *Verulamium: the King Harry Lane site* (London, 1989), no. 161.
20. Rashleigh, "Account of antiquities discovered at Southfleet in Kent", pl. VIII, no. 2; Brailsford, *Guide to the antiquities of Roman Britain*, pl. I, no. 7.
21. L. Hahl with V. von Gonzenbach, "Zur Erklärung der Niedergermanischen Matronendenkmäler", *Bonner Jahrbücher* 160, 1960, pp. 9–49; A. Böhme, *Schmuck der römischen Frau* (Stuttgart, 1974), pp. 18–19; Pfeiler, *Römische Goldschmuck des ersten und zweiten Jahrhunderts nach Christi, nach datierten Funden*, pp. 87, 96.
22. H. A. Cool, "A Romano-British gold workshop of the second century", *Britannia* 17, 1986, pp. 231–7.
23. Clarke, *Pre-Roman and Roman Winchester: Part II, the Roman cemetery at Lankhills*, grave no. 323, and p. 317.
24. Crummy, *The Roman small finds from excavations in Colchester 1971–9*, p. 19; Clarke, *Pre-Roman and Roman Winchester: Part II, the Roman cemetery at Lankhills* , p. 315.
25. L. Allason-Jones, *Women in Roman Britain* (London, 1989), p. 136.
26. H. Cool, "Roman metal hairpins from southern Britain", *Archaeological Journal* 147, 1990, pp. 148–82.

27. Brailsford, *Guide to the antiquities of Roman Britain*, fig. 14, no. 10; H. Tait (ed.), *Seven thousand years of jewellery* (London, 1986), no. 212.

28. From Mansion House; British Museum (P & RB), no. 1896.10-16.1. Unpublished.

29. Brailsford, *Guide to the antiquities of Roman Britain*, fig. 14, no. 11; Tait, *Seven thousand years of jewellery*, no. 213.

30. The larger pins are (1) (British Museum) Brailsford, *Guide to the antiquities of Roman Britain*, fig. 14, no. 9 and Tait, *Seven thousand years of jewellery*, no. 211; (2) Museum of London, reg. no. 559 (unpublished); the smaller example from Gloucestershire (3) is BM reg. no. 1883.10-30.1 (unpublished).

31. R. E. M. Wheeler, *London in Roman times* (London, 1930), fig. 32, no. 1; also the subject of a forthcoming article by C. Johns.

32. The Walbrook silver pin; Brailsford, *Guide to the antiquities of Roman Britain*, fig. 14, no. 12. For the symbolism, see P. Arthur, "Eggs and pomegranates", in *Roman life and art in Britain*, J. Munby & M. Henig (eds) (Oxford, 1977), pp. 367–74.

33. British Museum, Greek & Roman dept. no. 1898.11-21.3.

34. See Henig, "A glass ring from Shakenoak", p. 361.

35. Cool, "Roman metal hairpins from southern Britain".

36. Allason-Jones, *Women in Roman Britain*, pp. 133–4.

37. Crummy, *The Roman small finds from excavations in Colchester 1971–9*.

38. Unpublished. British Museum reg. no. P & RB 1934.12-10.20.

39. C. Johns,."A Roman silver pin from Oldcroft, Gloucestershire", *Antiquaries Journal* **54**, 1974, pp. 195–7.

Chapter 7

1. R. Hattatt, *Ancient and Romano-British brooches* (Sherborne, 1982), R. Hattatt, *Iron Age and Roman brooches* (Oxford, 1985), R. Hattatt, *Brooches of antiquity* (Oxford, 1987) and R. Hattatt, *Ancient brooches and other artefacts* (Oxford, 1989).

2. R. G. Collingwood, *The archaeology of Roman Britain* (London, 1930).

3. I should like to thank my colleague Val Rigby for her help in the matter of brooch typology.

4. Allason-Jones, *Women in Roman Britain*, pp. 109–14.

5. E. Fowler, "The origins and development of the penannular brooch in Europe", *Proceedings of the Prehistoric Society* **26**, 1960, pp. 149–77; Hattatt, *Iron Age and Roman brooches*.

6. B. Cunliffe, *The finds from the sacred spring*, vol. 2 of *The temple of Sulis Minerva at Bath* (Oxford, 1988), no. 48, pl. XVII.

7. H. E. Kilbride-Jones, *Celtic craftsmanship in bronze* (London, 1980), pp.170–83.

8. For examples of name-stamps from Aucissa brooches in Britain, see RIB II (3), 2421.

9. RIB 2421.50.

10. E. Ettlinger, *Die römischen Fibeln in der Schweiz* (Berne, 1973), pl. 11, no. 15.

11. Evans, "On two fibulae of Celtic fabric from Aesica"; R. G. Collingwood, "Romano-Celtic art in Northumbria", *Archaeologia* **85**, 1930, pp. 37–58; Megaw & Megaw, *Celtic art*, p. 229.

12. Collingwood, "Romano-Celtic art in Northumbria"; G. C. Boon & H. N. Savory, "A silver trumpet-brooch with relief decoration, parcel-gilt, from Carmarthen, and a note on the development of the type", *Antiquaries Journal* **55**, 1975, pp. 41–61.

13. *ibid.;* see also Megaw & Megaw, *Celtic art*, p. 230.

14. Collingwood, "Romano-Celtic art in Northumbria", p. 51.

15. K. Blockley, *Prestatyn 1984–5: an Iron Age farmstead and Romano-British industrial settlement in North Wales* (Oxford, 1989), pp. 183–7.

16. E. Keller, *Die spätrömische Grabfunde in Südbayern* (Munich, 1971).

17. E.g., see the illustration in J. Nantanson, *Early Christian ivories* (London, 1953), no. 4. The ivory is illustrated in many books on late Antique art.

18. Shelton, *The Esquiline treasure*, pl. 4.

19. Screw-threads were used in other late Antique jewels. The use of the screw in antiquity was the subject of an exhibition held in Germany in 1995, and the catalogue, B. Deppert-Lippitz et al., *Die Schraube zwischen Macht und Pracht: das Gewinde in der Antike* (Sigmaringen, 1995), is a valuable source of information, bringing together and illustrating examples from museums in Europe and America.

20. RIB 2421.43.

21. R. Noll, "Eine goldene 'Kaiserfibel' aus Niederemmel vom Jahre 316", *Bonner Jahrbücher* **174**, 1974, pp. 221–44.

22. Johns, Thompson, Wagstaff, "The Wincle, Cheshire, hoard of Roman gold jewellery", no. 4.

23. Potter & Johns, *Roman Britain*, fig. 90.

24. Heurgon, *Le Trésor de Ténès*, nos. 1 and 2.

25. Clarke, *Pre-Roman and Roman Winchester: Part II, the Roman cemetery at Lankhills*, pp. 257–63 and fig. 32.

26. Tait, *Seven thousand years of jewellery*, no. 498, p. 205.

27. Estimates of the recorded numbers of various types are based on Hattatt's published work, supplemented by the card-index of brooches compiled by Donald Mackreth, a copy of which is kept in the British Museum (P & RB department). The actual numbers found must be much higher, since so many go unrecorded, but there should still be some significance in relative numbers of various types.

28. For a particularly fine statuette, see C. Johns, "A Romano-British statuette of a mounted warrior god", *Antiquaries Journal* **70**, 1990, pp. 446–52.

29. Stead & Rigby, *Baldock: the excavation of a Roman and pre-Roman settlement*, fig. 49, no. 152.

30. Hattatt, *Brooches of antiquity*, p. 195.

31. Allason-Jones & Miket, *The catalogue of small finds from South Shields Roman fort*, no. 3.148.

32. R. Goodchild, "Romano-British disc brooches derived from Hadrianic coin types", *Antiquaries Journal* **21**, 1941, pp. 1–8.

33. Hattatt, *Ancient brooches and other artefacts*, no. 1648, p. 181; Henig, *The art of Roman Britain*, pl. 82.

34. A. Krug, *Antike Gemmen im Römisch-Germanischen Museum Köln* (Frankfurt, 1981), no. 82.

35. I. Stead, *Celtic art* (London, 1985); Megaw & Megaw, *Celtic art*.

36. See, e.g., the Clevedon torc-terminal, Stead, *Celtic art*, fig. 43; the Brentford horn-

cap, *ibid.*, fig. 20d; Tal-y-Llyn, Megaw, *Art of the European Iron Age*, fig. 358; medieval examples, see Megaw & Megaw, *Celtic art*, pp. 246–64.

Chapter 8

1. Ogden, *Jewellery of the ancient world;* J. Ogden, *Ancient jewellery* (London, 1992); Higgins, *Greek and Roman jewellery;* D. Strong & D. Brown (eds), *Roman crafts* (London, 1976); O. Untracht, *Jewelry concepts and technology* (London, 1982), and the technical chapter of Williams & Ogden, *Greek gold: jewellery of the classical world.*
2. CIL (*Corpus Inscriptionum Latinarum*), vol. VI, pt 2, Berlin 1882, no. 9437.
3. RIB 712.
4. J. Bayley & S. Butcher, "Romano-British plate-brooches: composition and decoration", *Jewellery Studies* **3**, 1989, pp. 25–32 (contains additional relevant references).
5. Blockley, *Prestatyn 1984–5: an Iron Age farmstead and Romano-British industrial settlement in North Wales*, pl. XIX; Henkel, *Römische Fingerringe der Rheinlande und der benachbarten Gebiete*, pl. 67 (nos. 1780, 1781).
6. I am indebted to Martin Henig for information on this object. It has the museum registration number 1929.747.
7. British Patent no. 1934.415181.
8. See the discussions of granulation in Ogden, *Jewellery of the ancient world* and in Untracht, *Jewelry concepts and technology*, pp. 348–63.
9. J. Ogden, "Classical gold wire, some aspects of its manufacture and use", *Jewellery Studies* **5**, 1991, pp. 95–105.
10. J. Ogden & S. Schmidt, "Late Antique jewellery: pierced work and hollow beaded wire", *Jewellery Studies* **4**, 1990, pp. 5–12.
11. The stages of manufacture are illustrated very clearly in Untracht, *Jewelry concepts and technology*, pp. 194–5.
12. A. Oddy, "The gilding of Roman silver plate", in *Argenterie Romaine et Byzantine*, François Baratte (ed.) (Paris, 1988), pp. 9–21.
13. S. La Niece, "Silver plating on copper, bronze and brass", *Antiquaries Journal* **70**, 1990, pp. 102–14.
14. A. Oddy & M. Bimson, "Tinned bronze in antiquity", in *Lead and tin: studies in conservation and technology*, G. Miles & S. Pollard (eds) UKIC Occ. Pap. 3, 1985.
15. S. La Niece, "Niello: an historical and technical survey", *Antiquaries Journal* **63**, 1983, pp. 279–97.
16. J. D. Bateson, *Enamel-working in Iron Age, Roman and sub-Roman Britain* (Oxford, 1981); Ogden, *Jewellery of the ancient world;* Sarnia Butcher in Strong & Brown, *Roman crafts*, ch. 3.
17. J. Henderson, "Technological characteristics of Roman enamels", *Jewellery Studies* **5**, 1991, pp. 65–76.
18. For example, Newman, *An illustrated dictionary of jewelry*, pp. 62–3 and 72.
19. Bateson, *Enamel-working in Iron Age, Roman and sub-Roman Britain*, pp. 86–98.
20. *ibid.*, pp. 92–3.
21. This method was suggested to me by Jennifer Price.
22. Bateson, *Enamel-working in Iron Age, Roman and sub-Roman Britain*, pp. 94–8.

23. Illustrated in colour in Potter & Johns, *Roman Britain*, pl. VIII.
24. Strong & Brown, *Roman crafts*, ch. 9; Ogden, *Jewellery of the ancient world*, pp. 128–33.
25. W. Gudenrath, "Techniques of glassmaking and decoration", in *5000 years of glass*, Hugh Tait (ed.) (London 1992), pp. 213–41, figs 36–58.
26. Price, "Romano-British bangles from East Yorkshire", p. 341.
27. Maaskant-Kleibrink, "Three gem-engravers at work in a jeweller's workshop in Norfolk".
28. This point was explained to me by Sir John Boardman.

Afterword

1. E. Hawkins, "Notices of a remarkable collection of ornaments of the Roman period, connected with the worship of the Deae Matres, and recently purchased for the British Museum", *Archaeological Journal* **8**, 1851, p. 44.

Appendix

1. Hawkins, "Notices of a remarkable collection of ornaments of the Roman period, connected with the worship of the Deae Matres, and recently purchased for the British Museum"; Walters, *Catalogue of the silver plate, Greek, Etruscan and Roman, in the British Museum,* nos. 183–7.
2. RIB 2414.36.
3. RIB 2422.9.
4. The full catalogue of the Snettisham hoard is in press.
5. The matter of technique and the identification of different hands is fully discussed in Maaskant-Kleibrink, "Three gem-engravers at work in a jeweller's workshop in Norfolk".
6. Johns & Potter, *The Thetford treasure: Roman jewellery and silver.*
7. C. Johns & R. Bland, "The Hoxne late Roman treasure", *Britannia* **25**, 1994, pp. 165–73 is a brief preliminary summary of the contents of the treasure. R. Bland & C. Johns, *The Hoxne treasure: an illustrated introduction* (London, 1993) contains the same material in a popular booklet with colour illustrations and without detailed references.
8. A. Curle, *The treasure of Traprain* (Glasgow, 1923).

Bibliography

Allason-Jones, L. *Ear-rings in Roman Britain* (Oxford, 1989).

Allason-Jones, L. *Women in Roman Britain* (London, 1989).

Allason-Jones, L. & D. M. Jones. Jet and other materials in Roman artefact studies. *Archaeologia Aeliana* (5th ser.) **22**, 1994, pp. 265–72.

Allason-Jones, L. & B. McKay. *Coventina's Well: a shrine on Hadrian's Wall* (Gloucester, 1985).

Allason-Jones, L. & R. Miket. *The catalogue of small finds from South Shields Roman fort* (Newcastle, 1984).

[Anon.] *The Mabinogion*, trans. G. Jones & T. Jones (London, 1949).

Arthur, P. Eggs and pomegranates. In *Roman life and art in Britain*, J. Munby & M. Henig (eds) (Oxford, 1977), pp. 367–74.

Atiya, N. *Khul-Khaal: five Egyptian women tell their stories* (Cairo, 1984).

Baratte, F. (ed.). *Argenterie romaine et Byzantine* (Paris, 1988).

Bastien, P. & C. Metzger. *Le Trésor de Beaurains* (Wetteren, Belgium, 1977).

Bateson, J. D. *Enamel-working in Iron Age, Roman and sub-Roman Britain* (Oxford, 1981).

Bayley, J. & S. Butcher. Romano-British plate-brooches: composition and decoration. *Jewellery Studies* **3**, 1989, pp. 25–32.

Behrens, G. Römische Fibeln mit Inschrift. In *Reinecke Festschrift*, G. Behrens & J. Werner (eds) (Mainz, 1950), pp. 1–12.

Birley, R. *Vindolanda, a Roman frontier post on Hadrian's Wall* (London, 1977).

Bland, R. & C. Johns. *The Hoxne treasure: an illustrated introduction* (London, 1993).

Bland, R. & C. Johns. A Roman hoard from Whitwell. *The Rutland Record* **14**, 1994, pp. 151–8.

Bland, S. & S. Boyd. *Handbook of the Byzantine Collection, Dumbarton Oaks* (Washington, 1967).

Blockley, K. *Prestatyn 1984–5: an Iron Age farmstead and Romano-British industrial settlement in North Wales* (Oxford, 1989).

Böhme, A. *Schmuck der römischen Frau* (Stuttgart, 1974)

Boon, G. *Silchester, the Roman town of Calleva* (Newton Abbot, 1974).

Boon, G. An Isiac intaglio from Wroxeter rediscovered. *Antiquaries Journal* **62**, 1982, p. 356.

Boon, G. C. & H. N. Savory. A silver trumpet-brooch with relief decoration, parcel-gilt, from Carmarthen, and a note on the development of the type. *Antiquaries Journal* **55**, 1975, pp. 41–61.

Brailsford, J. W. *Guide to the antiquities of Roman Britain* (London, 1964).

Bushe-Fox, J. P. *Fourth report on the excavations of the Roman fort at Richborough, Kent* (Oxford, 1949).

Chapman, H. Three Roman objects from the City of London. *Transactions of the London and Middlesex Archaeological Society* 25, 1974, pp. 273–7.

Charlesworth, D. Roman jewellery found in Northumberland and Durham. *Archaeologia Aeliana* (4th ser.) **39**, 1961, pp. 1–36.

Clarke, G. *Pre-Roman and Roman Winchester: Part II, the Roman cemetery at Lankhills* (Oxford, 1979).

Collingwood, R. G. *The archaeology of Roman Britain* (London, 1930).

Collingwood, R. G. Romano-Celtic art in Northumbria. *Archaeologia* **85**, 1930, pp. 37–58.

Comarmond, A. *Description de l'écrin d'une dame romaine trouvé à Lyon en 1841* (Lyons, 1844).

Connolly, P. *Hannibal and the enemies of Rome* (London, 1978).

Cool, H. A Romano-British gold workshop of the second century. *Britannia* **17**, 1986, pp. 231–7.

Cool, H. Roman metal hairpins from southern Britain. *Archaeological Journal* **147**, 1990, pp. 148–82.

Crummy, N. *The Roman small finds from excavations in Colchester 1971–9*, Colchester Archaeological Report 2 (Colchester, 1983).

Cunliffe, B. *The finds from the sacred spring*, vol. 2 of *The temple of Sulis Minerva at Bath* (Oxford, 1988).

Curle, A. The treasure of Traprain (Glasgow, 1923).

Curle, J. *A Roman frontier post and its people: the fort of Newstead in the parish of Melrose* (Glasgow, 1911).

Dalton, O. M. *Catalogue of the early Christian antiquities and objects from the Christian East in the Department of British and Mediaeval Antiquities and Ethnography of the British Museum* (London, 1901).

Deppert-Lippitz, B. *Goldschmuck der Römerzeit im Römisch-Germanischen Zentralmuseum* (Bonn, 1985).

Deppert-Lippitz, B. et al. *Die Schraube zwischen Macht und Pracht: das Gewinde in der Antike* (Sigmaringen, 1995).

Dio, C. *Roman history*, Loeb edn, trans. E. Carey (London, 1929).

Down, A. *Chichester Excavations III* (Chichester, 1978).

Ettlinger, E. *Die römischen Fibeln in der Schweiz* (Berne, 1973).

Evans, A. On two fibulae of Celtic fabric from Aesica. *Archaeologia* **55**, 1896, pp. 179–98.

Falk, F. (ed.). *Schmuckmuseum Pforzheim: von der Antike bis zur Gegenwart* (Pforzheim, 1980).

Finney, P. Senicianus' ring. *Bonner Jahrbücher* **194**, 1994, pp. 175–96.

Fowler, E. The origins and development of the penannular brooch in Europe. *Proceedings of the Prehistoric Society* **26**, 1960, pp 149–77.

Goodchild, R. Romano-British disc brooches derived from Hadrianic coin types. *Antiquaries Journal* **21**, 1941, pp. 1–8.

Gudenrath, W. Techniques of glassmaking and decoration. In *5000 years of glass*, H. Tait (ed.) (London, 1992), pp. 213–41.

Guido, M. *The glass beads of the prehistoric and Roman periods in Britain and Ireland* (London, 1978).

Guiraud, H. Un aspect de la bijouterie romaine: les bagues serpentiformes. *Pallas* **22**, 1975, pp. 82–7.

Guiraud, H. Bagues et anneaux à l'époque romaine en Gaule. *Gallia* **46**, 1989, pp. 173–211.

Hahl, L. with V. von Gonzenbach. Zur Erklärung der Niedergermanischen Matronendenkmäler. *Bonner Jahrbücher* **160**, 1960, pp. 9–49.

Hattatt, R. *Ancient and Romano-British brooches* (Sherborne, 1982).

Hattatt, R. *Iron Age and Roman brooches* (Oxford, 1985).

Hattatt, R. *Brooches of antiquity* (Oxford, 1987).

Hattatt, R. *Ancient brooches and other artefacts* (Oxford, 1989).

Hawkins, E. Notices of a remarkable collection of ornaments of the Roman period, connected with the worship of the Deae Matres, and recently purchased for the British Museum. *Archaeological Journal* **8**, 1851, pp. 35–44.

Henderson, J. Technological characteristics of Roman enamels. *Jewellery Studies* **5**, 1991, pp. 65–76.

Henig, M. Death and the maiden. In *Roman life and art in Britain*, J. Munby & M. Henig (eds) (Oxford, 1977), pp. 347–66.

Henig, M. A glass ring from Shakenoak. *Oxoniensia* **42**, 1977, pp. 260–61.

Henig, M. *A corpus of Roman engraved gemstones from British sites*, 2nd edn (Oxford, 1978).

Henig, M. Continuity and change in the design of Roman jewellery. In *The Roman West in the third century*, A. King & M. Henig (eds) (Oxford:1981), pp. 127–44.

Henig, M. An early Christian signet ring from the Roman villa at Moor Park. *Hertfordshire Archaeology* **9**, 1983, p. 184.

Henig, M. (ed.). *A handbook of Roman art* (Oxford, 1983).

Henig, M. Caracalla as Hercules? A new cameo from South Shields. *Antiquaries Journal* **66**, 1986, pp. 378–80.

Henig, M. The chronology of Roman engraved gemstones. *Journal of Roman Archaeology* **1**, 1988, pp. 142–52.

Henig, M. *The Content family collection of ancient cameos* (Oxford and Houlton, Maine, 1990).

Henig, M. Antique gems in Roman Britain. *Jewellery Studies* **5**, 1991, pp. 49–54.

Henig, M. *The art of Roman Britain* (London, 1995).

Henig, M. & H. Chapman. A Roman silver ring from London. *Antiquaries Journal* **65**, 1985, pp. 455–7.

Henig, M. & J. Ogden. A late Roman gold ring and other objects from Richborough. *Antiquaries Journal* **68**, 1988, pp. 315–17.

Henkel, F. *Römische Fingerringe der Rheinlande und der benachbarten Gebiete* (Berlin, 1913).

Heurgon, J. *Le Trésor de Ténès* (Paris, 1958).

Higgins, R. A. *Greek and Roman jewellery* (London, 1980).

Johns, C. A Roman silver pin from Oldcroft, Gloucestershire. *Antiquaries Journal* **54**, 1974, pp. 195–7.

Johns, C. A group of late-Roman jewellery from Owmby-by-Spital, Lincs. *Archaeology in Lincolnshire and South Humberside*, 1979, pp. 87–8.

Johns, C. A Roman gold ring from Bedford. *Antiquaries Journal* **61**, 1981, pp. 343–5.

Johns, C. *Sex or symbol? Erotic images of Greece and Rome* (London, 1982).

Johns, C. A Christian late-Roman gold ring from Suffolk. *Antiquaries Journal* **64**, pp. 393–4, 1984.

Johns, C. A Roman Christian ring from Brentwood, Essex. *Antiquaries Journal* **65**, pp. 461–3, 1985.

Johns, C. A Romano-British statuette of a mounted warrior god. *Antiquaries Journal* **70**, pp. 446–52, 1990.

Johns, C. Some unpublished jewellery from Roman Britain. *Jewellery Studies* **5**, pp. 55–64, 1991.

Johns, C. & R. Bland. The great Hoxne treasure: a preliminary report. *Journal of Roman Archaeology* **6**, pp. 493–6, 1993.

Johns, C. & R. Bland. The Hoxne late Roman Treasure. *Britannia* **25**, 1994, pp. 165–73.

Johns, C. & T. W. Potter. *The Thetford treasure: Roman jewellery and silver* (London, 1983).

Johns C., H. Thompson, P. Wagstaff. The Wincle, Cheshire, hoard of Roman gold jewellery. *Antiquaries Journal* **60**, 1980, pp. 48–58.

Jones, C. *Romano-British jewellery*. See Murdoch (ed.), 1991, p. 23.

Keller, E. *Die spätrömische Grabfunde in Südbayern* (Munich, 1971).

Kent, J. P. C. & K. S. Painter (eds). *Wealth of the Roman world* (London, 1977).

Kilbride-Jones, H. E. Glass armlets in Britain. *Proceedings of the Society of Antiquaries of Scotland* **72**, pp. 366–95, 1938.

Kilbride-Jones, H. E. *Celtic craftsmanship in bronze* (London, 1980).

King, A. & M. Henig (eds). *The Roman West in the third century* (Oxford, 1981).

Krug, A. *Antike Gemmen im Römisch-Germanischen Museum Köln* (Frankfurt, 1981).

La Niece, S. Niello: an historical and technical survey. *Antiquaries Journal* **63**, 1983, pp. 279–97.

La Niece, S. Silver plating on copper, bronze and brass. *Antiquaries Journal* **70**, 1990, pp. 102–14.

Lawson, A. Shale and jet objects from Silchester. *Archaeologia* **105**, 1976, pp. 241–75.

Lurie, A. *The language of clothes* (New York, 1981).

Maaskant-Kleibrink, M. *Catalogue of the engraved gems in the royal coin cabinet, The Hague: the Greek, Etruscan and Roman collections* (The Hague, 1978).

Maaskant-Kleibrink, M. *The engraved gems, Roman and non-Roman (Description of the collections in the Rijksmuseum G. M. Kam at Nijmegen)* (Nijmegen, 1986).

Maaskant-Kleibrink, M. Three gem-engravers at work in a jeweller's workshop in Norfolk. *Bulletin Antieke Beschaving* **67**, 1992, pp. 151–67.

McCarthy, M., T. G. Padley, M. Henig. Excavations and finds from The Lanes, Carlisle. *Britannia* **13**, 1982, pp. 79–89.

Marshall, F. H. *Catalogue of the finger rings, Greek, Etruscan and Roman, in the Departments of Antiquities, British Museum*, reprint 1968 (London, 1907).

Marshall, F. H. *Catalogue of the jewellery, Greek, Etruscan and Roman, in the Departments of Antiquities, British Museum*, reprint 1969 (London, 1911).

Mawer, C. F. *Evidence for Christianity in Roman Britain: the small finds* (Oxford, 1995).

Maxfield, V. *The military decorations of the Roman army* (London, 1981).

Megaw, V. *Art of the European Iron Age* (Bath, 1970).

Megaw, R. & V. Megaw. *Celtic art* (London, 1989).

Moscati, S. (ed.). *The Celts* (Venice, 1991).

Munby, J. & M. Henig. *Roman life and art in Britain* (Oxford, 1977).

Murdoch, T. (ed.). *Treasures and trinkets: jewellery in London from pre-Roman times to the 1930s* (London, 1991).

Nantanson, J. *Early Christian ivories* (London, 1953).

Newman, H. *An illustrated dictionary of jewelry* (London, 1981).

Noll, R. Eine goldene "Kaiserfibel" aus Niederemmel vom Jahre 316. *Bonner Jahrbücher* **174**, 1974, pp. 221–44.

Noll, R. Zwei römerzeitliche Grabfunde aus Rumänien in der Wiener Antikensammlung. *Jahrbuch des Römisch-Germanischen Zentralmuseums Mainz* **31**, 1984, pp. 435–54.

Oddy, A. The gilding of Roman silver plate. In *Argenterie Romaine et Byzantine*, François Baratte (ed.) (Paris, 1988), pp. 9–21.

Oddy, A. & M. Bimson. Tinned bronze in antiquity. In *Lead and tin: studies in conservation and technology*, G. Miles & S. Pollard (eds) UKIC Occ. Pap. 3, 1985.

Ogden, J. *Newsletter of Society of Jewellery Historians*, no. 9 (1980).

Ogden, J. *Jewellery of the ancient world* (London, 1982).

Ogden, J. Classical gold wire, some aspects of its manufacture and use. *Jewellery Studies* **5**, 1991, pp. 95–105.

Ogden, J. *Ancient jewellery* (London, 1992).

Ogden, J. & S. Schmidt. Late Antique jewellery: pierced work and hollow beaded wire. *Jewellery Studies* **4**, 1990, pp. 5–12.

Pfeiler, B. [= Deppert-Lippitz, B.] *Römische Goldschmuck des ersten und zweiten Jahrhunderts nach Christi, nach datierten Funden* (Mainz, 1970).

Piggott, S. Bronze, Britons and Romans: an early antiquarian problem. In *Between and beyond the walls: essays on the prehistory and history of North Britain in honour of George Jobey*, R. Miket & C. Burgess (eds) (Edinburgh, 1984), pp. 117–25.

Potter, T. W. & C. Johns. *Roman Britain* (London, 1992).

Price, J. Romano-British bangles from East Yorkshire. In *Recent Research in Roman Yorkshire*, J. Price & P. Wilson (eds) (Oxford, 1988), pp. 339–66.

Rashleigh, P. Account of antiquities discovered at Southfleet in Kent. *Archaeologia* **14**, 1803, pp. 37–9.

Riha, E. *Der römische Schmuck aus Augst und Kaiseraugst* (Augst, Switzerland, 1990).

Roman inscriptions of Britain, cited under individual numbers (RIB). The volumes are as follows:

   Collingwood, R. G. & R. P. Wright, vol. I, *Inscriptions on stone* (Oxford, 1965).

   Frere, S. S., M. Roxan, R. S. O. Tomlin, vol. II, Fascicule 1, *Instrumentum Domesticum*,

   RIB 2401–2411 (Gloucester, 1990).

   Frere, S. S. & R. S. O. Tomlin, vol. II, Fascicule 2, *Instrumentum Domesticum*, RIB 2412–2420 (Stroud, 1991).

   Frere, S. S. & R. S. O. Tomlin, vol. II, Fascicule 3, *Instrumentum Domesticum*, RIB 2421–2441 (Stroud, 1991).

   Frere, S. S. & R. S. O. Tomlin, vol. II, Fascicule 4, *Instrumentum Domesticum*, RIB 2442–2480 (Stroud, 1992).

Sax, M. & A. Middleton. A system of nomenclature for quartz and its application to the material of cylinder seals. *Archaeometry* **34**, 1992, pp. 11–20.

Schaad, D. et al. (eds). *Le Trésor d'Eauze* (Toulouse, 1992).

Shelton, K. *The Esquiline treasure* (London, 1981).

Stead, I. *Celtic art* (London, 1985).

Stead, I. The Snettisham Treasure: excavations in 1990. *Antiquity* **65**, 1991, pp. 447–64.

Stead, I. & V. Rigby. *Baldock: the excavation of a Roman and pre-Roman settlement* (London, 1986).

237

Stead, I. & V. Rigby. *Verulamium: the King Harry Lane site* (London, 1989).

Stevenson, R. B. K. Native bangles and Roman glass. *Proceedings of the Society of Antiquaries of Scotland* **88**, 1956, pp. 208–21.

Stevenson, R. B. K. Romano-British glass bangles. *Glasgow Archaeological Journal* **4**, 1976, pp. 45–54.

Strong, D. & D. Brown (eds). *Roman crafts* (London, 1976).

Tacitus, *Agricola*, Loeb edn, trans. M. Hutton (London, 1980).

Tait, H. (ed.). *Seven thousand years of jewellery* (London, 1986).

Tait, H. (ed.). *Five thousand years of glass* (London, 1992).

Taylor, G. & D. Scarisbrick. *Finger rings from ancient Egypt to the present day* (London, 1978).

Thomas, C. *Christianity in Roman Britain to AD 500* (London, 1981).

Untracht, O. *Jewelry concepts and technology* (London, 1982).

Walters, H. B. *Catalogue of the silver plate, Greek, Etruscan and Roman, in the British Museum* (London, 1923).

Watts, D. *Christians and pagans in Roman Britain* (London, 1991).

Wheeler, R. E. M. *London in Roman times* (London, 1930).

Williams, D. & J. Ogden. *Greek gold: jewellery of the classical world* (London, 1994).

Zienkiewicz, D. *The legionary fortress baths at Caerleon* (Cardiff, 1986).

Index